Ultimate Price

Ultimate Price

THE VALUE WE PLACE ON LIFE

Howard Steven Friedman

UNIVERSITY OF CALIFORNIA PRESS

University of California Press
Oakland, California

Library of Congress Cataloging-in-Publication Data

Names: Friedman, Howard Steven, author.
Title: Ultimate price : the value we place on life / Howard Steven Friedman.
Identifiers: LCCN 2019035374 (print) | LCCN 2019035375 (ebook) | ISBN 9780520343221 (cloth) | ISBN 9780520974685 (ebook)
Subjects: LCSH: Social values—Political aspects. | Equality.
Classification: LCC HM681 .F75 2020 (print) | LCC HM681 (ebook) | DDC 305—dc23
LC record available at https://lccn.loc.gov/2019035374
LC ebook record available at https://lccn.loc.gov/2019035375

Manufactured in the United States of America

25 24 23 22 21 20 19 20
10 9 8 7 6 5 4 3 2 1

To Junior. It is your turn now to try to make the world a better place.

Contents

1 Your Money or Your Life?

A cancer patient is denied the latest chemotherapy treatment because it costs over $30,000 a month. Should it matter if the patient is a Nobel Prize winner or a murderer, a wealthy CEO or a high school dropout?

Two murders, two convictions. One victim was a wealthy, middle-aged mother of three; the other victim was a poor, teenage illegal immigrant. Should the penalties be the same?

The acceptable level of arsenic in drinking water depends on the monetary value placed on each life saved by more stringent regulations. Government experts are tasked with providing that value, but putting price tags on life is not solely the responsibility of technical specialists. Many of us have made decisions about valuing life, such as when your life insurance agent asks, "How much money will your family need if you die tomorrow?"

A pregnant woman undergoing an amniocentesis knows that the test results may impact whether she continues the pregnancy or has an abortion. Or imagine you see a young boy run out into traffic. Your decision of whether or not to rush into the street to save him reflects the relative value you place on both his life and your own.

Each example above probes the deceptively simple question, "How much is a human life worth?" It is deceptive in that many find it impossible to say how much they would pay to save the life of a stranger, a friend, a lover, or a child, or even to save their own lives.[1] The answer's complexity resides in the fact that how we arrive at a price tag on life says a great deal about our priorities. These price tags are markers of what we define as just, infused with influences from economics, ethics, religion, human rights, and law. Our values as a society are reflected in both the methods used to develop these price tags and the prices themselves.

The methods used for valuing life depend on the purpose of the costing, what exactly the costs are meant to represent, and the perspective taken for the costing. A person estimating the amount of money needed to replace their income in case they die unexpectedly has a different purpose and perspective than a government trying to figure out how much lives should be valued to prevent incremental environmental risks, which in turn has a different purpose and perspective than a company trying to figure out how much money it should spend to improve product or worker safety. These different purposes and perspectives lead to the use of different calculation methods and, not surprisingly, produce different price tags.

This book uses a broad set of examples to explain a few critical points: (1) that price tags are routinely placed on human lives, (2) that these price tags have major ramifications on our lives, (3) that these price tags are often neither transparent nor fair, and (4) that this lack of fairness is critical since undervalued lives are left underprotected and more exposed to risks than more highly valued lives.

Many of us go through life unaware that price tags are constantly placed on our lives. We often have little recognition or understanding that many of our most important decisions are influenced by calculations or assessments of how much our lives are worth. These values affect nearly every aspect of our existence—from the air we breathe to the food we eat to the money we earn. They influence our daily decisions of how we spend our time and money. These price tags drive political decisions like whether to go to war or seek peaceful solutions. They drive legal decisions of criminal punishment and of awards in civil lawsuits. They drive personal decisions, ranging from life insurance to healthcare and from education investments to abortions. They drive decisions that impact nearly all aspects of life, from creating new life to delaying inevitable death. These values have been impacting us since the moment we were conceived, and when we die, the value we placed on our lives will impact the people we leave behind.

What do we mean by price tags and the value we place on human life? A price tag refers to how much money something costs.[2] We do not normally think of human lives as having price tags, yet this book demonstrates that dollar figures are routinely assigned to human lives. We will review methods used by economists, financial analysts, regulators, and statisticians to put price tags on human lives while scrutinizing some of the key assumptions and limitations of these methods.

The value of life is a more comprehensive topic than the dollar amounts found on price tags. Value can refer to monetary worth, but value can also refer to "the importance, worth, or usefulness of something" or "one's judgment of what is important in life."[3] These broader notions of value are reflected in the decisions we make both individually and as a society. This book will weave between these different notions of how value is expressed, in terms of both monetary price tags and nonmonetary expressions of importance.

Examining how life is valued requires us to identify the scope of exploration. At the most extreme end are the values placed on the creation and loss of human life. This includes actions individuals take as well as decisions that society makes about the relative value of different lives. Moving down on this scale are the values placed on health, a critical determinant of quality of life. Further along the continuum are personal decisions about how we chose to spend our time.

Examples of monetary values placed on loss of life include the compensation provided to the families of September 11 victims, the financial settlements in accidental death civil lawsuits, the spending limits on lifesaving medicines, and the economic benefits of lives saved due to stricter regulations. On a more personal level, price tags on life include the costs associated with having and raising a child and decisions about how much life insurance to purchase. Nonmonetary values of life and death are demonstrated in legal decisions, such as the punishments for murder and vehicular manslaughter.

We can observe society's assessment of the relative value of life in the varying level of attention and action in response to the loss of some lives versus others, such as the death of a wealthy singer or a famous politician versus that of a homeless person lacking status or kin. The legal status of abortion falls into this discussion of the relative value of life, as does the personal decision regarding for whom you would sacrifice your own life.

Assessing the value of your quality of life is only slightly less challenging than assessing the value of your life. Monetary examples related to the quality of life include payments to those injured on September 11, civil judgments for victims of injuries and negligence-caused infirmities, financial compensation for those wrongfully imprisoned, and the economic benefits of reduced illness due to new regulations.

Lastly, there are the decisions we make about how we spend our time. Examples of taking value of life into account in personal decision-making include tradeoffs we make in employment and choices we make about our lifestyle.

Not only are these price tags nearly ubiquitous, they are also often inevitable. Medical decisions are often based on profitability algorithms and affordability assessments. Is the treatment cost-efficient for the insurance company? Can the patient afford to pay out of pocket? It is essential to understand a basic truth: no health system could function without considering the costs and expected health benefits of care.

The same truth applies to parents. If they do not consider the cost of raising a child, parents may be unable to provide the basic necessities for their family. In some cases, such as cost-benefit analysis, the price tags are explicit. In other cases, the price tags are implicit, and we need to probe to find the underlying assumptions.

No company could implement every conceivable safety device and remain in business. They often rely on cost-benefit analyses to guide their decisions. Price tags are placed on the deaths associated with Phillip Morris's cancer-causing cigarettes, General Motors' faulty brakes, and Union Carbide's chemical storage tanks in Bhopal, India.[4] In the public sector, zero tolerance for any pollutant is both economically and technologically impossible; an acceptable level must be established for each toxin. This level depends on how expensive a given regulation will be to implement, the number of preventable deaths, when those preventable deaths will occur, and the monetary value of each lost life. If the benefits of an environmental regulation are not considered, businesses could be hurt with little public gain.

While price tags are constantly placed on life, few of us are aware of how these values are created. The methods that economists, regulators, business analysts, and healthcare and insurance companies employ to determine these values are often obscured behind technical language and legal jargon. The methods and price tags speak to our priorities as a society, reflecting our core values and what we define as being just. This book gives you access and insight into the methods of valuation and what they say about us.

Delving into the equations, one quickly learns that these price tags are sometimes unfair. Yet they influence our economy, our laws, our behaviors, and our policies. These price tags are infused with gender, racial, national, and cultural biases. They often value the lives of the young more than the old, the rich more than the poor, whites more than blacks, Americans more than foreigners, and relatives more than strangers. The September 11th Victim Compensation Fund paid some victims' families $250,000; others received $7 million, nearly thirty times as much.[5] Not too long ago, the U.S. Environmental Protection Agency proposed valuing elderly peoples' lives at a fraction of younger peoples' lives.[6] The justice system has repeatedly demonstrated that punishment is very much determined by the victims' backgrounds and identities.

This book takes a journey through many different aspects of valuing life. The discussion begins with purely monetary assessments—price tags. It then moves to areas that involve both monetary considerations and nonmonetary reflections of value. It finishes with topics that reflect relative values of life.

This is not a book of philosophy, theology, judicial theory, economic ideology, or policy prescription. Rather, it shares a multitude of ways that life is valued, showing that the methods used for valuing life can be readily grasped after they have been separated from their technical language. More importantly, given how critical these price tags are to everyone's lives, they must be discussed outside of the small universe of technical experts. We must understand these valuations, or else we risk having our lives undervalued and, consequently, underprotected.

Ignoring how life is valued leaves us susceptible to our health being placed at risk, our safety being placed at risk, our legal rights being placed at risk, our families being placed at risk, and ultimately, our lives themselves being placed at risk. It is only with knowledge and vigilance that we can ensure that all lives are treated fairly and sufficiently protected.

2 When the Towers Fell

September 11, 2001. The date immediately flashes images into every American's mind. Flames bursting from the Twin Towers. A plane crashing into the Pentagon. The "let's roll" rallying cry of United Airlines Flight 93 passengers making their final stand. The towers collapsing in massive plumes of dust, ash, and debris.

Nearly three thousand lives were lost that day in the most devastating terrorist attack to ever occur on American soil. Millions more were affected around the world. Nearly all the world's nations expressed solidarity with America. The shocking loss of civilian lives and the mass destruction pierced national boundaries and bridged rivalries. No peaceful society could rest comfortably in a world where terrorists could inflict this level of devastation. No government could allow this brutal criminal act to go unanswered. America briefly united across social, party, religious, racial, and ethnic lines. All agreed that America's safety must be ensured. All agreed that justice would prevail. Justice for the victims. Justice for the terrorists and their abettors. Justice for the families and friends of the victims. Justice for America.

The victims of September 11 died terrible deaths. Hundreds perished immediately upon impact. Others, trapped in the Pentagon or in the

North and South Towers, died of smoke inhalation or were crushed when the towers collapsed. Brave firefighters, police officers, and other heroes died trying to rescue those trapped. For the families of the victims, the cause of death is of little consequence.

The sudden loss of a life on September 11 left a permanent, daily sense of loss with the parents, children, relatives and friends of the dead. The empty seat at the dinner table, the missing laugh at the family reunion, and the uncelebrated birthdays and anniversaries will remain forever as emotional scars that can never fully heal.

But the damage was not just emotional. The victims had been building futures for themselves and others. Their absence caused immediate, concrete losses. The dependents of the September 11 victims would miss not just their loved ones but also their support in paying monthly bills, covering school expenses, caring for children and parents, and saving for retirement. In the practical world of dollars and cents, the loss for the dependents was not only emotional but also financial.

We can understand the ramifications more clearly by looking at the lives of four fictitious victims: Rick, Jim, Anitha, and Sebastian.*

Rick, a third-generation Italian American, grew up in Staten Island. He and his older brother were natural athletes, starring on the high school baseball team and each getting black belts in judo. Rick, a veteran firefighter, was off duty when he heard the emergency call on September 11, 2001. He rushed to his fire station and jumped on a truck headed to Lower Manhattan. His fiancée, Suzie, had just sent out the invitations for their Cancun destination wedding, planned for December. Rick and his brothers were remodeling the bathroom in their parents' house as a fortieth anniversary present.

Hard work, talent, and a few lucky breaks had helped Jim build a career that met his father's high expectations. Some people whispered behind his back the words "affirmative action" when they heard about his Dartmouth MBA, Goldman Sachs internship, and the fact that he was one of only two black managing partners at his investment firm. Jim worked hard to prove the whisperers wrong. He worked even harder to ensure that his two

*All characters appearing in this work are fictitious and have been developed for illustrative purposes only. Any resemblance to real persons, living or dead, is purely coincidental.

daughters went to the best prep school, practiced for their piano lessons, and learned flower arranging when they went to their summer cottage in Martinique. At forty-eight, Jim had already set aside enough money from his seven-figure annual bonuses to cover the costs of his daughters' private schools, tutors, and colleges. According to his will, the Miami condo would go to his younger daughter, while the older daughter would get the place in Martinique and his wife would inherit the four-family brownstone in Brooklyn Heights.

Anitha had arrived in America from Indonesia on a student visa six years earlier. Her parents' plan was for her to earn an undergraduate degree at Columbia University, marry a doctor, buy a McMansion in New Jersey, and have three kids, and then they would move to America to help raise them. But Anitha fell in love with baking sweets, hanging out in the West Village, and her American roommate, Ashley. After sophomore year, she dropped out of Columbia and began working part-time as a hostess at a restaurant in the North Tower, deflecting advances from business executives, while training on weekends at the International Culinary Center. Anitha and Ashley planned to open a little shop called A&A's Specialty Cakes in Ashley's hometown of Pittsburgh after graduating from culinary school.

Sebastian, an adorable six-year-old, was the joy of his mother, Amelia. The two had boarded a plane that morning in Boston, on the way to visit Sebastian's dad, who was working at the Bel-Air Country Club in Los Angeles. Sebastian loved soccer and baseball. Some days he pretended to be Ronaldo kicking a winning goal, while other days he was Pudge Rodríguez squatting down awaiting a fastball. Sebastian was the star striker in his soccer league, and whenever a teammate scored, no one shouted "Gooooooal!" louder than he did.

These four lives, separated by age, gender, race, education, nationality, and wealth, were permanently linked by the events of September 11. Total strangers who had never met, they died on the same day, victims of the terrorist attacks. Rick would never get married or finish renovating his parents' house. Jim would never retire or see his daughters grow up. Anitha would never finish culinary school or start her cake shop. Sebastian would never become a sports announcer or even celebrate his seventh birthday. Each left behind unfulfilled dreams. Each left behind hopes and plans for their future that would never be realized. Each left behind friends and family mourning their premature deaths.

Following the attacks that morning, the United States sputtered to take a definitive response. While the nation searched for explanations, consolation, protection, and vengeance, Congress passed the Patriot Act, and shortly thereafter America went to war.[1]

Americans in the military were quickly shipped to Afghanistan. National Guards were called for duty. Their families felt the short-term effects of September 11 as their loved ones were halfway around the world dodging suicide bombers and trying to calm the chaos in Afghanistan and later Iraq. Congress committed trillions of dollars to the ambiguously named War on Terror.[2]

Americans living near the sites of destruction in New York, Washington, DC, and Pennsylvania experienced long-term changes. The contaminated air, the cordoned-off areas, and the presence of military, investigators, government officials, media, and police continued. These Americans lived with the constant reminders of the terrorist attacks.

Millions of Americans lacked direct connections to September 11 victims, did not live near the sites of the attacks, and had no immediate contacts in the military. For them, life returned to mostly pre–September 11 conditions within a short time period. Stock markets recovered within a few months.[3] Unemployment rates ticked up somewhat, but overwhelmingly for these millions of Americans, the most visible reminders of the attacks and unfolding wars were the new security measures inconsistently implemented throughout airports.[4]

But for the families and friends of the victims of September 11, permanent emotional and economic gaps remained. There was the emotional gap due to the sudden loss of a loved one who would be missed forever. And there was the economic gap from the lost income and support that was no longer provided. Many of the victims had been earning salaries, contributing to the family income, paying expenses, and saving for retirement. Others had been performing unpaid labor, such as caring for children, elderly family members, and other dependents. Some were children who were still going to school but who would have eventually worked either paid or unpaid jobs.

The unprecedented destruction of September 11 prompted a similarly unprecedented response by the federal government. Previous terrorist attacks, such as the Oklahoma City bombing in 1995, the U.S. embassy bombings in Kenya and Tanzania in 1998, and the first World Trade Center terrorist attack in 1993, did not provoke the creation of a national compensation fund. Those tragic deaths did not spur the government to create a pot of money to be distributed to those most directly impacted. More important for our immediate purposes, those prior tragedies did not prompt the government to put price tags on the lost lives.

September 11 was treated very differently. Coordination between the struggling airline industry and government officials resulted in the Air Transportation Safety and System Stabilization Act.[5] This law sprinted through Congress and was signed on September 22, 2001.[6] It assigned billions of dollars to support the failing airline industry and billions more in compensation money for claimants, including the dependents of the victims of September 11. A primary purpose of the fund was to protect corporations from financial ruin. As such, families who accepted the compensation waived their right to sue any possible culpable organization, such as airlines, airports, security companies, or the World Trade Center. To induce families to accept the compensation offers and not file lawsuits, Congress limited the airline industry's financial liability to $6 billion and required that the payouts reflect the standards used in tort law.[7]

Kenneth Feinberg was appointed by Attorney General John Ashcroft as the Special Master of the September 11th Victim Compensation Fund.[8] Mr. Feinberg, a former federal prosecutor, had not only served as special counsel to Senator Ted Kennedy's Judiciary Committee but had also established himself as one of America's premier arbitrators when he settled the Agent Orange litigation case in the 1980s. Mr. Feinberg was given the task of creating price tags—the values placed on the economic and noneconomic costs due to death or injury.

The formula he created was a combination of noneconomic value, dependent value, and economic value. The noneconomic value was set at the same price for every victim, $250,000. The dependent value was the same for every dependent. If the victim had a spouse, $100,000 was added to the award, and an additional $100,000 was added for each other dependent.[9] The economic value was based on the victim's income, so it varied widely. It was calculated using the victim's expected lifetime income, benefits, and other compensation and then adjusted based on the victim's effective tax rate. The calculation included information about the victim's age, how many more working years they were expected to have, and how much their income was expected to increase over time. Mr. Feinberg placed a cap on the assumed annual income at $231,000 to avoid massive payouts to the families of highest earners.

The total was then reduced by the amount of compensation that was already going to be paid from some other source, such as life insurance, pension funds, or death benefit programs.

The total of the noneconomic value, dependent value, and economic value was adjusted upward based on medical and burial expenses. After all the numbers were crunched, the families would receive an offer. They could accept the offer, or they could appeal it. As discussed in detail by Mr. Feinberg himself in *What Is Life Worth?*, by the time this process was completed in June 2004, 97 percent of the families had agreed to receive a total of $7 billion, with an average payout for a death of around $2 million.[10] The range of awards, however, was vast. While the minimum award was $250,000, the maximum awards exceeded $7 million. Some lives were valued at nearly thirty times more than others.

Victims in the lowest income level, those who had been earning less than $20,000 at the time of the attacks, had their lives valued at $250,000 to $2.2 million, with an average award amount of less than $1 million. Victims in the highest income level, those who had been earning at least $220,000, had average awards of around $4 million.

The lives of Rick, Jim, Anitha, and Sebastian were priced very differently.

Computing the value of Rick's life was a complicated affair. It was assumed that firefighters and police officers received compensation from other sources, such as earnings from a second job, as well as their pension. Their price tags were reduced by survivor benefits, their children's social security benefits, and other insurance and payments that came along with the job. For Rick, this meant that his life was computed as having a value of $1,250,000—the sum of a noneconomic value of $250,000 and an economic value of $1 million. Rick's economic value of $1 million was calculated by subtracting his fireman survivor benefits of $1.7 million from his lost potential earnings of $2.7 million. Who would get this money? It was shared among his parents and his brothers. His fiancée, Suzie, did not receive anything because she was not legally a member of Rick's family at the time of his death.

Jim had annual earnings miles over the $231,000 maximum set out in the income formula. His family's payout was reduced to $4 million because of the extensive life insurance policy his company had purchased as part of his executive compensation package. His family could easily argue that this payout barely scratched the surface of his future earnings. After all, any formula that capped Jim's yearly income at $231,000 clearly had no relationship to the amount he was earning at his investment firm.

Anitha had been eking out a living at the restaurant while she attended culinary school, earning $19,000 a year. Her girlfriend, Ashley, was covering most of the rent and some of the tuition costs, although Anitha was also incurring loans. With no dependents and little income, the price tag on Anitha's life, at $750,000, was the lowest valued of the four. Despite sharing a studio, Anitha and Ashley had no legal status for their relationship, so Ashley received nothing. The compensation was sent directly to Anitha's family in Indonesia.

Sebastian, a first grader, was lumped together with the other victims below age eighteen. With no income and no dependents, these victims were all given the same the price tag, about $803,000. This number was computed based on the average income for American wage earners, and with in a bit of logical magic, the calculation assumed that these infants were actually twenty years old on September 11, 2001. The price tag for minors was hundreds of thousands of dollars less than the average award amount. Regardless of background, educational level, social status, race, sex, or any other factor, the life of each child victim was valued the same.[11] This equality in payouts for minors is strikingly different from the enormous compensation range applied to the other victims.

These four people all had their lives cut short. All had plans for the future. These four lives were valued very differently, with price tags assigned to their lives that varied widely. Price tags were identical for minors but ranged from $250,000 to over $7 million for adults. This wide range reflected the fact that most of the value assigned by Kenneth Feinberg was based on each victim's economic value—the money the person was expected to earn—and not on their noneconomic value.

The price tags were and still are controversial. They were loudly criticized by people across the political spectrum, from libertarians to liberals. Some protested the government stepping in to cover the airline's bills.

After all, the airlines had insurance coverage that would have paid the families. If sued, the airlines may have been found negligent for failing to detect the hijackers, allowing them to board, and letting them hijack the planes. In fact, the company Cantor Fitzgerald, which lost 658 employees on September 11, settled its case with American Airlines for $135 million.[12] Meanwhile, charities, a more traditional source of support, had quickly raised over $2.7 billion to assist those impacted by the attacks.[13]

Others argued that it was unfair that the government had provided any compensation to September 11 victims. This was neither the first terrorist incident in the United States nor the first terrorist incident where Americans were killed. And it will certainly not be the last. Many felt it was unjust for the government to pay the families of September 11 victims when government payments had not been organized for previous bombings, mass shootings, arson attacks, and other terrorist acts. There was no indication that victim compensation funds would be created as a standard practice for future terrorist activities. For example, the federal government did not compensate any of the victims killed or injured in the 2013 Boston Marathon Bombing or in the 2017 New York City truck attack that killed eight people. September 11 was treated as a one-time, special event despite the near certainty that Americans will continue to be the targets of terrorism in the future.

Practically, the fund had to draw some bounds around who would and wouldn't receive compensation, or else millions of people could have applied for compensation. Nonetheless, some protested that the compensation included only those who had been in what was called "the immediate vicinity." For example, it left out New Jersey residents living across the Hudson River from the World Trade Center, who had been subjected to massive plumes of toxic dust and smoke from the fallen towers. Their respiratory problems would not be compensated. Nor would compensation be provided to nonresponders who had waited more than three days to see a doctor about their injuries—the logic being that those who waited more than three days may have been presenting with injuries that were unrelated to the attacks.[14]

The compensation also favored families who appealed for a higher offer from the fund. Those who accepted the compensation fund's first offer were paid less, on average, than families who rejected the initial offer and appealed for additional compensation.[15]

Others protested that the price tag formula was unfair. Families of the highest earners felt that they were being shortchanged due to the capping of the annual earnings—after all, the decision to use $231,000 as the maximum annual salary was completely arbitrary. Some criticized those wealthier families for being greedy in a time of national tragedy. Because this price tag was dominated by income and not by noneconomic value or dependent value, all of the racial and gender inequities associated with income were compounded in these September 11 compensation packages.

None of the four people featured in this chapter were primarily caregivers, yet nationally a large part of the adult population devotes their time to raising children and caring for elderly parents and relatives. Since caregivers do not earn a salary, victims who were caregivers had no income in the compensation calculation. Stay-at-home parents offset the costs of day care centers or babysitters, yet this was not taken into account when their lives were valued.

In 2016, nearly one-third of all mothers stayed at home to take care of their children, and roughly 80 percent of stay-at-home parents were mothers.[16] There is also a gender imbalance in caregivers for the elderly, of which roughly two-thirds are women.[17] In caring for both children and the elderly, women are more likely than men to forsake income. As a result, the female victims were computed to have a lower economic value, and consequently lower price tags were placed on their lives. When the September 11th Victim Compensation program was completed, the average payout for female victims was only 63 percent of the average payout for male victims.[18]

It is clear that the September 11 compensation formula put a much lower value on the life of anyone who chose to devote more time to their family and less time to earning an income. Additionally, this formula punished people who chose professions that tended to have more social benefit but less compensation.

Beyond these issues, another problem lingers due to this price tag's reliance on income-wage gaps. Two working people with the same experience and education often do not receive the same payment. For example, whether comparing high school-educated, undergraduate-educated, or master's degree-educated adults, blacks earn about 25 to 30 percent less than whites.[19] Gender pay gaps, where women get paid less than men, persist even after accounting for differences in years of work experience, education, hours of work per year, industry, occupation, race, and marital status.[20] Wage gaps based on gender, race, or nationality are a sign of unfairness in the labor market. By estimating the economic value of a person's life using their current income, these gaps are multiplied over the decades they were expected to work.

The income-based methodology undervalues the contributions of people who are retired or not working. This was so apparent that the official Frequently Asked Questions document for the September 11th Victim Compensation Fund had an ominously vague statement that for these people, compensation would be based on "the economic value of replacement services using standard values as provided by relevant studies, or similar approaches."[21] "Replacement services" refers, for example, to a housewife performing tasks that could be done by a professional housekeeper or a professional cook. As it turned out, the average compensation for victims over sixty was less than half that of younger victims.[22]

Others noted that some injured survivors received over $8 million in compensation, more than any of the families that had received compensation for the loss of a life.[23] Any compensation program that allocates more for injuries than death is ripe for criticism.

We can see that there are many valid objections to the formula that was used to value the lives of the victims of September 11. What other approach might have been tried? There was—and, for future situations, remains—a simple alternative to the complicated algorithms that were developed: value all lives the same.

If, in order to determine compensation, a price tag needed to be applied to the lives lost, then why not set the same price tag for everyone? The logic behind this is straightforward. After all, the crime of murder is the same crime whether the victim was young or old, rich or poor, a man or a woman, an American or a foreigner. On paper, murder is murder, regardless of who the victim was. In America, the actual punishment for murder often depends on the race and socioeconomic status of the victim, but these biases in the legal system should not be replicated in compensating victims of terrorism unequally.

Human rights are supposed to be the same for all humans. The promises of life, liberty, and the pursuit of happiness are supposed to be extended to everyone, since we are all supposed to be "created equal." This principle is not limited to the United States of America's Declaration of Independence; it is stated clearly in the Universal Declaration of Human Rights as well: "All human beings are born free and equal in dignity and rights." If victim compensation is meant to be a human right, then why should it be driven by economic loss?

In 2004, Mr. Feinberg himself came to the same conclusion when he wrote that "a strong argument can be made that—if and when there is a next time and if and when compensation for terrorist victims is once again considered by Congress—all eligible claimants, however defined, should be given the same tax-free awards. Such a flat-payment approach would not only be easier to administer but would also minimize divisiveness among eligible claimants, who would no longer be able to argue that the loss of a loved one, such as a fireman, is being undervalued in favor of the loss of a stockbroker or banker."[24] A year later, Feinberg took an even stronger stand, stating that the formula was "defective" and that "individual wealth and the circumstances of surviving kin should play no role in the computation of awards."[25] And, indeed, the United States has a precedent for this method in the way it handles compensation for military deaths.

Since the government considered September 11 an act of war, it should have considered how military deaths are compensated. All active duty military deaths not involving misconduct are treated as line-of-duty deaths, whether they occurred in combat, in training, or as a result of something unrelated, like illness.[26] The compensation consists of immediate income assistance, transition assistance, and income replacement. The immediate income assistance is a $100,000 check, regardless of rank, so the families of privates and generals are paid the same. Transition assistance, such as medical and dental coverage, counseling services, and transitional housing, is also offered regardless of rank. The income replacement includes many programs, the two largest of which are the Servicemembers' Group Life Insurance (SGLI) and the Dependency and Indemnity Compensation (DIC). SGLI provides up to $400,000 in government-subsidized coverage and is nearly universally maximized for all active duty personnel, while the DIC is a monthly payment. Both programs pay fixed amounts regardless of the rank of the deceased.

There is another precedent. Over a decade earlier, the Civil Liberties Act of 1988 paid all Japanese Americans who were interned during World

War II the same amount, $20,000. The payment amount did not vary based on how much income each person lost during the time they were forced to move to internment camps. In this case, the compensation was for loss of opportunity and freedom, not for loss of life.

Valuing the lives of every victim of the September 11 attacks the same would have been simpler, less controversial, and consistent with how the federal government and international agencies typically do cost-benefit calculations. Federal agencies such as the Environmental Protection Agency (EPA) and the Transportation Security Administration (TSA) generally do their cost-benefit analyses using a fixed price tag, the same for everyone. These agency price tags do not vary depending on whether the person is rich or poor, black or white, young or old.

The agencies compute the expected costs of a program or regulation—say, to reduce a known carcinogen produced by industrial practices—and then compare them to the expected benefits. The benefits are based on the number of expected lives saved, which is in turn based on the concept called the Value of a Statistical Life.[27] The Value of a Statistical Life is computed based on reducing risk. It measures how much money people require to accept an incremental risk of death or are willing to pay to reduce a risk of death. Proponents of using the Value of a Statistical Life believe that the metric's focus on incremental risk is helpful in some cost-benefit calculations. It does not, they contend, attempt to fix the amount someone would pay to avoid certain death (an amount that is arguably incalculable) or the amount a group of people would pay to save a specific person (an amount that is certain to be riddled with biases).

Practically speaking, the value is routinely used for much more than calculating risk. Analysts use the estimates to represent the value of life itself, and it is a central input when computing the economic benefit of saving lives (not reducing risk) through enhanced regulations, improved safety, or other expenses.

In 1995, the Intergovernmental Panel on Climate Change (IPCC) used three different values for people's lives depending on whether they lived in a low-income, middle-income, or high-income country. The range was enormous, with the lives of residents of high-income countries valued at fifteen times more than those of residents of poor countries. The negative reaction to this violation of human dignity was immediate, and the scientists quickly backpedaled. By 2001, the IPCC was using a worldwide value of $1 million per life in computing the costs and benefits of greenhouse gas reduction.[28] This value was the same for all lives, irrespective of the country's wealth. By comparison, this $1 million value was far lower than that used by the Environmental Protection Agency (EPA), a reflection of the fact that the average U.S. income was much higher than the global average.[29] There is no consistent method used today. Some international researchers use values that are related to a nation's wealth, and others value all lives the same. For example, research papers have been published in *The Lancet* showing that there are high returns for investments in health and education in seventy-five low-income and middle-income countries. In these papers, the same value of life was used to represent the noneconomic value of these people's lives, regardless of the GDP per capita of the country they lived in.[30]

Under President George W. Bush, the EPA introduced the idea of two price tags on life, $3.7 million for people under the age of seventy and $2.3 million for people older than seventy, as part of the analysis for the Clear Skies Initiative. Criticism was immediate and scathing. The public reacted furiously to what advocates for the elderly labeled the "senior death discount."[31] This lower value for older people was deemed both highly inequitable and not defensible scientifically using the Value of a Statistical Life, which does not necessarily diminish with age.[32] The EPA soon backed off and reverted to using a single price tag for every life rather than assuming that some people are worth more than others.

In 2010, the EPA was using a value of $9.1 million per life in computing the cost-benefit associated with new regulations. The Food and Drug Administration used a fixed value of $7.9 million per life in 2010 and $8.3 million per life in 2011, while the Transportation Security Agency has recently used a value of $9.4 million.[33] All of these values vastly exceed the average future expected earnings, a metric that was previously used by agencies to value lives.[34]

While it may seem illogical that these agencies are all using different numbers, the fact remains that each agency is putting a single price tag on all lives saved, whether they are saved by regulating an airborne toxin, a foodborne illness, or airbags. Agencies are not pricing lives differently depending on whether someone has children, what their income is, or what age they are. This consistency in valuing lives is a positive aspect of the regulatory practice, regardless of the inconsistent values used across agencies or the questionable science behind the Value of a Statistical Life.

So where do these price tags come from? Here is where economists play god and try to "divine" prices for something that cannot be bought. There is no free market for life where economists can see how much people are charging to sell their lives and how much people with no financial constraints are willing to spend to extend their lives.

Imagine a crazed man decides that he wants to kill someone. He cannot purchase the right to commit murder. Similarly, slavery is illegal—one can't legally purchase someone as property. There is no legal market in America to buy the right to own or take someone's life.

Given that there is no market to purchase life, how do economists come up with this Value of a Statistical Life? One method involves asking hypothetical questions through surveys, while two other methods look at the economic and risk implications of actual decisions. The type of survey used in the first method is often called a contingent-valuation survey or a "stated-preference method." These surveys ask people to rate their willingness to pay for something or willingness to accept money for something. The other two methods look at actual decisions: one looks at the incremental amount people get paid to take on a riskier job (wage-based), and the second looks at the amount of money people pay to reduce their risk (revealed-preference). As we will soon see, these methods rely on false assumptions and routinely draw inconsistent conclusions

SURVEY-BASED METHOD OF ESTIMATING THE VALUE OF A STATISTICAL LIFE

The survey-based method is reminiscent of a classic joke. A robber points a gun at an old man's head and shouts, "Your money or your life!" The old man stares back at him, saying nothing. The robber shouts again, "I said your money or your life!" The old man replies, "I'm thinking, I'm thinking."

Economists can't simply ask people the question, "How much would you be willing to pay to not be killed?" and expect to get useful information back. The answer will likely be, "Everything I have and more," which is a poetic reply but not one that is particularly quantitative. Ask a parent,

"How much money are you willing to pay for your child to not be murdered?" and you will receive a similar answer. In the real world, people consider life to be precious and priceless. Many find the idea of putting a price tag on life repugnant, immoral, and often inconceivable. Most religions and philosophies thoroughly reject the idea of pricing human life. Yet doing so is at the heart of cost-benefit analysis and was the main task of the September 11th Victim Compensation Fund.

How do economists decide how much a life is worth? Since a straightforward question about the price people will pay for life will yield nothing, economists dance around the issue. They ask people questions that probe around the topic without asking direct questions about price tags. For example, they stop people in a shopping mall, call them on the phone, or contact them online to ask questions such as, "How much would you be willing to pay to avoid a one in ten thousand chance of dying from XYZ?" If the average comes out to $900, then the researcher would extrapolate that if ten thousand people paid that amount, then a total of $9 million would be spent to save, on average, one life. The $9 million would represent the amount that the population would spend to reduce the risk sufficiently to save a single life, and that number is called the Value of a Statistical Life. The flaws in this methodology are painfully obvious.

The survey-based method also suffers from selection bias. The population willing to spend time at a mall, on the phone, or online answering surveys like this is not representative of the general population. By definition, these people are willing to dedicate a significant amount of time to answering questions while receiving little or no apparent benefit.

Another major flaw is the completely abstract nature of the survey questions. Few people can really internalize and understand what the survey is trying to probe. As a result, the abstract questions often prompt baseless guesses, wishful thinking, and throw-away answers.

Researchers often adjust for this in a brutally unscientific manner by simply discarding the data points that they don't find convenient to analyze. A commonly rejected answer is, "I can't set a price on life." The fact that researchers have very clear notions about what responses are acceptable is clearly described by Value of a Statistical Life advocate W. Kip Viscusi: "Respondents should be willing to pay more for a safety policy as the magnitude of the risk reduction generated by the policy increases. . . .

More affluent respondents should be willing to pay more for a specified risk reduction than those with less adequate financial resources."[35] Discarding data that doesn't support your hypothesis violates basic science methods. Moreover, filtering out responses that disagree with the researcher's notions biases the computed Value of a Statistical Life to have specific attributes that agree with the researcher's preconceived notions.

Ask the same person a slightly different question related to this price tag and you could get a very different response.[36] As a result, a single individual may have a whole set of different Value of a Statistical Life estimates that vary depending on the exact risk they are trying to avoid, such as death by fire or cancer, the likelihood of that risk, or even simpler things, like the precise wording of the question or if, perhaps, they read about the risks of smog, *E. coli* in burritos, or an automobile recall in that morning's news.

Another concern about this method is that willingness-to-pay surveys are often conducted in isolation. This isolation means that respondents may not recognize how payments to address one problem will reduce the amount of money available to address other problems.

There is also the issue that paying and being paid are perceived very differently.[37] Just because someone says they would be willing to pay $900 to avoid a one in ten thousand chance of dying from XYZ does not mean that they would be willing to be paid $900 to increase the chances of dying from XYZ by one in ten thousand. This is not a specific issue with contingent valuation since it has been well established that across many areas, people's willingness to pay is often quite different from their willingness to accept payment.[38] Thinking about this another way, the chances that someone is willing to accept a payment for $100,000 to expose themselves to a certain degree of risk is not the same as someone being willing to pay $100,000 to reduce their risk by the same amount. Situations where people do not act like perfect risk calculators will be examined more in later chapters.

WAGE-BASED METHOD OF ESTIMATING THE VALUE OF A STATISTICAL LIFE

The wage-based method looks at how much more people get paid for working riskier professions. In economic theory, choosing a job involves an informed decision by job seekers in terms of what risk they will accept and how much they expect to get paid for accepting this risk. This theory assumes that job seekers have options regarding what jobs they would take; that they know the risk of death associated with each job and the corresponding incremental risk of different job options; and that they demand to be paid higher for jobs that have more risk. The ratio of the incrementally higher amount being paid for a risky job to the incremental risk is used to estimate the Value of a Statistical Life.

Numerous estimates have been developed based on this idea. The estimates are from different time periods, different countries, and different professions, and they have values ranging from tens of thousands to tens of millions of dollars.[39] Factors like the country used for the analysis, whether the employees were in unions, whether the employees were white collar or blue collar, and the employees' industry all influence the estimates. While there was a wide range of values estimated in different studies, cost-benefit analysts settled on a value of $6.1 million per life in 2000 using U.S.-based studies.[40]

This calculation is built on a number of false assumptions. Potential employees often don't have options but rather have to take whichever job is available to them. Potential employees often have little or no knowledge about the incremental risk associated with different jobs. Even if the employee has an accurate directional sense of the risk of acute injuries and death, they often don't know the exact risks. Moreover, employees don't take input information about precise estimates of these incremental risks, infer the missing data from nonacute risks, and then analyze the data to determine what is the necessary incremental compensation. Simply put, potential employees lack the information needed to make the informed decisions that this calculation assumes they are making, and often they also lack choice in employment options or salary negotiation opportunities.

They often don't even know the salary potential of jobs or have effective negotiating leverage, as evidenced by the fact that union organized labor is higher paid and thus has a higher Value of a Statistical Life estimate than nonunion labor.[41]

People have intrinsic risk tolerance. Some consciously avoid risk, while others knowingly take on higher risk. Smokers and drinkers tend to naturally take on more risk. Women on average are more risk averse than men, and so the calculated Value of a Statistical Life is higher for women than for men. People with fewer job options will take riskier jobs even without a lot of extra compensation because they lack alternatives. The inferred Value of a Statistical Life is lower for these people because they simply lack job options, the leverage needed to negotiate, or knowledge of the risks involved.

In spite of all of the logical and methodological flaws in the design, data acquisition, and computation of the Value of a Statistical Life, values are obtained through this method and used. These Value of a Statistical Life estimates have an enormous range and a high degree of variance depending on how exactly the value was estimated—and this high variance exists in spite of researchers' efforts to impose restrictions on which respondents' answers will be deemed acceptable for analysis.

A review of 621 labor-derived estimates of the Value of a Statistical Life that all leveraged the exact same occupational fatality data set showed that there was a nearly $34 million gap between the 95th percentile estimate ($35.7 million) and the 5th percentile estimate ($1.8 million). Another way to think about this is if you lined up these 621 estimates in order from lowest to highest, the 590th estimate (the 95th percentile, $35.7 million) would be about twenty times larger than the 31st estimate (the 5th percentile, $1.8 million).[42] This large range for U.S. estimates, and the other well-known issues, reminds us of the questionable scientific validity of this measure. Large ranges and highly counterintuitive trends (such as Pakistan having Value of a Statistical Life estimates that are more than fifteen times larger than those for Taiwan) are also seen in comparisons of international values.[43]

REVEALED-PREFERENCE METHOD OF ESTIMATING THE VALUE OF A STATISTICAL LIFE

The revealed-preference method can be thought of as the opposite of the wage-based method. Instead of analyzing how much more money people require to take on increased risk (willingness to accept), the revealed-preference method looks at how much people are willing to spend to reduce their risk (willingness to pay).

Imagine a study that looked at spending patterns associated with bicycle helmets. Economists could look at how much more people are willing to spend to buy a helmet that is more effective at reducing brain injury or possible death than a cheaper, less effective helmet. The ratio of the incremental amount being paid for the more expensive helmet to the incremental risk reduction would be an estimate of the Value of a Statistical Life.

Again, economists are assuming that purchasing a helmet is an informed decision based on an understanding of the reduced risk associated with the investment. Also, this analysis does not account for the fact that different customers have different amounts of disposable income, which means that some customers can easily spend more than others on safety devices. In reality, it is highly unlikely that the consumer knows about the precise differences in risk between the two helmets, and the decision of which helmet to buy is often based on both personal finances and factors utterly unrelated to safety, like a helmet's design and colors.

Economists can analyze the amount of money spent on home fire extinguishers or the time expended on buckling or not buckling seat belts. In both cases, these activities can be monetized and compared to the reduced rate of mortality. Again, economists are assuming that people are making an informed choice about the reduced rate of mortality, an assumption that is rarely true.

Whether one is using a survey-based, wage-based, or revealed-preference method for estimating the Value of a Statistical Life, the values obtained can vary wildly, and the calculations themselves are logically flawed.

One could use similarly flawed logic to create a much higher price tag on life by looking at the response to September 11 in terms of the War on Terror. Trillions of dollars have been spent on incremental internal and external defense and safety measures, purportedly as a response to September 11. These expenses include the creation of government agencies like the U.S. Department of Homeland Security, with its approximately 250,000 employees, and foreign wars such as those in Afghanistan and Iraq.[44] Dividing these trillions by the nearly three thousand lives lost on September 11, 2001, would yield a willingness to pay on the scale of hundreds of millions of dollars or more per life lost. Flaws in this type of calculation include the fact that American citizens have painfully little influence on these expenses and the fact that the impact of these measures on the risk of future terrorist events is highly debatable.

One could make a comparable calculation to estimate the massive number of life years spent by travelers in American airports taking on and off shoes—a response to the attempt by terrorist Richard Reid to ignite his shoes on board a plane. Economists could compute the amount of time spent on this defense procedure and monetize it by the annual earnings of the passengers to estimate the opportunity costs. This opportunity cost could be added to other incremental costs of security associated with the removal of shoes to obtain a total cost. This total cost could be compared with the expected number of lives saved by the procedure. This would produce another value of life, one that would also be methodologically flawed by the fact that passengers have not been given an option of whether or not to remove their shoes and that the reduced risk of death due to this safety procedure of removing shoes is questionable.

In short, every price tag method for determining the value of a human life is logically flawed. The analysis cliché of "garbage in, garbage out"[45] truly holds for estimating the Value of a Statistical Life, yet these methods are used to produce price tags. Despite the fact that these price tags are flawed and illogical, they are regularly employed, with substantial real-world implications.

Limitations aside, the use of the Value of a Statistical Life does have some very positive attributes. The value itself is much higher than most Americans' expected earnings, and so using this higher value offers greater protection than calculations based on lost income. Also, regulatory agencies use the same value for all lives, so the biases associated with using income-based values are avoided.

Because the September 11 compensation was designed to minimize lawsuits, it required financial losses to be considered. As a result, individuals' projected lifetime earnings were one of the inputs. As previously discussed, income is not a fair or appropriate barometer of an individual's worth. Imagine the preposterous conclusion that would be drawn if we used income to compare the value of the life of a hedge fund manager to that of a social worker, schoolteacher, police officer, fireman, or soldier. The suggestion that a top hedge fund manager, earning over $100 million a year, adds one thousand or more times value to society, to his family, and to his loved ones than these other hardworking individuals is ridiculous. Relying on income to estimate the value of someone's life produces this type of illogical conclusion, with its resulting immoral consequences.

Could the income-based method be used to assign an average income-based value to each person? Of course. This is exactly what Mr. Feinberg did for the September 11 victims who were minors. Yet the average of a logically flawed value is still flawed.

The fund was legally required to consider both economic and noneconomic values. But Congress did not need to force economic losses into the equation. After all, other government agency programs value lives the same. Had Mr. Feinberg been able to use a single value for all lost lives, as he suggested in 2004, he still would have needed to determine that value, but this would have greatly simplified the price tag formula. It would have meant that everyone had the same noneconomic value and that the dependent, economic, and benefit adjustment values would all have been set to zero.

This is not a perfect solution, and strong arguments can be made against it. Opponents of this solution can argue that this would excessively reward the families of lower-income victims while potentially creating hardship for families of high-income victims. They would argue that payouts of many millions of dollars to the families of victims who were either unemployed or working in low-paying jobs would be the equivalent of their winning the lottery. Meanwhile, they would point out that equal payouts would not recognize the effort that top earners had put into their educations, careers, and other controllable factors that helped drive their economic success. It would equate the saints with the sinners, the takers with the givers, Nobel Prize winners with homeless heroin addicts, the inventor of a lifesaving vaccine with a mass murderer.

While every system is subject to complaints, it is important to realize that, as with the results of Mr. Feinberg's formula, most of the complaints against using a single value would likely have come from the families of the highest earners. A sizable portion of the approximately 3 percent of families that rejected the government offer were in the situation of Jim's family. His annual income vastly exceeded the $231,000 maximum set by the fund. Those who found the salary cap unacceptable could have rejected the government offer and filed lawsuits instead of accepting the offer and waiving their rights.

So, how much should each family receive?

Rick, Jim, Anitha, Sebastian, and nearly three thousand other lives were lost on September 11. Hundreds of thousands later died in military actions during following years in Iraq and Afghanistan, many of them Iraqi or Afghanistan civilians. Each one of those victims was loved. Each one of those victims had a family. Each one of those victims had future plans. Each one deserves to be remembered and cherished.

Each of the nearly three thousand lives of those that died on September 11 was assigned a price tag, and these ranged massively, from $250,000 to over $7 million. Yet these lives could easily have been given the same price tag. While the actual number is debatable, a fixed amount, whether $3 million, $6.1 million, $10 million, or some other number, would have been the simplest and fairest way to compensate the families. Using the same value would have explicitly shown that humans all have value purely because they are humans, alive, and able to contribute to the life of family, friends, and society. While the U.S. military, federal agencies, and international agencies don't agree on which price tag to use, they are united in applying whatever price tag they select to all lives equally, with no life being valued more than any other. Using the same value is also consistent with Americans' intuitive feelings of justice—six out of seven Americans agreed that the September 11 compensation should have been the same for each family.[46]

In America, we proudly proclaim that everyone has the unalienable rights to life, liberty, and the pursuit of happiness. When that inalienable right to life is taken away, as it was taken from the September 11 victims, compensation should not favor the rich over the poor. Equal protection under the law, an idea enshrined in our legal system, certainly doesn't entitle the government to award wealthy families ten, twenty, or even thirty times the amount of compensation as poorer families.

The above discussion focuses on the amount paid to the families of the victims, but there is also the broader question of whether paying victims' families is a fair and appropriate use of taxpayer money. Terrorist attacks will continue to happen in the United States and throughout the world. As a result, some Americans will be killed. More generally, thousands of

American deaths occur annually from murders, accidents, and negligence. In 2001, there were more than five times as many people murdered or killed by nonnegligent manslaughter in the United States than there were people killed on September 11.[47] From the vantage point of this legion of dead Americans, the very existence of the September 11th Victim Compensation Fund is unfair. As tragic as that loss of lives was, it elevated the untimely deaths of that day to a different level than that of all of the other untimely deaths, whether due to accidents, homicides, terrorism, or negligence. The government program of redistributing taxpayer money for the families of September 11 victims forever opened the question of what other untimely deaths should invoke taxpayer-funded payments. It permanently posed a legitimate question: Since taxpayer money was distributed to pay the families of September 11 victims, why do other deaths not also deserve taxpayer-funded compensation?

Perhaps the large range of price tags on human life that occurred as part of the September 11th Victim Compensation Fund will remain the aberration for terrorism-related deaths. Following the 2013 Boston Marathon bombing, private donations poured in to a total of $60 million, but the government did not create a victim compensation fund. Mr. Feinberg was also the administrator of this privately funded victim compensation fund. This time, he determined that the families of those that died should be paid the same amount, regardless of the income of the victim or their number of dependents.[48]

Our government should not get into the business of creating victim compensation funds. That said, if our government ever decides to create another such fund, it could avoid many of the mistakes of the September 11 fund by implementing a very simple rule: all lives are worth the same.

The next chapter focuses on the courts—both civil and criminal—which are our normal recourse for justice. When human life is lost, the civil courts must assign price tags to those lives, while criminal courts are tasked with meting out justice on behalf of society. The courts are mandated to act in accordance with the Fourteenth Amendment's promise of "equal protection of the laws." As we will soon see, in practice, the justice system often reacts differently depending on whose life was lost.

3 Justice Is Not Blind

Famous homicide cases point to the American justice system's very different reactions to the deaths of different citizens: Mark Chapman shooting John Lennon, the O. J. Simpson trials, Officer Daniel Pantaleo choking Eric Garner, and George Zimmerman killing Trayvon Martin. The cases that went through the civil system placed price tags on the lost lives that reflected an assessment of how much money those lives were worth. All four cases went through the criminal system and had very different outcomes, a consequence not only of the circumstances of the cases themselves but also of how society valued the lost lives. These cases provide a window into the question of whether, from the viewpoint of the American justice system, some lives are valued more than others.

Mark Chapman has spent over thirty-five years in jail for murdering John Lennon. O. J. Simpson was tried twice for the deaths of Nicole Brown Simpson and Ronald Goldman. In the criminal trial, he was acquitted of first-degree murder. A civil court later found him liable for their deaths and awarded the plaintiffs a $33.5 million judgment. Eric Garner was choked to death by police officer Daniel Pantaleo after being accused of selling untaxed cigarettes. Officer Pantaleo was not indicted in spite of the video evidence and a coroner's ruling that Garner's death was a homicide, and he remained employed on the police force for over five years after the incident.[1] About a year later, New York City agreed to pay the Garner family $5.9 million rather than face a prolonged civil trial. Trayvon Martin was killed by community watch member George Zimmerman. Zimmerman was charged for Martin's death only after national media scrutiny and was acquitted the following year. The homeowners association settled with Martin's family for an undisclosed amount.[2]

The American justice system responded very differently in these four cases, where the victims represented a range of social statuses, wealth, and races. The resulting criminal trials produced both convictions and acquittals. The financial judgments and settlements reached in the various civil trials were also very different. Much could and has been said about the justice system's varying responses to these four murders. What I wish to highlight here is the fact that the two branches of the justice system take different views on the value of life.

The criminal courts look to punish people who have taken a human life either by murder or manslaughter. The state sits on one side of the courtroom seeking justice on behalf of the citizens, while the defendant sits on the other side of the courtroom. From our broader view of value as referring to "importance or worth," the Fourteenth Amendment's guarantee of equal protection implies that lives have equal value and, contrarily, that lives that are undervalued are underprotected by our legal system. Equal protection does not guarantee equal outcomes. But consistent patterns in inequality in investigations, acquittals, convictions, and death sentences suggest that the criminal justice system places different values of life on different victims and criminals.

The civil justice system does not hold jail time or death sentences as possible punishments. Instead, defendants risk losing money and possessions if they are forced to compensate for, say, an injury or the loss of a life. Civil trial judgments involving deaths provide a clear window into the price tags placed on human lives and the factors that influence those price tags. Both the civil and criminal justice systems shed useful light on how we value life, how we protect it, and with what degree of fairness we do so.

CIVIL JUSTICE

Civil trials are about money, pure and simple. No matter how much a plaintiff might claim that "the money isn't important" or that "money cannot bring back our loved one," these trials are specifically about money.[3] In wrongful death civil cases, the plaintiff is seeking compensation from the defendant, and the key decisions to be made are whether the defendant needs to pay the plaintiff and if so, how much? The award amount can be interpreted not only as an estimate of the personal loss the plaintiffs have suffered but also as a monetary measure of the value of the deceased's life.

People die every day. They die of natural causes or from accidents, or they are intentionally killed. Wrongful deaths are defined as those where a person dies or is killed due to negligence, misconduct, or the intent to cause harm. Wrongful deaths include those caused by medical malpractice, unsafe occupational exposure to dangerous conditions, automobile accidents, and criminal behavior. All civil trials for wrongful death must have a defendant—a party that can be sued. Civil trials involve specific, identified lives that have been impacted by either injury or death. This may be readily contrasted with regulatory agencies, which consider incremental risks to anonymous, statistical lives in their cost-benefit calculations.

When a wrongful death occurs, many different types of damages could be considered. They can include the victim's pain and suffering, funeral expenses, the loss of financial contributions and services the victim was providing and could have provided to his or her dependents, a spouse's loss of the victim's companionship, the trauma and bereavement suffered by the survivors, and the loss of the victim's life itself.[4] In a civil trial, however, the last two items, the survivors' grief and the deceased's life, are often ignored because in most states, civil law attaches no monetary value to life itself.[5] Civil trials focus on costs—both actual costs, such as those associated with the funeral of the victim, and opportunity costs, such as the victim's anticipated years of income and service in the household. This leads to the possibility for a civil judgment to draw the conclusion that no damages should be awarded in situations where money has been saved by the household because the victim is dead. Here, the fictitious Rick, Jim, Anitha, and Sebastian introduced in chapter 2 are once again useful. The life of Sebastian, our soccer-loving six-year-old, received a valuation very different from that of Jim, our financial analyst, which in turn received a different valuation from that of Rick, our firefighter. The September 11th Victim Compensation Fund required a minimum award of $250,000, so all lives had at least some non-zero price tag, in contrast to civil courts, where a value of zero can be awarded.

It is simplest to think of the damages awarded to survivors in a wrongful death lawsuit as belonging to one of three categories commonly used in tort law: economic damages, noneconomic damages, and punitive damages.[6] Economic damages represent the value of all of the financial contributions the victim would have made to the survivors had he or she not died. Lost financial contributions include the loss of the victim's expected earnings and benefits (such as pension plans and health care coverage), the medical and funeral expenses incurred by the death, and the loss of the services the victim would have provided. Economic damages usually dominate the judgments in civil trials, just as they dominated the September 11th Victim Compensation Fund. This is the primary reason why the payouts for the deaths of wealthy business people like Jim were so much higher than the payouts for low-income workers like the aspiring chef Anitha.

Noneconomic damages include the survivors' mental anguish, pain, and suffering and the loss of the love, companionship, care, protection, guidance, advice, training, and nurturing of the deceased.

Lastly, punitive damages punish the defendant financially. This is meant to send a message to the defendant and others and thereby deter similar misconduct in the future.[7] To have a deterrent effect, the award amount needs to be large enough so that, in the future, would-be wrongdoers will weigh a major financial cost against the benefits of committing a similar wrongful activity. Whenever higher price tags are placed on human life, there are more incentives for individuals, companies, organizations, and governments to protect those lives. In any particular case, there is an upper bound on punitive damages, since the Supreme Court has set limits on the allowable ratio of punitive damages to compensatory damages.[8]

In considering the American civil justice system, it is useful to look back to some of the origins of wrongful death judgments, starting with the Bible. Biblical law was extremely strict about wrongful death due to negligence. Exodus 21:29 states that if you knew an animal was dangerous yet let it roam loose and the animal killed someone, then you and the animal should be killed. Tellingly, Exodus 21:30 goes on to explain that the victim's family may accept payment to compensate for the loss of life. In a wonderfully short span of sentences, the principle—the value of a life is reflected in the stated right to take another life—is translated into a price tag—the value of a life is reflected in a price tag to be negotiated. Under biblical law, the victim's family is empowered to decide what retribution they will accept, whether "a life for a life" or "money for a life." Whatever else can be said about this system, the following seems clear: the victim's family holds significant influence over determining how much money a life is worth. If followed religiously, what these two verses from Exodus boil down to is: your money or your life.

English law, from which American wrongful death law traces some of its roots, introduces a crucial nuance. Nearly 1500 years ago, English law established that a killer had to pay the victim's family a compensation amount that was related to the victim's status.[9] The compensation for killing a knight was much higher than that for killing a peasant. In slightly more recent times, the English case *Baker v. Bolton* (1808) began solidifying the legal precedent for civil trials.[10] In that case, the plaintiff and his wife had been in a carriage accident, where the husband was injured and the wife fatally injured—she lingered in pain for a brief span of time before dying. In deciding the case, the jury was instructed that in determining the damages, they should consider only the plaintiff's injuries, the loss of his wife's companionship, and the grief he had suffered on her account from the time of the accident until her death. The life of the dead spouse, however, was left out of the jury's deliberation over a suitable price tag.

The jury instructions given in *Baker v. Bolton* influenced Britain's Parliament to pass Lord Campbell's Act in 1846, which stipulated that financial awards could not be made for the loss of life itself.[11] In America, many states passed similar laws.[12] Only five U.S. states—Connecticut, Hawaii, Mississippi, New Hampshire, and New Mexico—recognize loss of life itself as a damage in wrongful death cases.[13] The forty-five states that do not recognize loss of life as a damage are presenting a limited viewpoint of damages that undervalues the loss that the surviving relatives suffer.

In one legal system, biblical law, ascertaining the price tag of a lost life is left in the hands of the victim's surviving family. In another legal system, English common law, the compensation in a civil trial does not include a value for the loss of life itself. As guiding principles, each system points in the opposite direction of our commonly held notions of fairness.

Economic damages have a heavy influence on wrongful death awards. This can lead to counterintuitive conclusions that many would call inhumane or, at a minimum, that would strike many as being unfair. Consider the fact that the life of a child arguably could have a negative value since the costs of child-rearing, education, and other financial support given to children often exceed the economic value of their future services and the financial contributions the children later make to the family. Because the services and financial contributions of the children will often not be provided until far in the future, their value is weighed less in economic calculations. This concept, called discounting, will be discussed in the next chapter. For now, it is simplest to remember that $1,000 a parent spends on a child today is worth far more than $1,000 a child provides to a parent twenty years from now.

Courts have recognized the logic and moral flaws of determining that the wrongful death of a child incurs no penalty. They sometimes make significant efforts to justify a substantial award in a child death case while staying within the framework of the law.[14] Often, this means leaning heavily on noneconomic damages. Strict application of wrongful death award formulas would add the noneconomic damages (such as the survivors' mental anguish or pain and suffering) to the child's negative economic damages to produce a total that may be a shockingly low award amount. Precisely because it is difficult to accurately project a child's future financial contribution to the family, courts sometimes rely on statistical averages.[15] That the September 11th Victim Compensation Fund used just such a statistical average to assign values to the lives of children like Sebastian suggests the keen awareness that doing so was essential to maintaining appearances of fairness.

The focus on economic losses means that an adult's life can also be determined to have a negative value.[16] This inhumane outcome is not simply a theoretical artifact of civil law. *Thurston vs. The State of New York* (2013) provides an example of how this plays out in the real world.[17] Laurie Thurston's sister, Cheryl, was an inpatient at a state mental health institution. Cheryl was severely disabled and required one-on-one supervision while bathing. While left unsupervised in the bath, she had a seizure and was found unconscious. She died within a day. Cheryl, who was severely disabled and institutionalized, had no lost earnings. New York law allows for compensation for the victim's pain and suffering, but since Cheryl never regained consciousness it was assumed that she had neither felt pain nor suffered. The case was dismissed with no damages awarded. In so glaring an instance, the sense of unfairness was palpable enough for the judge to comment, "The ultimate scandalous irony is that, had Cheryl been chattel rather than a human being, Claimant could recover the lost value of her property. It is repugnant to the Court to have to enforce this law which places no intrinsic value on human life."[18]

Again and again we see the dangers in relying heavily on economic losses for monetary awards and then expecting transparent fairness. New York civil law, by not placing a monetary value on the loss of Cheryl's life, failed to protect her and is also failing to protect any other person who is not providing economic value to their family.

The same logic that prevented compensation for Cheryl's death can prevent compensation in the negligent death of any elderly person who is no longer working and is drawing financial support from his family. If we consider the lack of financial contributions of the elderly and the young, gender pay gaps that lead to men being paid more than women, and racial inequities that place white men most often on the top of the economic pyramid, we can see that focusing on economic losses leads to inequitable conclusions. The Cheryls of the world are more likely to go unattended while taking a bath if it is widely understood that their lives carry a price tag of zero. For many, the courts' reliance on economic losses suggests that a person's life is limited to a simple cash flow analysis, where victims with negative cash flows are not worthy of compensation. To many, this conclusion is inconsistent with basic principles of fairness and human dignity.

A solution seems obvious to anyone affronted by the conclusion that some victims are not worthy of compensation. If we recognized life's noneconomic value—the value we place on the survivors' grief and the loss of the love, companionship, care, guidance, and nurturing they received from the deceased—and the intrinsic value placed on life itself, it would become more likely that a court would conclude that a wrongful death resulted in a net loss to the victim's dependents and thus award financial damages. This solution of using higher noneconomic values and higher intrinsic values of life is not without limitations. Allowing judgments to be heavily determined by the noneconomic and intrinsic value of someone's life without a method for determining this value leaves justice open to the whims of the decision makers. This could create opportunities for prejudices and injustices to enter the judgment process. Applying the same noneconomic value to all lives would eliminate potential inconsistencies, but of course this brings us back to the same criticism that was directed at the option of assigning identical values of life to all September 11 victims: it fails to distinguish between the loss of a Nobel Prize winner and the loss of a convicted serial killer.

There is another way that the laws for wrongful death damages are very restrictive. Compensation is awarded only to survivors who are legally recognized as family.[19] If a person had an expected income but lacked dependents or a spouse, then economic losses are not considered.[20] Unmarried adult victims without children can be left without claimants unless their parents or siblings successfully sue.

Consider our fictitious fireman Rick. At the time of the September 11 attacks, he was engaged to be married that December, but since the wedding had not taken place, his fiancé received nothing after his death. Similarly, Ashley and Anitha, as a same-sex couple, could not be legally married in New York State at that time. Moreover, Ashley was not a dependent of Anitha and was not receiving any financial support from her. After Anitha was killed on September 11, the compensation went to Anitha's family in Indonesia, and Ashley received nothing.

Information about civil suits are often unavailable to the public, but it is well established that awards can vary greatly by jurisdiction and that juries can often attach great values to minor aspects of victim's lives. For example, there is no legal basis for why victims who enjoyed outdoor activities may be valued more than those who preferred watching television at home.[21]

There is yet another way that allowing court settlements to determine a life's value admits a lack of fairness. Some amount of the civil trial judgment is related to the quality of the legal representation. Affluent individuals and companies can afford a team of legal specialists to help identify jurors and legal arguments most predictive of a large award. Imagine two identical legal cases, one where the plaintiff has substantial funds and more skilled lawyers, and the other where the plaintiff is impoverished and employs a less skilled lawyer. It seems reasonable to presume that, on average, better lawyers are more likely to get better judgments. Most tort lawyers work on commission, so a plaintiff with a strong case should be able to find legal representation, but there is no guarantee that this legal representation will be any good. Could we consider a legal system fair if it leaves some significant percent of the task of arriving at the value of life up to legal counsel when the contrast between the quality of legal support for the indigent and the wealthy can be stark?

High-profile cases garner massive amounts of public attention and media scrutiny. The defendants are often challenged to make their case both in civil court and in the court of public opinion. In these highly publicized cases, the settlements no longer reflect just the criteria previously listed. A generous settlement that resolves the case quickly is often a better outcome for the defendant than a drawn-out trial that exposes them to other lawsuits or further reputational damage.

Consider the death of Sean Bell in 2006. Bell and two friends were shot at fifty times by New York City police officers on the morning of Bell's wedding to the mother of his two children. Rather than go to trial, the city settled with Bell's family for $3.25 million. Because Bell was murdered before his wedding, the money could go only to his children.[22] His fiancé was not directly entitled to any part of the settlement. Indeed, Bell's case is an example of the many ways we currently value life, and it raises questions of fairness. The award amount far exceeds the expected earnings of Bell, an unemployed twenty-three-year-old man, and the city would have probably settled the case for a much lower amount absent extensive media attention. On the criminal side of the law, none of the police officers involved were convicted of any crimes, including the officer who shot thirty-one times.[23]

Other high-profile cases have followed a similar pattern. The $5.9 million settlement in the Eric Garner case bears no relation to the expected earnings of the forty-three-year-old man, who was out of jail on bail for selling untaxed cigarettes.[24] Freddie Gray was a twenty-five-year-old with over twenty criminal court cases at the time of his death while in police custody.[25] His death sparked days-long protests and riots in Baltimore. When concerns were raised about the $6.4 million settlement amount, Baltimore's mayor responded by stating, "The purpose of the civil settlement is to bring an important measure of closure to the Gray family, to the community and to the city and to avoid years and years of protracted civil litigation."[26] In short, it was largely untethered to any effort to come up with a just valuation of Gray's life.

Those amounts pale in comparison to the $33.5 million awarded to the families of Ronald Goldman and Nicole Brown in the O.J. Simpson civil trial. The judgment consisted of an $8.5 million award to the Goldman family for compensatory damages and a $25 million award to the Goldman and Brown families for punitive damages. The wrongful death judgment was influenced by a California law stating that the defendant's ability to pay may be considered in the award calculation.[27] The judgment was more money than Simpson had been worth, so it may be considered mostly symbolic.

Wrongful death suits are somewhat unique in presenting clear examples of how life is valued. Consider wrongful imprisonment, where someone was wrongfully convicted and later proven innocent. With the advent of DNA exonerations, such miscarriages of justice are increasingly being identified, and in each case society has robbed a citizen of their freedom, deprived their family and friends of their company and support, and crippled the wrongly convicted of their ability to develop themselves professionally. After release, these individuals are often without money, housing, insurance, or prospects. States that have allowed these wrongful convictions to occur should provide compensation; support for basic necessities like food, transportation, and housing; and social services assistance to get these innocent people back on their feet. This too is a measure of how we value life, in this case how we value the quality of life. But as it turns out, seventeen states do not have compensation laws.[28]

The government sometimes creates limits on liability to financially protect defendants. Recall that following the September 11 attacks, Congress limited the airline industry's financial liability to $6 billion. State governments also can institute limitations on how much they can be held liable for in specific situations, such as wrongful convictions. State-level variations in how wrongfully convicted prisoners are compensated are striking. In Texas, the compensation for a wrongful conviction is $80,000 per year plus an annuity set at the same amount. In 2017, Florida allowed $50,000 annually up to a maximum of $2 million. Louisiana's maximum payment is $250,000, regardless of how many decades the person was wrongfully imprisoned.[29]

Just like high-profile wrongful death cases, high-profile wrongful imprisonment cases have exceptionally high settlements. New York City settled with Barry Gibbs for $9.9 million. Framed by a corrupt police officer, Gibbs spent nearly two decades in prison.[30] A settlement for $21 million was reached in 2019 in California for a man who was wrongfully imprisoned for thirty-nine years.[31] These large payouts can be contrasted with the North Carolina maximum of $750,000, which was awarded to Henry Lee McCollum and Leon Brown, who had both spent over thirty years in prison due to a wrongful conviction.[32]

Like the wrongly convicted, the wrongfully injured are still alive and offer a different window on price tags and principles related to the quality of life. While there is no uniform database to examine injury-related civil judgment patterns, there are interesting observations related to the value of life that can be made from looking at these cases. In most states, the goal of personal injury statutes is to make the victim whole. This can be contrasted with wrongful death statutes, where the goal is to compensate the victim's dependents. In some circumstances, a grievously injured person requiring a lifetime of medical treatment and incapable of working again can receive a price tag that eclipses those of the wrongly killed. Once again, the September 11th Victim Compensation Fund is instructive, for its highest payout was to a severely injured survivor.[33] It seems counterintuitive and somewhat unjust that an award for an injury can be greater than an award for a loss of life, yet this is a consequence of the law placing no value on life itself.

Morally objectionable outcomes are not the only results of wrongful death statutes not accounting for the full value of what is lost. Another is that some people's lives are less protected. The consequence of undervaluing and underprotecting lives is that more wrongful deaths occur than what economists would dispassionately call "optimal." While the idea of there being an optimal number of wrongful deaths sounds cruel, the reality is that these types of deaths will occur, and the civil court's role is both to provide compensation to the families of the victims and to discourage others from causing similar deaths. When the court arrives at an insufficient price tag for life, companies and governments are not sufficiently induced to invest in safety measures.

CRIMINAL JUSTICE

Civil trials pit plaintiffs against defendants, while criminal trials pit the government against defendants. A critical difference is that in a criminal trial, the government must convince the jury that the defendant is guilty "beyond a reasonable doubt."[34] In examining how the criminal justice system responds to murders and vehicular homicides, we can gain insight into how much society values human life in noneconomic terms of importance. From the viewpoint of valuing life, a critical question is whether justice is truly blind. When a murder occurs, does the prosecution proceed irrespective of who the victim was and who committed the crime? Numerous scholars and social critics have tracked the disparities in the American criminal justice system. Inequities in how America treats accused murderers speak to how we value life and specifically to which lives are valued more than others.

For the criminal justice system to punish a murderer, several things have to happen. Evidence must be gathered to determine that the death was indeed a murder rather than an accidental death or suicide. Once the case has reached this stage, an investigation must identify the suspect. Then the suspect must be charged, tried, convicted, and punished by the court. Between the murder and the eventual punishment, many things can impede or influence the severity of punishment. These factors include the ability to identify a suspect, the decision to charge the suspect, the ability to convict, and the variability in sentencing upon conviction. All of these variables influence how criminals are punished. They also speak to how the criminal system values life.

America has a homicide rate that vastly exceeds that of other wealthy countries. Of the thirty-six countries in the Organisation for Economic Co-operation and Development (OECD), only Mexico has a higher homicide rate than the United States.[35] Canada, France, and the United Kingdom all have homicide rates that are one-third to one-fifth that of America's. Firearms are far more available in the United States than elsewhere, far more Americans own firearms, and firearms were used in roughly two-thirds of the nation's homicides.[36] Only one OECD country has a rate that is even half as high as America's gun ownership rate. One inference is that Americans value the right to gun ownership more than they do the cumulative value one could attach to the lives lost to guns annually.

Who you are, who you know, and where you live impact your chances of being killed in America. Homicide rates vary depending on many demographic factors. In America, people aged eighteen to twenty-four have homicide rates that are more than double that of other age groups, and men are more than three times as likely to be killed as women.[37] This pattern of higher homicide rates for younger adults and for men is generally seen in other countries as well.[38] From 2010 to 2012, the homicide rate for black Americans (19.4 per 100,000) was more than three times the rate for Hispanics (5.3 per 100,000) and nearly eight times the rate for whites (2.5 per 100,000).[39] These factors of race and sex combine so that black men are nearly twenty times more likely to be killed than white women.[40] Nearly 15 percent of homicides in America are committed by family members, and nearly 30 percent are committed by friends or acquaintances.[41]

The vastly higher murder rate in the United States in general and in specific communities within the United States raises countless questions, which have inspired numerous authors, investigative journalists, and criminal justice reformers. Here, however, my interest is limited to the following question: What does the criminal justice system tell us about the alignment of principles when it comes to valuing life, both of the murderer and the victim?

American criminal law and biblical law agree that all murders are not equal. Biblical law discusses the value of a slave's life in Exodus 21:20–21, where it is stated, "When a man strikes his slave, male or female, with a rod and the slave dies under his hand, he shall be avenged. But if the slave survives a day or two, he is not to be avenged, for the slave is his money." The conclusion is straightforward. If an owner beat his slave so that the slave died immediately, then the owner was to be killed. If the slave lived a day or two and then died, then the owner was not killed and did not even pay compensation. One interpretation of this distinction between dying immediately and dying a few days afterward is that perhaps the Bible was trying to separate intentional killing (where the victim dies immediately) from unintentional killing (where the victim dies one or two days later).[42] If this interpretation is correct, it is reflected in our modern laws, which provide harsher penalties for premeditated murder than for manslaughter.

Similarly, in the eyes of American law, all murders are not the same. First-degree murder is an unlawful killing that is both willful and premeditated. Second-degree murder is an intentional killing that was not premeditated, a killing caused by dangerous conduct, or a killing caused by the offender's obvious lack of concern for human life.[43] Manslaughter, a lesser crime than murder, is divided into two categories: involuntary (a killing caused by negligence) and voluntary (a killing committed in the heat of passion and in response to adequate provocation).[44] State laws also vary, with types of homicide defined differently in different states. While such distinctions matter little to the murdered, they matter profoundly to the murderer. The penalty for a conviction of manslaughter is different than that for a conviction of murder in the first degree. How numerous questions are answered helps distinguish among types of murders and determine the corresponding charges and punishment.

There is the question of intent. Did the killer intend to murder, or was it an accident? If it was an accident, was the killer negligent? Was the murderer seized by a fit of anger and rage, or was the murder premeditated?

Then, there is the question of whether the murderer had the capacity to make a rational decision. Was the killer mentally ill or disabled? Did the murderer have the cognitive capacity to choose to kill someone? Was the killer of a sufficient age to comprehend the concept of murder?

There is also the question of justification. Was the killer protecting himself or another person?

There is the question of the victim's political status. Was the victim an internationally protected person, such as a foreign diplomat or official? If so, the crime may be elevated from a state crime to a federal crime, as those individuals are more valued by governments and thus receive both greater protection when alive and more severe justice is meted out if they are killed.[45]

Finally, legal status and procedural questions are considered. Was the murder committed in Nevada, where 6 percent of convicted murderers are put on death row, or in one of the twenty-one states where the death penalty is not allowed?[46] From a legal standpoint, it is clear that all murderers and all murders are not viewed the same. Other factors that influence the charges filed and the sentencing include how many people were killed, where the killing occurred, and the killer's background. There is some logic to this hierarchy of homicides, but it inevitably leads to uneven applications of the law. Every step along the way—from the criminal investigation to the last parole hearing or the execution—is open to judgment calls that provide opportunities for potential discrimination based on who the defendant is and who the victim was. Being impartial to the race, sex, lifestyle, socioeconomic class, and family status of the victim and the defendant is difficult, and consistent biases indicate that some lives are more valued, and consequently more protected, than others.

The killing of a homeless heroin addict is not treated the same as the killing of a leading politician, a wealthy businessperson, a famous artist, or some other leading member of society. People who are in vulnerable situations, associate with criminals, or are offenders themselves have higher risks of victimization.[47] It is also the case that the police may perceive these victims as less deserving of their attention.[48] Victims who elicit the most sympathy and the most policing include those who are weak, those who were involved in a respectable activity at the time of the crime, those who were in a respectable or safe location at the time of the crime, those who were attacked by a stranger, those who were attacked by someone considered bad, and those who have been identified as a victim by the community.[49] The perception that some victims are more deserving of police attention than others has been supported by anecdotal evidence from interviews with homicide investigators, who stated that they consider a "true victim" to be someone who just happened to be in the wrong place at the wrong time. This was contrasted with those who were killed while involved in criminal acts in dangerous locations.[50] While this type of anecdotal evidence should be taken lightly, there is statistical evidence to support the fact that clearance rates are significantly lower when the victim was a gang member, drug dealer, involved in illegal activity, or had a criminal record.[51] These lower clearance rates may partially reflect the perception that those lives are less valued by society.

More generally, it is difficult to underestimate the role of the media in generating interest in the deaths of certain individuals and the corresponding reaction by police departments in terms of the manpower allocated to solve the crimes that are most visible in public's eye. Consider the case of Karina Vetrano, an attractive young white woman who was raped and murdered while jogging near her home. Her murder received far more media coverage than nearly any of the other 334 murders that happened that year in New York City. The New York City Police Department responded to this public interest by creating a task force of about one hundred detectives for the case, according to trial testimony that resulted in a criminal conviction.[52] This murder exemplified many of the aspects of those cases that elicit the most policing attention; many of the hundreds of other murders that occurred that same year received only a fraction of the police effort expended on solving Vetrano's murder.[53]

To summarize the clearance rate data, cases involving women and children victims have the highest clearance rates, though some of the difference in the rates is likely due to the circumstances of the murders. There is inconclusive evidence as to whether there is inequity in the clearance rate by race, but investigators are far less likely to solve crimes involving victims whose lifestyle indicated a history of risk-taking, crime, or drug use.

Once the police have identified a suspect, the government needs to decide whether to prosecute and if so, what charges to file. If the homicide is considered to be justified, such as in cases of self-defense or defense of someone else, then no charges are filed. Justifiable homicide is the formal recognition that it is reasonable and legally acceptable for you to value your own life more than the life of someone who is threatening you with potentially fatal consequences.

Florida has a stand-your-ground law that allows a person to use deadly force and does not require a person to retreat if he or she reasonably believes that using force will "prevent death or great bodily harm." This law was originally invoked when Florida elected to not charge George Zimmerman with the murder of Trayvon Martin. Public reaction to the evidence that Zimmerman had ignored police dispatcher instructions made many question whether he had "stood his ground" or rather had instigated an incident with Martin based on racial profiling. While we will never know for certain, it is possible that the case may have been decided very differently if it had occurred in a state that did not have a stand-your-ground law.

Unjustified homicides can result in charges ranging from involuntary manslaughter to first-degree murder. Vehicular homicide is a crime where an individual, other than the driver, dies as a result of either criminally negligent or murderous operation of a vehicle. In a vehicular homicide, the victim could be either a passenger in the vehicle with the offender or a person not in the car with the offending motorist (such as a pedestrian, bicycle rider, or another motorist or passenger in another vehicle). This means that the victim is likely to be somewhat more random than a murder victim and more likely to be considered a "true victim" who just happened to be in the wrong place at the wrong time.

Despite the higher level of randomness associated with being a vehicular homicide victim, inequalities still exist. Shorter sentences are handed out to drivers when the victim is black or male.[54] Shorter sentences are also handed out when the victim is unemployed. This last observation is consistent with the fact that a civil judgment associated with the accidental death of someone who is unemployed will be less than that for someone who is gainfully employed, since lost income is a primary consideration in determining price tags. In terms of vehicular homicide, the lives of blacks and the unemployed are less valued and less protected.

The death penalty is controversial, with many passionate advocates and opponents in the United States. Internationally, the death penalty is not the norm, with the vast majority of countries either not allowing the death penalty for any crime or not executing its citizens in practice.[55] In 2017, twenty-three countries in the world recorded executions. The United States had the eighth highest total, with the list being topped by China, Iran, Saudi Arabia, and Iraq.[56] The United States was the only member of the Organization of American States (with thirty-five member countries) and one of only two members of the Organization for Security and Co-operation in Europe (with fifty-seven member countries) to carry out executions. Clearly, America is an outlier from other high-income countries in its attitude toward the death penalty.

In the United States, the death penalty is legal in thirty-one states. In these states, the justice system is empowered to weigh the value of allowing the convict to continue living against the benefits of terminating a human life. When the death penalty is invoked, the state has concluded that society benefits more from ending the convict's life. This is not to say that the state is saving money by pursuing the death penalty versus life imprisonment. In fact, a number of studies have demonstrated that the costs are substantially higher when the state pursues the death penalty than in comparable cases where the death penalty was not sought. The incremental costs in death penalty cases are due to increased expenses associated with the prosecution, defense, and appeals.[57]

The death penalty is usually applied for murder, though some states have laws allowing it for capital drug trafficking, capital sexual battery, kidnapping, aircraft hijacking, and rape of a child.[58] Capital punishment can be applied to federal crimes even if the state does not have the death penalty. This was the case in the trial of Dzhokhar Tsarnaev, one of the Boston Marathon bombers. Though the crime was committed in Massachusetts, a state that has no death penalty, he was sentenced to death in federal court in Boston.

Many studies have shown that the death penalty is far more likely to be applied in situations where the murder victim was white and the murderer was black.[59] Nationally, the highest death sentence rate is for black defendants where the victim was white, with the next highest rate for white defendants where the victim was white. The lowest death sentence rate is for black defendants where the victim was black.[60]

A higher death penalty rate may be driven by disparities between cases in any or all of the following: the grand jury's decision to indict, the prosecutor's decision to charge the defendant with capital murder, the district attorney's decision to pursue the death sentence, and the jury's decision to impose the death sentence.[61] Texas is the most appropriate place to analyze these four steps, since that one state accounted for approximately one-third of all executions in America between 2011 and 2014.[62] Harris County (Houston) is the epicenter for death penalty cases in Texas, with 116 executions carried out between 1976 and 2015.[63] Harris County's district attorney was more likely to pursue the death penalty when the victim was white than when the victim was Hispanic or black.[64] This racial disparity in pursuing the death penalty occurred despite the fact that black victims were more likely to have been killed in multiple murders than other victims. This further supports the fact that the threshold for pursuing death penalties was higher for black victims than for white victims.

In Ohio, 15 percent of homicides where the murderer was a black male and the victim was a white woman resulted in a death sentence.[65] This 15 percent rate can be contrasted with no death sentences in the twenty cases in which the murderer was a white female and the victim was a black male. More generally, statistical analysis shows that death sentences were more likely when the victim was female or white or when the victim was a child (twelve or younger). When the murderer was a stranger, the chances of a death sentence were also higher.

Analysis of North Carolina murders showed similar results.[66] Murders involving white victims were more likely to result in the death penalty.

Additionally, the death penalty was rarer if the victim was involved in a crime. Both observations are consistent with the clearance rate data.

These observations regarding the racial imbalances in sentencing are supported by the fact that blacks are disproportionately wrongly convicted. In the specific situation of murder convictions, the National Registry of Exonerations has reported that "innocent black people are about seven times more likely to be convicted of murder than innocent white people," and that among prisoners who have been convicted for murder, black prisoners are about 50 percent more likely to be innocent than other prisoners.[67]

The racial imbalances lead to the clear conclusion that despite the end of slavery over 150 years ago, the civil rights movement, historic legislation, and now ubiquitous declarations of equality of justice for all American citizens, black lives are still not protected as much as white lives by the criminal justice system.

These are statistical observations based on a large number of observations, yet there will always be prominent exceptions. O. J. Simpson, despite being a black man accused of killing a white woman and man, was acquitted of first-degree murder charges. His high-priced law team created an elaborate defense case that the plaintiffs, who were relying on public defenders, could not hope to replicate.

It is also true that the state often transparently signals that certain lives are more valuable than others and hence worthy of greater protection. Consider that police, fire fighters, and elected officials are afforded special rights and privileges. In California, the penalty for murdering a police officer is more severe than the penalties for other murders, while in Connecticut, special provisions protect the lives of law enforcement officers, sheriffs, Department of Correction employees, and fire fighters in the line of duty.[68] The additional legal protection provided to people in these occupations may reflect the idea that these people, because of their occupation, may be at greater risk or may indicate that their lives are valued more than others by society. The greater penalties for murdering these people indicate that their deaths are deemed a greater loss to society than the deaths of educated professionals not working in those select professions, including schoolteachers, social workers, doctors, and nurses. The higher levels of protection placed on the lives of these agents and representatives of the state may be due to their vital function in society or have some other explanation. Regardless of the justification, the fact remains that society places different levels of legal protection and, correspondingly, different values on the lives of people depending on the job they perform. Legally mandating that the lives of those working in certain professions are afforded additional protections than lives deemed by the state to be less worthy of protection and hence less valuable directly challenges the notion that justice is blind.

Not only are the lives of these agents and representatives of the state valued more than other lives, but the violent actions they take are far less likely to be punished. In 2018, it was reported that 998 people were shot and killed by police in the United States; similar numbers were reported in 2015, 2016, and 2017.[69] Homicides committed by police officers are rarely prosecuted. Between 1977 and 1995, no New York City police officer was convicted on homicide charges for an on-duty shooting.[70] Of the more than one hundred cases where police killed unarmed black people in 2015, only one officer has received jail time.[71] Often, this is due to the killings being deemed justifiable. There are far more situations where a policeman can legally and justifiably use deadly force than situations where an ordinary citizen can.

Another reason why so few police are convicted of killing citizens in the line of duty is the conflict of interest that occurs when a district attorney charges a police officer.[72] After all, district attorneys must work closely with police officers to do their job, so prosecuting an officer could impede their ability to work effectively in the future. Given America's systematic devaluing of certain lives—principally those of the poor and nonwhite—it is not surprising that Officer Pantaleo was not indicted for causing Eric Garner's death despite the coroner's report that the death was homicide or that none of the officers involved in Sean Bell's death were convicted.[73] Pantaleo's legal punishment would likely have been very different if he had choked someone whose life was valued more by society, such as a famous, wealthy, white rock star, instead of a poor black man.

It is clear that both sides of the justice system—the civil side and the criminal side—do not value all lives the same and, as a consequence, do not protect all lives equally.

Civil court judgments value some lives more than others, and some lives are even given negative values. Plaintiffs in higher profile incidents get higher payouts, and payouts vary by state. Families of top earners receive more than families of low earners. White American households have an average net worth that is estimated at around thirteen times that of black households, and white households have median incomes that are over 60 percent higher than those of black households.[74] The racial inequalities in income and wealth predict that on average, a civil trial award for the death of a black person will be substantially lower than that for the death of a white person. In other words, the fact that whites earn more than blacks indicates that, all other variables being equal, civil trial judgments tend to place higher price tags on the lives of whites than on the lives of blacks.

On the criminal side, the law explicitly favors the lives of police and other actors of the state. Beyond that, the law reads as though it is blind to the victim's gender, race, social status, and criminal history, but the reality is that justice is not blind. Equal protection may be the written law of the land, but data clearly shows that a prosecutor's decision regarding how to charge a crime and the criminal punishments meted out depend on who the victim was and sometimes on who committed the murder. All actors in the legal system, including police, prosecutors, judges, and juries, play a role in this inequity that results in some lives being valued and protected more than others.

Civil and criminal judgments reflect the justice system's assessments of the monetary and nonmonetary value of life, which in turn reflect the degree to which fairness and equality are in fact that system's governing principles. Similarly, regulatory agencies such as the Environmental Protection Agency and the Federal Aviation Administration develop cost-benefit analysis where key inputs reflect the country's regulatory system's assessments of both human price tags and the degree to which all citizens' lives are equally valued. As we will see in the next chapter, both the justice and the regulatory system demonstrate how parts of our government incorporate price tags into their work and how both leave some lives undervalued and underprotected.

4 A Little More Arsenic in Your Water

ACME is a fictional coal-fired power plant located in Michigan, a state that still relies on coal for roughly half of its electricity.* ACME is a medium-sized plant built in the early 1970s that relies on coal brought in by rail from Wyoming. The plant employs a full-time staff of forty-five. In spite of declining profit margins, the owners, fourth-generation Michiganders, continue to support the local women's ice hockey team. Their business outlook is uncertain due to pricing pressures from natural gas competitors and looming new regulations from the Environmental Protection Agency (EPA). The EPA's regulatory decisions have implications for the health of everyone living near ACME, as well as for the livelihoods of ACME's owners, employees, and their families. Regulations that add substantial costs will reduce ACME's profitability and may result in the owners shutting down the plant, moving the plant to another location, or laying off workers. Those same EPA regulations are meant to have benefits, including preserving the health and improving the longevity of those affected by ACME's pollutants.

*All characters and entities appearing in this work are fictitious and have been developed for illustrative purposes only. Any resemblance to real persons, living or dead, or entities is purely coincidental.

The EPA and other regulatory agencies use cost-benefit analysis to identify if the benefits that are gained from stricter regulations outweigh the costs. Nowhere are the risks of lives going insufficiently protected by virtue of their being insufficiently valued more opaque than when it comes to federal regulations. Whether we are talking about coal plant emissions or the amount of arsenic allowed in drinking water, price tags on life are built directly into the daily work of America's regulatory systems. Debates about balancing corporate short-term profits with public safety often pit industry regulators against industry advocates. Other common battles are between different industries, which can be helped or hurt by a potential regulation, and between established industry leaders and disruptive newcomers. When these debates rise to public awareness, the calculations that go into deciding whether a regulation is cost-beneficial or not are often portrayed as rock-solid science. In truth, cost-benefit analysis can be readily manipulated through either unconscious or deliberate choices. These choices may produce conclusions that either overestimate or underestimate the value of a regulation; these are known as biased estimates. Deliberate efforts to produce biased estimates, called gaming, and unconscious choices can both influence the outcomes of the analysis. The real-world consequence of these deliberate and unconscious choices is that lives are often exposed to unnecessary risk.

The dollar amount used for the Value of a Statistical Life and assumptions about the relative value of current versus future lives are often two of the most important considerations in many of these regulatory calculations. To ensure that lives are being suitably protected and not merely gambled on for the sake of maximizing corporate profits, public advocacy, consumer watchdog groups, and the public must vigilantly monitor the arguments and evidence put forth by regulators and industry advocates. This chapter arms you with the basic insights necessary to do precisely that.

Federal regulations, regardless of the industry they regulate, are generally held to similar scientific standards and focus their cost-benefit analyses on impacted populations rather than on known, identified individual lives. As a result, the business cases used to justify a regulation, whether it is issued by the Food and Drug Administration, the Federal Aviation Administration, the Occupational Safety and Health Administration, or the Environmental Protection Agency, all tend to follow a similar method of analysis.[1] Draft regulations and the implementation of government-wide policies are often overseen by the Office of Information and Regulatory Affairs (OIRA), a part of the executive branch's Office of Management and Budget. Part of OIRA's mandate is to "account for benefits and costs, both quantitative and qualitative," while "recognizing that some benefits and costs are difficult to quantify."[2] This mandate (Executive Order 12291, issued during the Reagan Administration) has since been modified by Executive Order 12866, issued by President Clinton, and Executive Order 13563, issued during the Obama Administration.[3]

This official guidance from OIRA of accounting for benefits and costs sounds perfectly logical and fair. The problems lurk in the details, where special interest groups often have undue influence. Cost-benefit analysis can easily be manipulated, leading to distorted results, depending on the influence of politicians, bureaucrats, industry experts, and special interest advocates. Simply put, different people hold different assumptions that reflect their own priorities and interests. As a result, key assumptions and inputs into cost-benefit analysis can vary widely across agencies, researchers, and vested interests. For example, ACME's owners have a clear interest in discouraging the introduction of costly environmental regulations, while those living downwind of the ACME plant have a clear interest in encouraging the introduction of this type of legislation, as they wish to breathe air that does not damage their health.

Cost-benefit analysis is allowed to consider equity, quality of life, and other factors that are difficult to quantify. But precisely because they are difficult to quantify, these factors often get little consideration and are sometimes ignored completely. Instead, quantifiable values, such as the number of preventable deaths and the Value of a Statistical Life, are often key drivers of the benefits in regulatory cost-benefit calculations.

To better understand how cost-benefit analysis can be influenced by special interest groups, it is necessary to understand the intricacies of the analysis. Part of the American regulatory toolbox since the 1930s, cost-benefit analysis is a systematic process for computing and comparing the costs and benefits of a decision, project, or policy.[4] The standard methodology for cost-benefit analysis is well established and follows these clearly defined steps:[5]

1. Identify the possible regulations being considered (including the no regulation / do nothing option)
2. Decide who has standing (whose costs and benefits need to be considered)
3. Select measurement indicators and catalog the costs and benefits
4. Predict the costs and benefits quantitatively over time
5. Monetize all the impacts by assigning dollar values to all costs and benefits
6. Account for the passage of time by discounting the costs and benefits to obtain the present value of each cost and benefit
7. Compute the net present value of each possible regulation by summing the items in step 6
8. Perform a sensitivity analysis
9. Make a recommendation

In reviewing these steps, we will highlight concerns with the standard methodology, including the role that price tags play, equity considerations, and what aspects of the analysis can be influenced by special interests. Some of the most important decisions regarding cost-benefit analysis happen in the first few steps. In identifying the possible regulations, the breadth of options is defined. For example, if the regulation defines the allowable levels of a toxin in drinking water, then the set of possible regulations included in the scenarios would relate to different possible allowable levels. If the possible regulations being considered range from requiring less than 5 part per million, less than 10 parts per million, or less than 20 parts per million, then more restrictive regulations, such as requiring less than 0.1 part per million, are not in the scope of what is being considered. The possible regulations are compared to the status quo—the current state of regulations.

Imagine you are working for the Environmental Protection Agency and are charged with developing a cost-benefit analysis to determine acceptable levels of carbon, sulfur dioxide, and nitrogen oxide in coal and gas power plant emissions. You should identify a set of possible levels of emissions, including timelines to reach those levels, to test in your cost-benefit analysis. These possible new regulations should be compared to the current level of emissions allowed. This analysis does not happen in a vacuum. Power plants fund lobbyists and researchers who try to influence the analysis in favor of their industry. In addition to the power plants, there are other groups that can be affected by the regulation, including the children with asthma living near power plants, the coal miner in Wyoming who is trying to feed his or her family, and the employees of competing gas-fired power plants.

Given the power plant industry's goal of minimizing costly regulations, its advocates will argue that increased regulations will result in prohibitively expensive costs and deliver minimal benefits. These industry advocates can try to tip the cost-benefit analysis in their favor in various ways, such as by trying to limit the number of people who have standing (the people who might benefit from reduced harmful coal plant emissions), providing the EPA with overestimates of the costs of introducing the sweepers and carbon capture methods more stringent regulations would demand, challenging the science that supports the health benefits of improved air quality, suggesting low estimates of the Value of a Statistical Life, and applying large discount rates so that the costs (incurred in the short term) have more weight than the benefits (reaped further in the future).

Once the set of possible regulations has been specified, regulators need to decide whose costs and benefits should be included in the analysis. Analysis can be performed at a local, state, regional, national, or international level. The choice of who has standing is important. If defined too narrowly, groups who are harmed or who benefit may be left out of the analysis.

This issue of ignoring groups who are impacted is clearly seen when the negative consequences of a practice—coal emissions carried by the wind, for example—cross national borders. National regulations that result in transnational environmental impacts are always sources of controversy. When a factory emits pollution that negatively impacts the health of citizens in a neighboring country, those impacts are considered only if those foreigners have standing. If the analysis does not give them standing, the damage to their health and the increased risk of mortality are completely ignored.

ACME's factory is near the Canadian border. When Canadians are given standing in the cost-benefit calculation, both the Canadian and American lives saved by enhanced regulations appear on the benefits side of the equation. This results in a greater estimate of benefits, and as a consequence, a greater justification for the higher costs of more stringent regulations. When Canadians are not given standing in the cost-benefit calculation, the benefits of the enhanced regulation are smaller, and it is more difficult to justify the higher costs of more stringent regulations.

ACME is fictional. Consider now an actual example. Today, many of the people negatively impacted by climate change are not accounted for in cost-benefit analyses because they live outside of the countries emitting the most greenhouse gases and therefore lack standing in national cost-benefit analyses. Standing should be based on who is affected by a program or regulation, which means that a regulation may sometimes need to be analyzed at local, state, national, and international levels.

After determining who has standing, the analyst identifies all of the inputs and outputs, with only the impacts on people who have been established as having standing being included in the analysis. This is a critical moment in the cost-benefit analysis, since inputs and outputs that are not listed do not directly count in the analysis. Inputs and outputs should include a regulation's impacts not only on financial items, like incomes and the consumption of goods and services, but also on more diverse items, including the environment, health, crime, and quality of life.

After identifying the possible regulations, who has standing, and the inputs and outputs, the analyst then has to quantify the impacts over time for each possible regulation. In considering whether the regulation should restrict pollution levels to 5 parts per million, 10 parts per million, or 20 parts per million, the inputs needed and the resulting outputs are estimated for these three possible options, as well for the current legal level.

Usually, projecting the costs of implementing the steps to meet a new regulation is easier than projecting the impacts of that new regulation, since the steps associated with implementing a regulation are often clearer than the potential impacts. For example, if the regulation aims to lower the levels of acceptable emissions from power plants like ACME, then the costs of implementing and operating carbon capture mechanisms and sweepers must be estimated. However, if the suggested regulation is new or there are no previous relevant examples from which to draw assumptions, then estimating the costs is more difficult and often less accurate. The cost estimation is one step where vested interests often lean on the scales. Those who do not want the regulation in place are inclined to advocate that the maximal possible costs and minimal possible benefits be assumed by the regulator, often by exaggerating the economic hardship that a regulation would incur. Those in favor of the regulation are inclined to minimize the estimated costs and maximize the assumed benefits of the regulation.

A majority of the time, the costs of implementing a regulation are overestimated.[6] This may be because analysts fail to anticipate advances in technology. However, overestimations may reflect the influence of industry lobbyists, who, such as in the case of ACME, have much to gain from the costs of reducing air pollutants being overestimated. It is easy to see how industry lobbyists might obtain undue influence over this process. After all, many of America's largest companies pay more to lobbyists than they do to the federal government in taxes.[7] Companies view lobbying activities as business investments meant to influence policy and decision-making, investments that often yield high returns.[8]

On the benefits side, impacts are generally less transparent and usually more challenging to articulate and quantify.[9] The projected benefits need to include not only monetary benefits but also nonmonetary benefits related to improved health, improved quality of life, reduced risk of mortality, protection of biodiversity, and broader environmental impacts. The more complex or unique the regulation, the more difficult it is to accurately forecast its consequences. Generally speaking, the further into the future a forecast is projected, the less clarity there is about cause-and-effect relationships and the accuracy of the size of the effects, so it becomes more difficult to causally and accurately link the benefits to the regulation. Imagine the challenges an analyst faces in trying to develop any reasonably accurate estimate of the impact that a new regulation on bike lanes or carbon emissions will have on citizens' health twenty or thirty years in the future.

After all of the regulations' impacts over time have been predicted and quantified, each of these impacts needs to be monetized. Certain impacts, such as economic growth, are already measured in dollars. While there is uncertainty in the projections, there is no need to convert them to monetary units. In the case of the coal and gas plant regulations, the costs of emission control technologies like scrubbers are already measured in dollars.

In contrast, the impacts on human health and life need to be monetized. These impacts require price tags. This is where the Value of a Statistical Life appears again, though as we will see, not in the way economists often portray. Recall that the Value of a Statistical Life was supposed to represent the amount a population would be willing to pay to reduce a risk of death. This price tag, whether it is $9.1 million or some other value, is estimated using the concept of risk. In estimating that number, economists specifically do not directly ask people to value life (or death) itself. Yet analysts routinely ignore the distinction between the risk of death and death itself when they are performing cost-benefit analyses.[10]

The way this issue should be handled is unambiguous in the Office of Management and Budget instructions. Agencies are told to apply the benefits not from the moment the risk of death is reduced but rather from the moment an expected death is avoided. An avoided death is much further out in the future than a reduction in risk.[11] This switch between how the Value of a Statistical Life is defined and how it is actually applied is a good example of a technical issue that, underneath the equations, has substantial implications. By applying the Value of a Statistical Life only at the moment an expected death is avoided, analysts have pulled a major switch. Risk reduction (the basis for the Value of a Statistical Life estimate) happens immediately, while prevented deaths occur often many decades in the future. By delaying the recording of the benefits for decades, the total benefits of the regulation are greatly reduced due to the application of discounting, a concept that values $1,000 today more than $1,000 in the future.

As mentioned previously, different U.S. government agencies use different price tags, many of which are in the $8–10 million per life range.[12] These varying price tags highlight not only the many theoretical and practical limitations with estimating this value but also the fact that estimates can vary by sex, income, race, occupation, union membership, personal risk tolerance, and when the estimate was made.[13] Given all of the sources of variance associated with estimates of the Value of a Statistical Life, it would be more logical and defensible for the government to use a single value across agencies, a point supported by former OIRA administrator Cass Sunstein.[14]

Ensuring that all agencies use the same price tag would also prevent regulators from trying to assign different values of life to different sectors of the population. The previously mentioned "senior death discount" is a prominent example of this behavior. In their 2004 book *Priceless,* Frank Ackerman and Lisa Heinzerling discuss the time when the EPA tried introducing price tags that valued the lives of people older than seventy less than the lives of younger people. This inequity was stark and not supported by any facts—the elderly do not value their lives any less than younger people do. The EPA backed off amid public furor. Similarly, the Intergovernmental Panel on Climate Change tried establishing values of life that varied depending on a country's wealth until they were pushed to back down.[15] The use of price tags that vary for different segments of the population results in greater protection for the higher-priced lives, since saving these lives results in greater financial benefits than saving the lives of those who have lower price tags. Imagine a proposed regulation that can save either five hundred lives that are valued at $10 million each or six hundred lives, half of which are valued at $10 million each and half of which are valued at $5 million each. The first option saves one hundred fewer lives but would still be the recommended cost-benefit option since the total price tag of the lives in option one exceeds that in option two. This consequence of valuing lives differently is highly unjust. Not only is using the same value for all people the simplest and most logical choice, it also prevents some of the negative consequences that can be justified if analysts are allowed to value some segments of the population more than others. This conclusion is consistent with the one reached by Kenneth Feinberg of the September 11th Victim Compensation Fund, who stated that all lives should be valued equally when determining how to disperse future funds.

More generally, the exact price tag used as the Value of a Statistical Life in these calculations plays a critical role in cost-benefit analysis conclusions. Those wishing to discourage regulations tend to advocate for using the smallest value possible so as to minimize the projected benefits, while those in favor of regulations are more likely to advocate for using higher values.

The Value of a Statistical Life is applied to human mortality, but there are other impacts on human lives that should be considered in cost-benefit analysis, including reduced morbidity, reduction in injuries, reduced anxiety, and improved quality of life. The health and productivity-related benefits, including premature deaths prevented, as well as reduced rates of emergency room visits, hospital admissions, and lost workdays, should be monetized.[16] Other outcomes of regulations, such as environmental impacts, should also be quantified and monetized.

Looking more broadly, nonhuman species—including spotted owls, bald eagles, whales, and less beloved animals—are impacted by environmental regulations. All of these impacts need to be monetized and included in a cost-benefit analysis.

Cass Sunstein starts his book *The Cost-Benefit Revolution* by identifying the strengths of cost-benefit analysis. By the end of the book, he concludes that there are substantial limitations to cost-benefit analysis, including issues handling very large or small numbers of lives saved; unemployment effects; the impacts of small economic losses on large populations; intense emotional reactions; benefits such as increased convenience and ease; situations involving incomplete knowledge; difficult to quantify aspects such as dignity, equity, and fairness; and actions where a practice can cause irreversible harm.[17]

Recall that some economists estimate the Value of a Statistical Life by examining how much people are willing to spend to reduce their risk. This method has clear limitations, yet it is often used to monetize the value of protecting flora and fauna. If estimates show that there is no willingness to pay to preserve a certain species, then the value of protecting that species will be nil in a cost-benefit analysis. Willingness to pay reflects the priorities and values of the people who are surveyed today, not the priorities and values of future generations. Since we can't travel decades into the future, ask people's opinions, and then travel back to today, economists usually assume when running a cost-benefit analysis that today's values are the same as the future's values.[18]

It is worth spending a moment to reflect on this limitation of taking a human-centric perspective that uses today's priorities. This entire book is written from a human's perspective—that is, even when we are discussing appropriate price tags to put on other forms of life, the value of that life is based solely on how much humans value it. It is assumed that the animals themselves have no intrinsic value. Perspectives, priorities, judgments of fairness, and values change over time. Many of the attitudes and standards of behavior that were generally acceptable a few decades ago, let alone a few centuries or millennium ago, are now considered narrow-minded, unacceptable, or even barbaric. Likewise, the human-centric perspective of valuing animal lives may be looked on by future generations as similarly primitive. Future generations may question why some animals, such as panda bears, polar bears, dogs, and tigers, were considered so much more important than the millions of other animal species.

Cost-benefit analysis suffers from an inherent flaw in that not every important impact can be quantified or monetized. This is a critical limitation that results in important items being either ignored or undervalued. Cost-benefit analysis is left with very few tools when the impact cannot be quantified (e.g., How many terrorist attacks will a new regulation prevent?) or the quantity cannot be monetized (e.g., How much is it worth to enhance the quality of life of a specific group of Americans?). In these situations, analysts can perform a breakeven analysis. This entails computing how much the benefits would have to be to justify the regulation. Using a breakeven analysis is a much weaker argument for supporting a regulation since it produces a threshold for the benefits rather than a specific dollar estimate of the net present value. Intuitively, it is clear that a breakeven analysis is far less compelling than an analysis where the impact can be quantified precisely and the quantity can be monetized. Because of this weaker supporting evidence, regulations involving key impacts that cannot be monetized and thus necessitate the use of breakeven analyses are less likely to be supported through cost-benefit analysis.

A cost-benefit analysis should always include a detailed sensitivity analysis. Sensitivity analysis involves systematically identifying the relationships among a range of key input parameters and assumptions, such as the discount rate and the corresponding cost-benefit analysis conclusion. The regulator examines a range of plausible assumptions for inputs and then computes the range of results from the analysis. This systematic sensitivity analysis allows the regulator to present how robust the analysis is and to specifically identify under what set of inputs and assumptions the proposal would be justified or not justified from a cost-benefit perspective.

After monetizing all identified and quantified impacts, analysts can then estimate the dollar values of costs and benefits as a function of time. The exact timing of when the costs are incurred and when the benefits are reaped is critical. Imagine you have two investment options, both of which cost $10,000 and pay back $11,000. The first investment option pays you $11,000 ten years from now. The second option pays $11,000 next year. Clearly, the second option is better, since in a mere year, rather than a decade, you will have $11,000 to spend or reinvest. Without doing any math, it seems obvious that the second option allows you to earn a lot more from your original $10,000 than the first option. While intuition is a good starting point, it is important to use discounting to fairly compare investments and cash flows with different costs and payments over time.

Discounting is applied in a large number of areas, from cost-benefit analysis to corporate financial projections to personal investment planning.[19] Discounting is a standard method for comparing investment options where the financial costs and benefits are distributed over time. The application of discounting to cost-benefit analysis is extremely important to the analysis' conclusions.

Discounting is the opposite of compounding, an idea we are all familiar with from savings accounts. If we put $1,000 in a savings account that pays 3 percent interest compounded annually, after one year there will be $1,030 in the account. We earned $30 of interest on our original $1,000. After the second year, there will be $1,060.90 in the account. Between the first and second year, we earned an additional $30 on our original $1,000 and $0.90 of the interest from the $30 of interest earned in the first year.

From this example of compounding interest, it is clear that $1,000 received today is worth more than $1,000 received in one year, since today's $1,000 can be invested. That leaves us with the question of what exactly $1,000 received in one year is worth today. By using the same formula we used for compounding, we can discount the $1,000 received in one year at a rate of 3 percent to calculate that it is worth approximately $970.87 today. That $970.87 today is the present value of the future cash flow of $1,000 received in one year.

Discounting the predicted costs and benefits puts all of the cash flows that occur over time into a single unit of measure, the present value. When we discount, we are mathematically adjusting the value of future cash flows to represent the time value of the money. The further we go out in time, the more impact discounting has on the present value. At a 3 percent discount rate compounded annually, $1,000 received in one year is worth about $970 today. Using the same discount rate, $1,000 received ten years from now is worth about $744 today, and $1,000 received twenty years from now has a present value of only around $554 dollars.

More generally, the further out in the future the benefits are received, the lower the present value of the benefits. Using discount rates has major policy impacts. For instance, using a discount rate "implies that it never pays a society to spend even a tiny amount today in order to avert an environmental disaster that will destroy the economy as long as the disaster occurs sufficiently far into the future."[20]

Table 1 Relationship between Present Value, Discount Rates, and Years in the Future

	Years in the future		
Discount rate	*10*	*50*	*100*
1%	$905.29	$608.04	$369.71
4%	$675.56	$140.71	$19.80
7%	$508.35	$33.95	$1.15
10%	$385.54	$8.52	$0.07

Changing the discount rate has profound impacts. Recall that $1,000 received in one year has a present value of $970.87 when we apply a 3 percent discount rate. Raise that discount rate to 5 percent, and the present value drops to around $952. Drop the discount rate to 1 percent, and the present value becomes roughly $990. The present value is very sensitive to the discount rate; the higher the discount rate, the lower the present value. And the longer the time horizon, the more critical the discount rate becomes. Similarly, the future amount of your savings account is driven by the interest rate and the length of time your money is invested. Table 1 summarizes the present value of $1,000 received ten, fifty, and one hundred years in the future with a discount rate of between 1 and 10 percent.

Discounting mathematically reaffirms our intuition about which of the two investment options mentioned above is better. It reflects the general idea that a given amount of resources available today is more valuable than the same amount available in the future.

Discounting is not without uncertainty. One of the most basic concerns is selecting an appropriate discount rate. There are a number of discount rates that could be used in this calculation, each with its own justifications and limitations.[21] Since the choice of the appropriate discount rate is open for debate, it is important to pay attention to how that discount rate affects the present value. We have seen that using larger discount rates decreases the present value of benefits that occur further out in the future. This means that the higher the discount rate, the more likely that regulations with near-term benefits will be supported, and the less likely that regulations with only long-term benefits will be supported. Put a simpler way, the higher the discount rate, the more short-term the thinking. ACME's industry lobbyists may encourage higher discount rates so that benefits from improved health and lives saved due to cleaner air that accrue decades in the future appear far less impactful than if a lower discount rate is used. That said, regulators tend to have standard default discount rates, so this may not be an area of major leverage for lobbyists.

When discounting is applied to a financial decision, such as making business investments, the application is elementary, straightforward, and necessary. In that situation, the analyst is faced with investment choices, so incorporating discounting permits investment options that have different timings of costs and benefits to be compared on the same scale, the present value. Analysts who ignore discounting and simply sum the costs and benefits, regardless of when those costs and benefits occur, would ignore the time value of money. This would be a mathematical error that would yield false answers.

Using discounting as part of the decision-making process for business investments is mathematically correct and morally uncontroversial—it represents nothing more or less than putting all of the costs and revenues into the same unit, the present value. What is controversial is when we are no longer speaking about flows of money but rather human lives. While it is clear that $1,000 today is worth more than $1,000 ten years from now, are one thousand lives today worth more than one thousand lives ten years from now? When regulators measure the benefits of a regulation in terms of the lives saved and then insert the Value of a Statistical Life to monetize the impacts, they have converted those saved human lives into a series of benefits, measured in dollars, over time. When regulators discount these monetized values of life, they are comparing not alternative financial investments but rather the present value of preventing deaths in one time period with the value of preventing more deaths in a later time period. The present and future value of money simply does not translate to the present and future value of life, yet this translation is made routinely when a price tag is inserted to represent the value of life and then discounting is applied. Despite issues with discounting the monetary value of human life, this mathematical magic is frequently used as part of the regulatory decision-making process, the outcome of which impacts who is more likely to live a long, healthy life and who is more likely to die a premature death.

Consider two regulations that cost the same amount. The first regulation would save eight hundred lives in the first year it is introduced but no other lives in subsequent years. The second regulation would save one thousand lives ten years after its introduction but none before and none after. Which one would you choose? At a 3 percent discount rate, a cost-benefit analysis would favor the first option. At a 1 percent discount rate, a cost-benefit analysis would favor the second option. To value all lives the same, irrespective of whether the lives are saved this year, next year, or ten years from now, a 0 percent discount rate would be used. In that case, the second regulation would clearly produce the greater benefit. This 0 percent discount rate can occur either as an explicit assumption in the modeling, as part of the sensitivity exploration, or in situations where the assumed value of life increases at the exact same rate as the discount rate.[22]

By applying a non-zero discount rate to the benefits associated with saving lives, a cost-benefit analysis is explicitly assuming that the lives of people in the future are worth less than the lives of people today. This is a dangerous assumption, one that automatically leads to shortsighted decisions that ignore the interests and welfare of future generations. At a 3 percent discount rate, the death of about five thousand people today is equal to the death of one hundred thousand people a century from now—or put another way, at a 3 percent discount rate, the lives of people today would be valued roughly twenty times more than the lives of people one hundred years from now. Increase the discount rate or the time horizon, and the ratio gets even more extreme. This calculation points to the general conclusion that with a positive discount rate, any regulation where the benefits are far enough in the future will be difficult to justify through cost-benefit analysis, since the present value of those distant future benefits will be greatly reduced by discounting.[23] Additionally, the discount rates do not represent the priorities of future generations but only those of current generations.

While there is no perfect solution to discounting after the Value of a Statistical Life has been inserted into the benefits, there are some reasonable approaches.[24] A standard approach to test how sensitive the cost-benefit analysis results are to the discount rate is to vary the discount rate and see how the results are impacted. Another approach is to use a discount rate that declines over time rather than a constant discount rate. This will not eliminate the issue of future lives being valued less than current lives, but it will reduce the impact of the issue.

After discounting all the future monetized values so that each cost and benefit is measured in its present value, analysts then add up these values to obtain the net present value. Regulations that have large positive net present values are said to be financially viable, while regulations that have large negative net present values are not likely to be supported. These net present values are often presented as very precise estimates with detailed explanations of how the estimates were computed.

Sensitivity analysis can be thought of as a systematic exploration of how the uncertainty in the values of important parameters and key assumptions built into a cost-benefit analysis affects the net present value. This is a critical step, since some inputs and assumptions may be very precise, while others may be little more than educated guesses. The range of inputs and assumptions used in the sensitivity analysis is based on the level of uncertainty. The higher the uncertainty, the wider the appropriate ranges in the sensitivity analysis.

Examining how the net present value changes when the cost-benefit analysis uses discount rates of 0 percent, 3 percent, 5 percent, and so on is a standard sensitivity test. This sensitivity lets the regulator understand how important the discount rate is to the cost-benefit analysis conclusions, but it does not address the concern of valuing current lives more than future lives. In order to address this concern, it is recommended to explore the use of two discount rates, one for the costs and benefits that are always measured in dollars and one for the benefits that are measured in dollars only because human lives saved have been monetized.[25] The discount rate for the benefits tied to saving lives should be fixed at zero so that future lives are valued the same as current lives. Sensitivity analysis should be performed only on the discount rate that is applied to costs and benefits that are always measured in dollars. This method allows true flows of money to be treated appropriately from a financial point of view while at the same time not devaluing future lives. Cost-benefit analysis performed this way encourages longer-term planning and favors regulations that could save many lives further in the future.

We have focused on the issues associated with discounting, but it is important to also examine the Value of a Statistical Life. Given the strong concerns about the way this estimate is derived and the very wide range of estimates, a sensitivity analysis should examine the relationship between the assumed Value of a Statistical Life and the net present value. Regulators can report the net present value of a proposed regulation as a function of changes in the Value of a Statistical Life. For example, the regulator could incrementally increase the default Value of a Statistical Life by 25 percent, 50 percent, and so on and report how the resulting net present value changes. The regulator can then incrementally decrease the default Value of a Statistical Life by 25 percent, 50 percent, and so on and again report how the net present value changes.

There is often substantial uncertainty in estimates of how emissions regulations will impact the risk of, for example, cancer deaths. As a result, there is uncertainty in the number and timing of the expected lives saved associated with a new regulation. The scientific literature is mined to identify the level of uncertainty in the impact estimates, and this information is then used to guide the ranges of sensitivity used in the analysis.

Within a cost-benefit analysis, there are clearly a vast number of inputs and assumptions that could be tested using sensitivity analysis. It is reasonable and appropriate to focus on only the inputs and assumptions that are most critical to the net present value calculation. But it is also useful to perform an extreme-case analysis. An extreme-case analysis tests whether there are combinations of reasonable assumptions and inputs that could reverse a net present value calculation, for example, causing a regulation that initially appears to have a negative value to have a positive value.[26]

The goal of cost-benefit analysis is to identify the option with the maximum net present value. The analysis pays little to no attention to who benefits the most and the least from proposed regulations. In the example of coal plants, we know that the poor are more likely to be living nearby and downwind of ACME's power plant. As a result, poorer people are more exposed to ACME's pollutants and health risks than wealthier people.[27]

When equity considerations are not explicitly brought into the calculation, a cost-benefit analysis will not only ignore concerns about social and economic inequality but might even reinforce them. Equity concerns can be represented in the analysis by weighing the costs and benefits experienced by low-income or other at-risk groups differently. Weighing different groups differently is inherently contentious. A more transparent means of ensuring that the regulations take equity into consideration is to produce cost-benefit estimates for specific populations, such as high-risk and low-income groups. This way, the analysis is from the point of view of a specific population and reflects only their costs and their benefits. Population-specific analysis makes it clear who is truly reaping the benefits from a regulation and who is truly paying a price, in dollars and in lives.

Regulators have a daunting task. They seek to defend the public good against some of the dangers of unfettered capitalism. Regulators need to develop regulations that are fair, feasible, and protect both the current world and the future world. At the same time, they need to demonstrate that the regulations do not create undue harm to business. Their work is performed under major restrictions, and regulators have to defend their recommendations through an analysis of costs and benefits, a method that we have seen is filled with potential for undue influence, false assumptions, and major uncertainties in even the least biased analysis.

The well-meaning regulators' goal of defending the public good is all the more difficult given the substantial means at the disposal of certain industries and interest groups. Industry special interest groups seek to maximize the profits of their clients. They often have a stated or unstated goal of minimizing regulations while either ignoring the costs associated with the damages their products may cause or passing the cleanup bill to the public.

For example, the EPA issued an order to limit the emissions of mercury, arsenic, and acid gases from coal-fired power plants in 2012 and later performed an analysis to determine the allowable emissions standards. Industry groups representing power utilities and roughly half of the nation's states sued the agency.[28] The case went to the Supreme Court, where it split straight down party lines.[29] The court concluded that the EPA's analysis must take costs into consideration before issuing regulations. When the EPA did run their cost-benefit analysis, it estimated that the benefits of the regulation would prevent up to 11,000 premature deaths and 130,000 asthma cases annually. It valued these benefits at between $37 billion and $90 billion, a tiny fraction of the costs of the regulation. However, the calculations performed by the EPA and the industry lobbyists were very different. Industry groups estimated that far fewer lives would be impacted and valued the benefits at merely a few million dollars a year. Two different groups, the EPA and the industry lobbyists, performed analyses of the same regulation and developed two radically different estimates of the benefits.

The powerful influence of special interest groups can sometimes lead to regulatory capture, a form of political corruption where a regulatory agency advances the concerns of the industry interest groups it is charged with regulating rather than acting in the public interest.[30]

Regulators can also be heavily influenced by more senior members of their own administration. After the September 11 attacks, the White House reviewed and changed EPA statements about the public health risks in New York City, specifically for those living and working near Ground Zero.[31] Reassuring statements were added, and warnings such as cautions to asthma patients, the elderly, and people with existing respiratory diseases were removed.[32] The goal of this whitewashing was to "reopen Wall Street." Protecting the health of people living and working near Ground Zero was apparently less important, another tradeoff of dollars and lives.

These examples demonstrate many of the issues and flaws of cost-benefit analysis. The method is subject to the influences of interested parties trying to game the system in their favor. These analyses are politicized, with industry experts seeking to overestimate the costs and underestimate the benefits and activists try to do the opposite. This is sometimes euphemistically called *strategic bias*. Given the influence that industry lobbyists wield over the government, public advocacy and consumer watchdog groups must vigilantly watch the details in the analysis. Industry often brings vast resources to its efforts to influence cost-benefit analyses, with the goal of maximizing short-term profits and minimizing regulations while ignoring negative externalities in its business models.

Although the flaws in cost-benefit analysis are rampant, it is still defended by its advocates as a dispassionate means of determining the best way forward. Regardless of its limitations, cost-benefit analysis will continue to be used as a standard tool, meaning that it is critical to know its flaws and the ways it can be used as well as misused. At a minimum, public advocacy and consumer watchdog groups should understand the key issues and limitations in cost-benefit analysis identified earlier in this chapter in order to keep both industry advocates and regulatory agencies honest. Moreover, by understanding the details, public advocates and consumer watchdogs can encourage this method to be used to support regulations that provide more equitable outcomes.[33] Opportunities generally exist for the public to express opinions, since Executive Order 13563 states that agencies, "where feasible and appropriate, should seek the views of those who are likely to be affected."[34]

One of the flaws of cost-benefit analysis is the fact that it often relies on the Value of a Statistical Life as a primary input. We have already seen that this price tag on life is subject to vast amounts of theoretical and practical problems. That said, a strength is that Value of Statistical Life estimates are substantially higher than most people's expected earnings, so the benefits associated with this value are much higher than if the analysis were simply based on average financial impacts.

A second flaw is that analysts generally insert the Value of a Statistical Life not to represent when the risk increases but rather to represent when a death occurs. This ignores the fact that the Value of a Statistical Life is supposed to represent increased risk of mortality, not mortality itself. The consequences of this switch are substantial. Following this switch, the benefits appear much further in the future and are greatly diminished once discounting is applied.

A third flaw is related to how discounting is used. After the Value of a Statistical Life has been inserted, human lives have been monetized. Those lives are now treated as though they are financial investments that have compounded interest. Discounting the value of these lives results in analysts valuing lives in the future much less than lives in the present.

A fourth flaw is that within cost-benefit analysis, important factors that cannot be quantified or monetized are often either ignored or have minimal influence.

A fifth flaw is that there is an asymmetry in that the cost elements are usually relatively complete and commonly overstated, while the benefit elements are often incomplete and understated.

A sixth flaw is that cost-benefit analysis often does not pay attention to equity, ignoring the question of who would benefit the most and who would lose the most from the implementation of a new regulation.

A seventh flaw is that cost-benefit analysis is subject to gaming, as evidenced by how much the estimated costs and benefits of a regulation vary depending on the interests of the group conducting the analysis.

I certainly do not advocate for ignoring cost-benefit analysis. A mechanism needs to be in place to examine the costs and benefits of regulations to prevent implementing regulations that provide little or no benefit but incur huge costs. The government is, and should continue to be, required to provide justification for regulations so as to ensure that citizens are protected and industries are not crippled. This should be true not just for environmental or transportation regulations but for all major government programs and expenditures. The government needs to ensure that there is maximal transparency in all of its cost-benefit analyses, where the assumptions and sensitivity analyses are easily available for review and, when possible, equity considerations are clearly examined. At the same time, regulations should do their best to guarantee that industries are paying the costs associated with their operations rather than passing these bills on to the public.

Imagine if government decisions and investments, from military expenditures to airline security, were subject to the same level of scrutiny as environmental regulations. We have seen the detailed and heated exchanges associated with government regulations that impact industry's profitability, but regulations related to national security are often readily implemented with little or no analysis. Often, there is little consideration given to how many lives will be saved or need to be saved to justify the incurred military or security expenses. Some would argue that this is due to the difficulty in computing the benefits of these expenses, yet the same argument could be made for many other expenses and proposed regulations. Others would make the case that investments in national security are absolutely necessary for the continuing viability of the country, so they should never be subject to cost-benefit analysis. The more cynical would say that the comparatively lower level of scrutiny for national security expenses is a ramification of America's military-industrial complex and the extremely tight relationship between the security industry and government officials.[35]

Regardless of the explanation, the reality is that large swathes of government are empowered to act irrespective of the costs or projected number of lives saved or lost. Simultaneously, other government agencies, like the Environmental Protection Agency and the Federal Aviation Administration, are required to present detailed analyses littered with numerous technical and practical limitations before they can enact any regulation.

But for all of its shortcomings, cost-benefit analysis has the merit of forcing analysts to explicitly declare the inputs and assumptions that were made. This guarantees some level of transparency and accountability. Additionally, it gives independent review committees the ability to scrutinize the analysis. Sensitivity analysis must always be performed on key inputs that affect the impact estimation. The standard practice of exploring the sensitivity of an analysis to different discount rates should be extended to exploring the impact of changing the discount rate for the flows of money while setting to zero the discount rate associated with the lives saved. This method would force analysts to reveal the conclusions of the cost-benefit analysis when future lives are valued as much as current lives and flows of money are treated appropriately.

There needs to be a standard practice of performing a vigilant review of all benefits that are not quantified or not monetized to ensure that they aren't simply ignored. Equity considerations must be front and center, not pushed off to a sideline exercise that is occasionally explored.

The objectivity, validity, and robustness of cost-benefit analysis should not be oversold. Cost-benefit analysis allows for a large range of possible net present values depending on the analysts' preferences and predispositions. Anyone performing or presenting this type of analysis should do so with transparency and humility so that the media and the public are not given the mistaken impression that it is a precise science.

Cost-benefit analyses are also performed by financial experts within companies, though the perspective and the scope of these analyses are different, and in these applications it is often referred to as "financial analysis." The next chapter discusses two very different aspects of how business values human lives: cost-benefit analysis and labor markets.

5 Maximizing Profits at Whose Expense?

In the late 1960s, Ford Motor Company decided to introduce a low-price car, the Pinto, into the American car market. To meet deadlines, the time from design to distribution was compressed, and this rush to production created opportunities for mistakes. Ford crash tests showed that the Pinto did not meet the safety standards being proposed at that time by the National Highway Traffic Safety Administration (NHTSA) to reduce fires from traffic collisions. These standards were supposed to be introduced in 1972, with the safety level to be further raised the following year. The crash tests also showed that minor modifications to the Pinto design, such as adding a rubber bladder in the gas tank, would make the car safe enough to meet the upcoming NHTSA standards.

Ford prepared a cost-benefit analysis for submission to the NHTSA. This analysis, infamously known as the Ford Pinto Memo, was specifically prepared to dissuade regulators from passing new safety standards. The analysis monetized the options of modifying the Pinto to make it safer or introducing the car unchanged, including the costs of incremental injuries and deaths.[1,2]

Cost-benefit analyses performed by businesses, in this case Ford, use a price tag for human life to evaluate business decisions that may result in injury or death. Companies seek to maximize profits by optimizing the trade-off between business costs and lives saved. The labor market represents an alternative window into how businesses value lives, as there is an explicit trade-off of an employee's time in life versus money. The labor market spans a broad range of circumstances, with the extremes defined by slaves on one end and free-will employees on the other end. In all these circumstances, a price tag is placed on each employee's time, a price tag that may be infused with inequities.

BUSINESS DECISION-MAKING USING COST-BENEFIT ANALYSIS

Regulatory agencies and for-profit companies both perform cost-benefit analyses, but there are key differences in how they do it. Regulatory agencies conduct social cost-benefit analyses that must account for the total costs to society, including both private costs and external costs. Companies conduct private cost-benefit analyses focused on their own bottom lines. A company's costs are limited to those reflected on its income statements, known as private costs, so cost-benefit analyses conducted by a company are specifically from the perspective of that company. Costs that are incurred not by the company but by society are known as external costs. External costs are ignored when companies perform cost-benefit analyses. Cost-benefit analysis is intrinsic to the decision-making process of companies, and analysts are tasked with helping companies maximize profits by choosing between alternative strategies.

Imagine you are an executive at a car manufacturing company. You have data that shows that one of your car models has a design flaw so that ordinary traffic collisions have a high chance of causing a fire. As the decision-maker, you need to choose between either recalling the model so that the cars can be fixed or ignoring the problem despite knowing that this issue will likely cause some people to die or be injured. A recall will result in some short-term bad press as people will fear purchasing your vehicles, and it will damage your company's short-term profits. Ignoring the design flaw may lead to the death of innocent people as well as the risk of future lawsuits and damage to the company's brand.

It is naïve to think that for-profit companies exist primarily for the benefit of society. These companies seek profits by providing goods or services, a pursuit that often enhances the lives of their customers, but the company's fundamental purpose is to make money. This is not a vilification of for-profit companies but rather a reminder of what defines their priorities. Given this primary purpose, it is unrealistic to expect companies to ignore profitability concerns when making decisions about valuing and protecting lives. This does not suggest that companies are all heartless organizations blindly pursuing profits. Companies sometimes make business decisions that are driven by the moral or ethical standards of their executives and not purely by profits, but a company that continuously makes decision without regard to profitability may soon be out of business.

While some might want car companies to invest in eliminating every potential risk to drivers, passengers, and pedestrians, this idealism is both naïve and unrealistic. Although these statements about the priorities of for-profit companies are somewhat obvious, revelations of the details that companies use to drive their cost-benefit analyses often invoke strong, negative reactions from the public and from jurors in civil court cases.

Major problems that greatly increase the risk of accidents, injuries, or deaths are most critical to our hypothetical car company. But how large does the increase in risk need to be to prompt a company to take an action such as a recall? No car company could stay in business if it issued recalls for every possible flaw and concern. One way for the car company to reach an informed decision is to conduct a cost-benefit analysis that compares the net present value of at least two scenarios: in this case, recalling the structurally flawed cars or ignoring the issue and settling lawsuits and paying regulatory fines later. Of course, the car company has information on customers' willingness to pay for safety features and other market research that can be used to inform the cost-benefit analysis.

Comparing these two options involves similar steps to those taken by the EPA when it examined the net present value of adjusting emissions regulations, but as noted before, there is a key difference: car companies perform cost-benefit analyses with a focus on their own revenues and costs. This reflects the car company's narrower mandate to generate financial returns for its owner. Two important steps within a company's cost-benefit analysis are quantifying the impacts over time and monetizing those impacts. To quantify the impacts, the car company needs to estimate the expected number of accidents, injuries, and deaths over time attributable to the structural flaw of the car in question. For example, the company might estimate that due to this flaw, there will be ten injuries and five deaths annually. To move from this impact quantification to monetization, the company now has to insert a cost for each injury and for each death. These costs reflect the company's best estimate of what it would have to pay in a civil case if found guilty. Additionally, the company will include some estimate of the sales lost and the damage to the company's reputation due to negative publicity.

The company could hire researchers to comb through similar cases to obtain a reasonable estimate of the price being placed on people killed in wrongful deaths lawsuits where the car company was found to be at fault. But many of these settlements are sealed, so this would provide only a glimpse at the total number of cases; researchers would be right to be concerned that the estimated price tag from so limited a sample would be biased. The company could also get insight into expected judgment amounts by holding mock trials. Mock trials often take place in rooms decorated to look like courtrooms, with lawyers arguing for both sides and statisticians analyzing the factors influencing the mock jury's judgments.[3] Mock trials are often useful in helping identify the factors that influence jury decisions, but the financial judgments in a mock trial may not be representative of the amounts determined in a real-world trial.

Cost-benefit analyses involving issues where human health or lives are put at risk will require the company to put a price tag on life. In addition to the costs associated with lost health and lost lives, the company needs to weigh factors related to brand identity and the potential negative impacts on future sales of issuing a recall or of ignoring the safety issue, as well as any potential regulatory fines. A sensitivity analysis should be performed before a decision is made. This sensitivity analysis is similar to the one performed by regulatory agencies in which a range of possible values for key assumptions, such as the risk to the public and the price tag on life, are explored and the resulting net present values are computed. The higher the assumed price tag on life—in this case the expected amount the car company would need to pay per victim—the more likely it is that the car company will perform an immediate recall to protect lives and avoid the costs of future lawsuits. The less the lives are valued, the more likely it is that the company will ignore the structural flaw and wait to see how much it will need to pay in lawsuit settlements and regulatory fines. This is another situation where the lives that are less valued are left less protected.

The car example is not theoretical. The decision to invest more in safety devices or fix technical issues is faced routinely by car manufacturers and more broadly by any company creating products that pose risks. The Ford Motor Company's experience with its Pinto subcompact represents a classic case of business ethics and exemplifies how companies incorporate price tags on life into their decision-making process.[4]

Modifying the Pinto to improve safety would incur design and production costs and delay the product's rollout, thus giving foreign companies more time to capture domestic market share. The redesigned Pinto would meet the safety standards set to be introduced and consequently put fewer people at risk. Introducing the car unchanged would save the company money in the short term but increase the risk of costs the company would likely have to pay later. Those who ended up suffering because of the structurally flawed vehicle—the victims of preventable injuries and the families of those who died unnecessarily—may sue the company for damages. Regulators may issue fines to the company for failing to adequately disclose and resolve safety issues. The Ford brand would likely be hurt by the negative publicity, which would impact sales of other Ford cars. Also, when NHTSA's new regulation was passed, the improvements would need to be made anyway to meet the new safety standards. In summary, Ford needed to make a business decision. Would it incur the immediate costs of a recall and repair the affected vehicles or delay the recall and pay out settlements and other expenses sometime in the future?

Key inputs into Ford's calculation included the costs of the modifications; the impact of the time delay on sales; the increased risk of accidents, injuries, and deaths; and the value of a human life. For this last input, the company had guidance other than mock trials and prior settlements. At the time, most federal agencies were using a price tag of $350,000 for each human life, though the NHTSA was using a price tag of $200,000 for a human life and $67,000 for a burn victim.* By using

* Note that all values reported in the Ford Pinto example are in 1972 dollars and have not been adjusted to current values.

the lower value, Ford was able to reduce the projected benefits of fixing the design flaw. Ford assumed that the cost of repairing each vehicle would be $11. Other companies (including Goodyear) later suggested the repair could have been done for about half of that price. Selecting the higher unit repair cost resulted in higher assumed costs for fixing the design flaw. Not surprisingly, Ford computed that the total costs of the repairs would vastly exceed the economic benefits of the lives saved and that it would be financially sensible to not implement the repairs.[5]

In 1974, the Center for Auto Safety petitioned the NHTSA to recall Ford Pintos, but no action was taken until 1977, when *Mother Jones* released a scathing article about the car. The article immediately caught the nation's attention. Ford issued a recall in 1978, ahead of an NHTSA order to do so.

For many Americans, this case was their first clear glimpse into how human lives were monetized and how deaths were treated as a "cost of doing business" by some companies. In general, many Americans continue to be unaware that price tags are routinely placed on their lives and are disturbed when examples of this type of activity come to their attention. Moreover, in the short news cycles of American media, examples of deaths being treated as a business expense fade very quickly from the public's attention. The dollar amount Ford used for a human life triggered more public interest in economic valuations of human life. The public awareness and concern for how human lives are monetized and how these price tags are used spurred more scrutiny and research into the subject.

Ford was not interested in a theoretical calculation about the economic value a human life adds to society. The company specifically cared about how much it would need to pay per victim and had estimated that it would be $200,000 per preventable death. As it turned out, the civil trial damages were much more than Ford had assumed. In the case of *Grimshaw v. Ford Motor Co.*, the California Court of Appeal upheld compensatory damages of $2.5 million and punitive damages of $3.5 million against Ford.[6]

What about the regulation that the NHTSA had been proposing to implement in 1972? Lobbying by Ford and other car companies delayed the adoption of NHTSA crash standard until 1978. The car industry leveraged their collective government influence to extend short-term corporate profits by delaying the need to implement improved safety standards.

Delaying the implementation of stricter regulations may have made good financial sense for Ford, but it resulted in more lives being put at risk of injury and death.

As in many other industries, the car industry's lobbying activities could have generated a very high return on investment for Ford. If the 1977 *Mother Jones* article had not galvanized public interest, many more lives would have been sacrificed based on Ford's questionable cost-benefit analysis assumptions. Not only did the company have to pay legal damages, but its reputation suffered, and the case has become a textbook example in business ethics classes. One year after the *Mother Jones* article was published, Henry Ford II fired the company's president, Lee Iacocca.[7]

The Ford Pinto example is not an isolated case. More recently, major car companies, including Toyota, Volkswagen, and General Motors, have drawn negative press, Department of Justice investigations, and numerous lawsuits for delaying the recall of faulty parts that caused unnecessary risks and sometimes deaths. Safety, profits, and the value of human life are routinely balanced by companies in many different industries, as these companies are incentivized to produce short-term profits, sometimes at the expense of human lives. Because many of the key inputs and assumptions used in cost-benefit analyses have wide ranges of uncertainty, there is room for analysts to potentially develop different conclusions depending on their motivations and incentives.

Multibillion-dollar companies are rarely naïve, and they have vastly greater assets and political influence at their disposal than all but the wealthiest individuals. Companies usually identify their options, assess the costs and benefits, and then make informed decisions. Roughly forty years after the Ford Pinto case, car executives continue to protect the corporate bottom line by making assumptions about how much their companies would have to pay in the future for lives damaged or lost as a result of their products.

In the case of General Motors, the Department of Justice concluded in 2005 that more than one hundred deaths were tied to faulty ignition switches that the company delayed recalling.[8] More damning was the fact that this fault had first been identified by the company's own engineers in 2003.

Toyota was not only aware of the fact that its vehicles had acceleration issues but also hid the data. The company knowingly allowed injuries and deaths to occur during the period between first recognizing the issue to when the recall occurred. The company admitted criminal conduct and agreed to pay $1.2 billion in damages.[9]

Volkswagen made a different business decision that pitted profitability against environmental damage and human lives. It installed software in millions of its diesel cars that allowed the cars to pass emissions tests. The software was programmed to deactivate the emission controls once the cars were out of the laboratory, resulting in the cars spewing emissions at up to forty times the allowable level.[10] In total, about 11 million cars were designed to cheat the emissions tests.[11] The environmental damage and negative health impacts attributable to this fraud are likely to be substantial.

In each of these situations, the car company, whether it was Ford, Toyota, General Motors, or Volkswagen, knowingly placed human health and lives in jeopardy to further their narrow interests of enhancing corporate profits. These billion-dollar companies are well equipped with analysts who are tasked with performing cost-benefit analyses and giving management recommendations as to how it should proceed. These situations highlight the critically important public function of regulatory agencies. These agencies balance the scales of fairness by trying to ensure that lives are sufficiently protected, yet they must be sufficiently staffed, funded, and supervised to be effective.

In all of these examples, there was a known risk. The companies were aware of the problem and still made business decisions that resulted in avoidable deaths. When corporations conduct cost-benefit analyses, they identify and then analyze the possible business options. In the case of a defective product, options include major efforts, such as recalling the product and providing a complete replacement, and minor efforts, such as offering a limited set of repairs, ignoring the defect, or, as in the case of Toyota, intentionally hiding data regarding safety defects.

Companies then need to decide who has standing, meaning who exactly should have their costs and benefits considered. As seen in the previous chapter, the decision of who has standing is critically important. When standing is defined too narrowly, people who are harmed may be ignored in the analysis. Anyone impacted by the decision should have standing, but there are different types of impacts—direct and indirect. In the case of a defective car that results in injuries or death, those who are directly impacted are the people injured or killed, and those who are indirectly impacted are the affected family and friends. The estimate of the total impact—direct plus indirect—is a crucial piece of a cost-benefit calculation. If the total impact of the defect is underestimated, then the cost-benefit analysis will be biased toward the option of ignoring the defect and paying lawsuits and fines later.

After quantifying the scenarios, including identifying the expected number of people impacted through injuries or death, all items have to be monetized. In the Ford Pinto case, the value placed on life was lower than the figure regulators in other agencies were using. Unsurprisingly, the lower the price tag a company puts on life, the less likely the company will try to protect those lives and the more likely it will be to pursue short-term profits by ignoring the risks placed on the health and life of the public. If civil trial verdicts place a very high price tag on human life, that high price tag will appear in corporate cost-benefit calculations, and the result will be that companies will need to invest more in safety and will be less likely to ignore a known safety risk.

The Value of a Statistical Life, with all of its logical and computational flaws and limitations, is often the price tag used by regulators. Companies are more concerned with how much they will lose in potential lawsuits, so they do their best to estimate expected civil suit judgments and use that value as the price tag on human life. The choice of price tag demonstrates the difference between a cost-benefit analysis performed by a regulatory agency, which is focused on the total impact on society, and one performed by a company, which is focused only on the costs that impact the company's bottom line (private costs) and ignores external costs.

Companies have greater incentives to address safety risks that pose immediate dangers for two reasons—causality and discounting. Causality refers to the relationship between the safety issue and the resulting damage. In general, the shorter the time period between the safety issue and the resulting damage, the easier it is to prove that the company was at fault. If the engines of a certain brand of car spontaneously catch on fire and passengers die, it doesn't take a lot of investigation time to mount a case against the company that produced the cars. On the other hand, if the damage doesn't appear for decades, then causality is more difficult to demonstrate. Consider the relationship between smoking tobacco and the increased risk of lung cancer. The long lag between smoking and developing lung cancer allowed tobacco companies to misdirect some people into thinking that other factors were causing lung cancer in smokers, not their product.

The length of time between the introduction of a dangerous product and the appearance of resulting damage from that product also relates to discounting. A consequence of discounting in financial calculations is that a profit of $100 million today more than offsets $100 million in losses in a civil trial in ten or twenty years because of the time value of money. The longer it takes to prove a company was at fault, the more motivation that company has to not correct the safety issue.

There is another incentive not to act when it is assumed that it will take decades to establish the link between a dangerous product and the resulting damages: the corporate executives involved in the original decision to ignore the risks are unlikely to still be at the company ten or twenty years later when the long-term health consequences are exposed. They may be long retired at that point and well insulated from any financial losses and legal responsibilities when the company is forced to settle or plead guilty. By comparison, safety risks that pose immediate threats can affect executives' corporate bonuses, their reputations, and the company's short-term bottom line.

Balancing profits and safety happens in many industries. Companies cannot simply build 100 percent risk elimination into every part of every product. Defects in design, manufacturing, and labeling can and do occur in a broad set of industries and products, including drugs, medical devices, toys, and household products. Industries would grind to a halt if they were expected to eliminate all risks associated with their products without paying any regard to the likelihood of a defect causing harm or to the severity of that potential harm. Safety investments are always balanced with the expected cost of repairs or recalls. Given that companies cannot eliminate every possible risk, regulators play an important role in ensuring that certain specific risks are not ignored by companies and, more generally, that lives and health are fairly protected. Without appropriate safety regulations, companies that invest in developing safer products may get pushed out of the market by companies that produce riskier but less expensive goods. One of the roles of regulations is to fix this type of market failure by ensuring that minimum standards exist and are enforced.

The ethics of corporate executives also affect corporate decision-making, but morality considerations are often subjective and insufficient for running a company. In situations where corporate executives knowingly deceived the public and regulators about the safety of their products, it is a rare event for those executives to ever be charged with, let alone convicted of, committing a crime. A consequence of decision-makers being de facto insulated from prosecution is that it is increasingly important for public advocates to try to influence the inputs used in cost-benefit analyses, such as by encouraging the use of large price tags on life and ensuring that all affected people have standing.

The balancing of profitability with safety and human lives occurs across industries where companies are acutely aware of litigation risks and potential losses. The Union Carbide disaster in Bhopal, India, took the lives of roughly four thousand people and produced a similar number of severe and permanently disabling injuries.[12] It was settled in 1989 for $470 million, a price tag of roughly $60,000 per victim.[13] In 1989, the average income of people living in India was less than one-twentieth that of Americans.[14] The comparatively low price tag placed on the loss of these lives may have reflected the fact that these victims were not high-income earners. It is safe to speculate that the payout would have been substantially higher had the accident occurred in the United States, where incomes are much higher and the financial penalties for failing to protect lives is far steeper.

The fashion industry has seen similar tragedies. Fashion companies often outsource production to lower-wage countries like China, India, Bangladesh, and Vietnam. In 2013, a factory complex collapse in Bangladesh resulted in roughly 1,100 deaths and 1,500 injuries. The International Labor Organization established a victims' compensation fund financed by the fashion companies that had produced their products at the complex. A total of $30 million was raised, which corresponded to less than $40,000 per death.[15] The workers in Bangladesh earned only a fraction of the income of American workers. Just as with the Union Carbide disaster, a consequence of these victims not being high-income earners was that the price tag placed on their lives was low. Again, there is little doubt that the compensation would have been significantly higher had the collapse occurred in a wealthier part of the world, such as the United States or Europe, where worker safety is more vigilantly protected.

Morality and ethical considerations are not sufficient for corporate decision-making, but they should play a role alongside financial and legal restraints. The corporate approach to valuing human lives through cost-benefit analysis may have reached a moral nadir with the infamous 2001 report commissioned by Phillip Morris then developed and written by the consulting firm Arthur D. Little International.[16] The report's cost-benefit analysis made the business case that the government of the Czech Republic should encourage smoking because the premature deaths of smokers are revenue-positive for the government. While this was not the first business case to argue that premature deaths due to smoking are good for public coffers, it attracted the most attention.[17] The Wall Street Journal quoted Professor Kenneth Warner as saying, "Is there any other company that would boast about making money for the public treasury by killing its customers?" The same article quoted Phillip Morris's spokesman defending the work by stating, "This is an economic-impact study, no more, no less."[18] In reaction to the criticism from the public and politicians, Philip Morris soon issued a formal apology for the report, stating that financing and distributing the study "exhibited terrible judgment as well as a complete and unacceptable disregard of basic human values."[19]

Arthur D. Little's cost-benefit analysis focused on the Czech Republic's public finances, specifically the country's national and municipal budgets and the budgets of health insurance companies in 1999. Their analysis did not include the private costs of smoking, the private costs of any of the social impacts of smoking, or the private costs of the early deaths attributable to smoking. The firm's accounting exercise was conducted from the point of view of public finances. The analysis recorded direct positive effects due to government revenues from excise taxes, value-added taxes, corporate income taxes, and customs duties. The negative effects of increased smoking included the increased health care costs of first-hand smokers and those exposed to second-hand smoke, the lost income tax due to premature deaths, absenteeism-related costs, and smoke-induced fire costs. These items seem relatively innocuous and would raise few eyebrows. What aroused attention was the fact that the indirect positive effects were identified as savings to the government because the premature deaths would result in the state paying less for health care costs, pensions, social security, and housing for the elderly due to early smoke-related mortality.

The researchers used a discount rate of 6.75 percent without performing any sensitivity analysis. This discount rate emphasizes the positive cash flows earned immediately from taxes from the sales of the cigarettes while minimizing longer-term costs and benefits.

This calculation assumed that life itself had zero standing or intrinsic value. The only value a smoker represented in the scope of this analysis was as a contributor to the government's coffers. The calculation was designed specifically to advocate to the government that early deaths should be encouraged as long as government revenue from Phillip Morris's product exceeded the financial costs. The scope of the analysis was designed to ignore all of the other financial and social impacts of the premature deaths. It represented human lives as being valued only as cash machines generating financial inflows and outflows to the government. By limiting the scope to only the government's financial flows and by choosing such a high discount rate without any sensitivity analysis, the analysis was biased in favor of the tobacco company that funded the study. More problematic than the bias of the study was its disregard for the sanctity and intrinsic value of human life. Representing humans as nothing more than cash flows that governments should optimize by encouraging early smoking-related deaths is immoral and, in Phillip Morris own words, displays a "disregard of basic human values."

LABOR AND THE VALUE OF LIFE

The labor market provides insight into how money is exchanged for time in an individual's life. Compensation for labor is critically important to the discussion of price tags, since income is a driving factor in determining the monetary value placed on human lives in civil trials and played a crucial role in the September 11th Victim Compensation Fund.

A starting point for discussing labor is first recognizing that there is a vast spectrum of rights, free will, and choice in the world of employment. At one extreme is slavery, where the slave has few to no rights or options except the choice of whether or not to keep living. At the other extreme is the free-will employee who pursues one of several jobs, negotiates her salary and benefits, and has enough financial security to choose whether to change employers without legal or financial constraints. In between these extremes are employees who have varying degrees of legal or practical restrictions on their options, including indentured servants and employees living paycheck-to-paycheck, who may be practically, though not legally, bound to their employer.

Slavery

Price tags on life and their influence on labor markets is most evident at the extreme examples of labor—slavery and indentured servitude.

Not everyone has the freedom to choose their work. Neither historically nor now have all workers made labor agreements that protect their basic human rights and are based on exercising their free will. Brutal forms of employment have always existed in which workers toil in violent, inhumane conditions, profits are maximized, and few if any considerations for the health and well-being of the workers are made. Slavery holds a prominent place among these brutal forms of employment.

Slavery, which is when people are owned, bought, and sold as commodities, has existed in various forms throughout history and in diverse cultures throughout the world. Humans have been enslaved as punishment for crimes, as payment for debts, during wars, by entrapment, and for hereditary reasons. The enslaved person is subjected to constant threats to her survival, safety, health, and dignity. The repugnant practice is transparent in one respect: slavery provides a clear view into how slaves' lives are valued by those participating in the market of buying and selling human lives.

Slaves and all their descendants in pre–Civil War America were property that could be legally traded in public markets. Slave auctions allowed buyers and sellers to openly place price tags on people's lives. A slave's value was driven by how much the buyer expected the slave to earn minus the costs of the slave's upkeep, such as food, clothing, and shelter.[20] Slaves were investments, and the price tag on a slave's life was a reflection of the projected cash flows. Buyers paid more for slaves who could provide the highest returns on investment and the least for those who represented low returns. Factors that influenced a slave's potential revenue included the slave's sex, age, health, capacity to work, and marketable skills. Young adult men had the highest price tags, a value justified by their strength and ability to work more than older men. Young children had lower price tags, since prospective owners would have to support them during their early years, when the costs may have exceeded expected revenue. Women of childbearing age were valued not only for their labor but also for their ability to produce children. Older and weaker slaves were worth less. Slaves with marketable skills, such as blacksmiths and carpenters, were worth more, since owners could make higher revenue by selling their products than the revenue associated with the work of a field hand.

The perverse extremes of putting price tags on people's lives for the purposes of labor are seen where slavery exists. The modern definition of slavery includes human trafficking, forced labor, debt bondage, forced marriage, and hereditary-based slavery.[21] Nearly all countries have national laws criminalizing at least some forms of modern slavery, yet humans are still bought and sold daily. The reality of modern slavery was brought into international focus in 2014, when ISIS released guidelines on capturing and keeping slaves.[22] Around that time, the United Nations confirmed that ISIS had a price list for captured children, ranging from hundreds to thousands of dollars per child.[23]

Indentured Servants

Indentured servants represent an explicit trade-off of a period of time in a life versus money, where an individual agrees to work for a fixed period of time to pay off a debt.

A key difference between indentured servants and slaves is that there is a fixed time period during which an indentured servant is owned. After that time, the servant is freed and able to exercise the rights and privileges of a free person.[24] Slaves, on the other hand, are owned for their entire lives, as are all their descendants.

Indentured servitude played a major role in American history and still occurs in the form of human trafficking. Human traffickers demand a certain number of years of labor to pay back the cost of transporting and smuggling a person into a country. Globally, the human trafficking industry impacts millions of lives and is estimated to be valued at over $30 billion annually, with many trafficked migrants finding themselves trapped in commercial sexual exploitation.[25] The return on such investments is high for the trafficker. For example, in 2006, it was estimated that traffickers could earn up to $50,000 per person trafficked, where the amount earned depends on the victim's place of origin and destination.[26] This large range in the costs and profits associated with human trafficking reflects the fact that in the human trafficking business, as in other business, prices are driven by supply and demand.

Compensated Labor

Slavery and indentured servitude are hidden from most people's view, while compensated labor, an exchange of the employee's time for the employer's money, is a fundamental part of our day-to-day existence. Compensated labor involves a value being placed on the employee's time, where that value is derived by the marketplace, though this marketplace is not completely free. This price tag defined by employment is so intrinsic to our daily lives that we often do not notice that this is yet another transaction where an interval of life is being priced. This is true whether that employee is a low-wage, hourly salaried restaurant employee, like Anita from chapter 2, or a high-income business executive, like Jim, whose compensation is mostly driven by profit-sharing agreements and annual bonuses.

From the employer's point of view, all things being equal, given the choice between two similar employees who cost the same, the employer should prefer the one who generates more profit. Likewise, given the choice between two similar employees who generate the same profit, the employer should prefer the employee who costs less. The employee is sitting on the other side of this transaction. The employee wants to maximize her compensation, both monetary and nonmonetary. This includes salary, health insurance, retirement plans, paid leave, family benefits, and other benefits.

There are a multitude of factors that influence compensation. These include, but are not limited to, education, skill set, experience, the industry, union membership, race, sex, location, and the risk of the job. Some factors, like education, are controllable, so an individual can, through concerted effort, change her circumstances and potentially earn more money.

Other factors are uncontrollable yet still can impact how someone's time is valued.[27] In summary, compensation is driven by the expected amount the company can earn from the worker's output, the supply and demand of the worker's skill, and other factors.

Let us start with an example of two people at different ends of the pay scale by comparing the compensation of two hospital workers: a radiologist, who interprets images from mammograms, ultrasounds, magnetic resonance imaging, and other sources, and a janitor, who mops the floors. The radiologist earns many times more than the janitor, and few people would argue that these two should earn anywhere near the same amount. The hospital values the time of the radiologist much more because of the income it can generate by having an employee with this expertise. Hospitals are businesses that pay for skills that can be sold to customers, in this case patients. The total compensation of the radiologist includes salary, health insurance benefits, a pension plan, and six-weeks of vacation time, as well as other possible perks, like education grants for the radiologist's children and payment for malpractice insurance. The total package could easily reach $500,000 a year, which, assuming a typical workload, comes out to around $250 an hour.[28] The hospital willingly pays this amount because it can earn substantially more money from the radiologist's billings. The amount the radiologist can earn for the hospital depends on the number of services she can provide and the revenue the hospital receives per service. If she receives an offer that pays substantially more per hour, the radiologist may want to take that higher-valued position.

The janitor who mops the floors is paid minimum wage. He receives his health insurance through the hospital and gets two weeks of paid vacation. His total compensation is less than $10 an hour. The hospital tracks his work time, monitors his location in the hospital, and has him pass through a security checkpoint upon exiting due to concerns about theft. He has little ability to negotiate salary with the hospital and is constantly reminded that he can be readily replaced. The hospital views the services he provides as a necessary operating expense but not a profit center, and it strives to minimize costs by looking for lower-priced alternatives whenever possible, including automation opportunities. The salary for mopping the floors will always be kept comparatively low because mopping is a low-skill job with competition from a large supply of potential workers.

Contrast that with the job of the radiologist, a high-skill position with a limited supply of potential workers. Clearly, the radiologist should be compensated more than the janitor. But how great should her hourly earnings be, and how should this salary difference be fairly determined?

The salaries of the radiologist and the janitor are both determined by the marketplace, with all of its transparency and obscurity, fairness and bias. If the hospital can find another radiologist who can generate the same revenue but will accept less compensation, it may have little incentive to continue paying $500,000 a year. It is interesting to note that the value of the radiologist's time, and her corresponding salary, is inflated by limiting the supply. An outside organization—the American Medical Association (AMA)—influences the labor market to ensure the radiologist's high price tag. By controlling the number of physicians licensed to practice, the AMA helps maintain the level of American physicians' salaries.[29] Similarly, outside constraints such as minimum wage laws and unions seek to influence the labor market to ensure that the janitor's price tag does not fall below a certain level.

The columnist Thomas Friedman declared, "The world is flat," by which he claimed that thanks to the Internet, global competitors have equal opportunities regardless of their location.[30] Despite Friedman's famous assertion, the world is not yet flat, and location still matters a great deal in many industries. If human geography didn't matter, then there would be little income disparity across countries for similar tasks that can be done remotely. If location didn't matter, then computer programmers, legal document reviewers, certified accountants, and even radiologists would earn about the same, whether they worked in America or in India. Yet there are vast differences in incomes around the world. Jobs that can easily be outsourced to lower-income countries tend to pay less domestically and be less stable. Jobs that are subject to domestic competition from low-skilled immigrant labor usually pay low wages.

In comparing the radiologist and the cleaning crew member, we can identify many factors that influence their relative salaries, including the professional requirements for the job, such as educational achievement, certifications, accreditations, and technical skills. There is usually a smaller supply of qualified potential employees for positions with major professional requirements, so those who have invested the time and money to gain these requirements are often rewarded with higher salaries. Starting salaries in New York City for lawyers are over $150,000, while starting salaries for physicians in the United States range from around $130,000 for infectious disease doctors to over $500,000 for neurological surgeons.[31]

In addition to placing value on professional requirements, companies usually put a premium on relevant experience. The logic is that, on average, an experienced employee should add more value to the company's bottom line than one without experience.

Another factor that can affect compensation is the amount of power that employees have to negotiate with their employer. Rick, from chapter 2, benefited from being part of the Uniformed Firefighters Association of New York, a strong union that negotiates generous pensions and lifelong medical coverage for firefighters and their families.[32] Unions, through collective bargaining, advocate for the rights and benefits of workers. Successful union negotiations lead to higher compensation and, correspondingly, higher valuations of workers' lives. The United States has a lower rate of unionization than most wealthy countries.[33] It is not a coincidence that America also has a lower minimum wage than other wealthy countries. Minimum wage workers in America earn about 25 percent of the GDP per capita, one of the lowest ratios seen among wealthy countries.[34] America's comparatively low minimum wage reflects our society's sense of fairness.

The industry itself is also a major factor in compensation, even after controlling for skill set and education. For example, data modelers working with hedge funds often receive compensation that is many times more than the compensation of people with similar skill sets and educational backgrounds working in academia, health care, retail, and other data-intensive industries.

There are controllable factors that individuals can influence that can impact their compensation. For example, compensation increases with education. Those with a master's degree earn about 20 percent more than those with only a bachelor's degree, and those with a bachelor's degree earn about 65 percent more than those with only a high school degree.[35] This increasing trend is logical since higher education reflects the acquisition of more advanced skills needed for certain jobs and also serves as a filter or certification that is necessary to enter specific jobs. It also appeals to our sense of fairness since those individuals have invested time and effort to increase their marketability.

The return on education depends on what was studied. Those with undergraduate degrees in engineering or computer science have much higher returns on the costs of their college education than do students who majored in arts and humanities.[36] The differences in salary are linked to the profitability that a company can generate from an employee's contribution.

When employees are aware that a job places their health and life at greater risk, they may be able to negotiate higher compensation if they have a clear understanding of the incremental risk, have choices in their employment opportunities, and have the capacity to negotiate salaries. As we saw previously, one method of estimating the Value of a Statistical Life computes the wage premium associated with working in riskier industries, such as mining and commercial fishing. International civil servants also receive additional compensation for working in locations that are considered dangerous.[37] What is the fair amount that someone should receive to take on extra risk? Looking at the compensation patterns of risky and nonrisky jobs is a starting point, but that does not necessary give an accurate estimate of the risk premium. Factors that can work against there being an accurate risk premium, if any risk premium is being paid at all, are numerous. These factors include the asymmetry of information and power; the fact that a job's risks are often unknown to the employee; the absence of choices afforded to those who often end up working risky jobs, such as illegal immigrants and people with language barriers; and the fact that people working in risky jobs often are less risk averse, have few or no job options, and have limited capacity for negotiation.

I have listed a number of factors that impact compensation that are both comprehensible and easily defensible, such as education, special training and certification, and job experience. These factors are all proxies for an employee's ability to earn money for a company; employees who can generate more profit for a company have a higher compensation or price tag placed on their time. This higher price tag for more profitable employees is similar to the observation that the price paid for a slave was based on how valuable the slave's labor was to his master. This is not to conflate compensated labor and slavery but rather to simply point out the fact that in both situations, the employer is willing to pay more in anticipation of higher profits earned from the employee's time.

After controlling for those factors, there are still disparities related to factors such as gender and racial pay gaps. These pay gaps are fundamental inequalities that have major ramifications. Income is a critical factor in determining the compensation paid in civil suits, and it played the main role in determining the compensation in the September 11th Victim Compensation Fund. More generally, these pay gaps are inequalities that are compounded in any valuation of life that uses salary as an input. A consequence of these racial and gender pay gaps is that the lives of women and some minority groups are undervalued and, consequently, underprotected.

The gender pay gap refers to the average difference in compensation between a man and a woman after controlling for factors that are relevant to compensation. The highly touted factoid "women make $0.77 for every $1 a man earns" is misleading in that it reflects a population average and fails to account for education, job experience, industry, occupation, and time taken off by women who have children.[38] After accounting for those factors, a gender pay gap persists, though it is much smaller: women are paid roughly 10 percent less than men with similar qualifications and experience to do the same job.[39] A similar order of magnitude was seen in graduates one year out of college, with women earning roughly 6 percent less than men after controlling for occupation and experience.[40] In the parlance of valuing life, after controlling for major factors relevant to worker productivity, employers tend to value a woman's time less than they value the time of a man. The ramification of this gender pay gap is that when income is used to determine the economic value of someone's life, women tend to have lower price tags than men.

The racial pay gap refers to the fact that after controlling for factors related to employee productivity, black employees are paid less than white employees. Black men earn less than white men and black women earn less than white women across all levels of education.[41] This racial pay gap is substantial—for example, black employees earn about 25 to 30 percent less than white employees, whether we are comparing employees with master's degrees, undergraduate degrees, or high school diplomas.[42]

The range of legal compensation is enormous. The low end of the compensation scale is defined by the government, although many jobs in the informal sector pay wages below this rate.[43] In the United States, the federal minimum wage is $7.25 an hour, with no guarantee of health benefits, a pension, paid vacation, or other benefits. Migrant farm workers are paid even less, with no benefits. These informal economy jobs not only pay poorly but are also often more dangerous as they operate below the radar of legal worker protections. Even more extreme low salaries are seen in prison labor, with prisoners often being compensated at pennies an hour.[44]

A living wage is the theoretical wage level that would allow the earner to afford adequate shelter, food, and the other necessities of life. The ratio of minimum wage to living wage in the United States declined from 94 percent in 1968 to 57 percent in 2003, meaning that minimum wage workers in 2003 were earning only a little more than half of what was necessary for a decent standard of living.[45] The fact that the minimum wage in America can be roughly half the living wage speaks to high degree of unfairness in how people are compensated and, correspondingly, the low price tags placed on the lives of minimum wage workers.

At the opposite end of the wage scale are the top earners. In the United States, the CEOs of the 350 largest firms earned over three hundred times more than average workers at their companies in 2017.[46] This represents a vast increase over the 1978 ratio of thirty to one. Although the ratio of CEO-to-worker compensation is globally higher now than it was in the 1960s and 1970s, the United States is an outlier, with wealthy countries such as Australia, Sweden, Japan, and the United Kingdom all having much lower ratios.[47]

Viewing compensation as a tradeoff of time in life versus money, the extreme ratios in the United States indicate that companies value the time of their CEO hundreds of times more than that of their average workers. We expect that CEOs will earn more than average workers, and it would feel unfair to have them earn the same amount. After all, CEOs need to have experience, advanced skills, knowledge, education, and other specialized expertise that enables them to successfully lead a company. But these extreme differences in the compensation of CEOs versus average workers leads to the conclusion that, in situations such as civil trials, the price tags on their lives are vastly different. In the case of the September 11th Victim Compensation Fund, Mr. Feinberg specifically implemented his vision of fairness by setting a minimum price tag for any victim and a maximum income to be used in his price tag calculations. The net result was a range, where the ratio of the highest to the lowest payout was about thirty to one, an order of magnitude lower than the range found in the national ratio of CEOs' salaries to average workers' salaries.

In general, capitalism and its pursuit of profits can be the engine of powerful economic growth and development. Capitalism can help drive improvements in health, education, and wealth. But it also has the potential for destruction. Not the creative destruction touted in business magazines, but true destruction. Brutal pursuit of profits, unfettered by legal and moral restraints, can lead to unnecessary suffering and deaths, destruction of the environment, and a pathologically short-term perspective. Hence the need for laws, regulations, and other restrictions to harness the positive aspects of capitalism while controlling the negative aspects.

How many more lives would be lost if it weren't for legal restrictions, regulatory agencies, vigilant journalists, consumer advocacy groups, public watchdogs, nongovernmental organizations, and citizen activists acting as a counterweight to some of the dangers associated with the brutal and blind pursuit of profits?

The next chapter discusses how individual decisions also play a prominent role in deciding whether to purchase life insurance as well as in determining the coverage amount—a self-assessment of one's own replacement value—in dollars.

6 I Want to Die the Way Grandpa Did

The caption below an image of a crying baby reads, "Why didn't you plan for me?" This life insurance advertising campaign is targeted, emotional, and effective. What parent could possibly look at that poster without wondering if they need life insurance? Parents who have insurance will wonder, is it enough? Uninsured parents will not be able to avoid feeling guilty after seeing that crying baby. This ad works well because we all value the baby's innocence and appreciate its vulnerability. It connects with us on an emotional level and has undoubtedly prodded many people to purchase life insurance to provide some security to their family. A far less effective, yet more honest, caption might have read: "What is a fair valuation of your life such that were you to die tomorrow I'd be financially stable?"

Life insurance is an important topic in any discussion of the value placed on life, since for many people, this is the most obvious situation where human price tags appear. Life insurance is distinct from the other examples of price tags discussed so far in that it is purchased in a competitive market where the price tag is decided by the consumer. Also, individuals can choose whether or not to purchase life insurance, as well as how much coverage to purchase.

Equity plays less of a role in determining the price of life insurance than it does in determining the values of the other types of price tags discussed so far for a few reasons. First, the price tag is determined by the consumer and not by some other person, such as an economist, corporate financial analyst, or a regulator. If the consumer thinks they should purchase more coverage then, provided that they can afford it, that is their choice.

Second, there is a competitive market for life insurance. This means that economists do not need to develop price estimates. Unlike the Value of a Statistical Life, where valuations are inferred through surveys or estimated from people's willingness to pay, life insurance costs are well known.

Third, the cost of life insurance is based on the risk of mortality. The mathematics behind determining someone's risk of mortality is based on life tables, a straightforward concept that has been well understood for hundreds of years.

Lastly, companies that sell life insurance are not motivated by concerns about equity and do not have a mandate to ensure that their products are fairly distributed. They are generally for-profit companies whose goal is to maximize profits while competing on prices and products with many other competitors. In the United States, life insurance is a multitrillion-dollar industry.[1] The face value of individual life insurance policies in the United States in 2017 totaled $12 trillion—roughly two-thirds of America's gross domestic product that year.[2,3] In 2017, there were roughly 289 million policies in force in the United States, nearly one policy for every American.[4,5] Insurance companies create powerful marketing campaigns to stimulate demand for their products, and customers seeking life insurance can easily find price quotes either online or through a broker.

This is not to say that there are no equity considerations in life insurance. As we will discuss, equity considerations come up in relation to the factors these companies can legally use (and the ones they choose to use) in determining risk or mortality. Moreover, the pricing of life insurance policies reflects the values of both society and the company. These restrictions and choices open up questions of what is fair and unfair in this valuation of life. Equity also plays an indirect role in that pay gaps due to factors such as gender and race impact an individual's ability to purchase life insurance.

CONSUMER DECISIONS

The amount of insurance coverage that a consumer purchases—a value of life developed for the purposes of life insurance—is very different from other price tags. This valuation is a self-appraisal, driven by the insurer herself. It is not estimated by a separate group of people, such as the jurors in a civil trial, or by economists' estimations based on some calculation, such as a statistical valuation.

When considering whether to purchase life insurance, you need to answer a number of questions, the most important ones being: Do you need life insurance? What type of life insurance should you purchase, term or permanent?[6] Who will be your beneficiaries? How much coverage do you need? That last question is a direct assessment of the value of your life.

The question of whether you actually need life insurance depends on some key information, including whether you have dependents, what their financial needs are, and the value of your assets that are readily available to pay for those needs.

Critical decisions you must make to arrive at a valuation of your life include identifying your beneficiaries and the amount each beneficiary should receive. Often, the beneficiary is a direct relative of the policyholder, such as a spouse or a child who is financially dependent. That said, there are generally no restrictions on who can be named a beneficiary—you could choose a beloved alma mater or even a surviving pet. Of course, if you cannot think of anyone who should be your beneficiary, then you probably do not need life insurance.

Finally, there is the question of how much insurance you should purchase. This decision depends not only on need and the necessary replacement value but also on the cost of the insurance. While you could simply pick a round number that "sounds good," like one million dollars, it is better to make this decision with a specific goal in mind. There are a few ways you can decide how much life insurance coverage you need.

If your goal is to make sure the lifestyle of your dependents would not change were you to die prematurely, then your life insurance coverage should be at least the amount of the economic contribution you would have made were you still living. This is called the replacement income need. It is similar to the way economic value was determined in the September 11 victim compensation calculation. To estimate your replacement income need, you should consider not just your salary, benefits, and retirement savings but also the tasks you do that your beneficiaries would need to pay someone else to do if you died. If you earn a salary and also drop your kids off at school, the need for both earning an income and dropping off the kids would continue were you to die. This rather grim part of the process of purchasing insurance is important in estimating valuation, and it might include tasks such as child care, housecleaning, cooking, and driving. Of course, since you would not be around, you wouldn't be spending money on yourself, so you should subtract out your personal consumption, such as the money you spend on your clothing, entertainment, travel, and food. This is a sobering and detailed calculation that provides clarity regarding the coverage your family would need to replace all your contributions.

Because this calculation includes income as a major input, all of the inequalities previously discussed that are associated with income (such as race- and gender-related income inequalities) are magnified by it. Stay-at-home parents who are not earning an income but are providing unpaid services like taking care of children, cooking, cleaning, driving, and other domestic support have a replacement income need, too. This replacement income need reflects the total amount that would be needed to pay for the services a stay-at-home parent provides. Similarly, someone who is not earning an income but is actively engaged in caring for an elderly parent would have a replacement income need that reflects the amount of money that it would cost to care for the parent.

The results of a replacement income need calculation are readily apparent. Those who earn more have a higher replacement income need and require a higher coverage than those with lower incomes.

Calculating your replacement income isn't the only approach you could take. You could also estimate the coverage appropriate for your beneficiary's needs from the opposite perspective. Rather than starting with what you currently contribute (supply), you could work from the point of view of the survivors (demand). This approach is called the survivor-needs calculation. For this method, you compute how much money your survivors would need to enjoy a certain level of income and lifestyle. This might include the costs of paying for the mortgage or rent, health insurance, food, clothing, and college until your survivors are able to earn enough to pay their own bills. The more dependents you have, the higher the results of the survivor-needs calculation estimate will be. Lifestyle expectations impact this calculation. A parent who doesn't expect their children to go to college need not consider college costs in the survivor-needs calculation, whereas a parent who is committed to paying for her daughter to graduate from medical school should add these costs to the estimate.

The survivor-needs calculation draws the conclusion that individuals with survivors who are anticipated to have more expensive lifestyles and more expensive future expectations require more support than those who have more modest needs to fulfill.

Once you have determined the coverage amount needed, you compare this total to your liquid assets, defined as assets that can be quickly converted into cash. If your liquid assets, such as stocks, bonds, and cash, exceed the coverage amount needed, then life insurance may not be necessary. Illiquid assets, such as houses and cars, cannot be easily converted to cash and would almost certainly require substitutes if you did end up selling them. For example, it may take a long time to sell your house, and once it is sold, your survivors would still need a place to live, meaning that they would need to pay rent or another mortgage. Often, one does not have enough liquid assets to meet the computed need. This is the situation where it makes sense to buy life insurance.

Both calculation methods—the replacement income needs calculation and the survivor-needs calculation—try to answer the question of how much money it would take for your dependents to live a certain lifestyle if you were not alive to provide for them financially (via your income) and with services (by dropping off the kids, etc.). This can be considered a partial price tag on your life in that it focuses only on the direct benefits received by your dependents. No one else and nothing else is considered. It doesn't reflect contributions you make to people other than your dependents, such as the contributions you make to your society, as well as any other interactions that you didn't monetize.

The average face value of new life insurance policies purchased in 2016 was $153,000.[7] This is a small fraction of the estimates used for the Value of a Statistical Life—a stark reminder that different methods and purposes of valuing a human life result in very different values. In the case of life insurance, the focus is on assisting one's beneficiaries financially in the case of one's untimely death, whereas in the regulatory sector, the focus is on controlling population risks in a cost-effective manner.

The need for life insurance generally increases with wealth, although at the extremes of very low and very high wealth the need may decrease. Not surprisingly, households with incomes over $100,000 are nearly twice as likely to own life insurance as households with incomes less than $50,000. Similarly, adults sixty-five years or older are more than twice as likely to have life insurance as adults younger than twenty-five, a likely consequence of wealth, family status, and life expectancy at that age.[8]

It is worth revisiting our fictitious September 11 victims to gain some perspective on this issue by looking at how they might have approached these life insurance questions, since they spanned a range of ages and socioeconomic classes.

Rick, the firefighter, had a solid middle-class income. He owned a $100,000 life insurance policy through the fire department, but since he had no dependents he designated his two brothers as the beneficiaries. His plan was to increase the coverage to the maximum amount of $500,000 after getting married and change the beneficiary to his wife. His basis for choosing the figure $500,000 was simply that this was the highest amount easily available through the department's subsidized life insurance program.[9]

Jim, a corporate executive, had a wife and twins relying on his income to fund their lifestyle. Jim had a multimillion-dollar life insurance policy paid for by his company as part of his executive compensation package and had already set aside money for his daughters' private schools, tutors, and college. If his family burned through all of that money, Jim figured they could sell some of the property he had purchased. Jim's wife did not earn a salary, do housecleaning, or drive a car, but she made all the family's meals and helped take care of the children when they weren't in school, so Jim had figured that it would be a reasonably good statistical bet to take out a $500,000 policy on her to replace the babysitting, tutoring, and cooking services that he would need to purchase if she passed away.

Anitha had been barely scraping by and would have been out on the streets if not for the financial support of her girlfriend, Ashley. Neither of them had remotely considered taking out life insurance. It simply wasn't a consideration for young people such as themselves with such little money and a narrow focus on paying the next month's rent.

Sebastian's father and mother both earned incomes. His father brought in around $35,000 a year from the Bel-Air Country Club and sent nearly $1,200 to Sebastian's mother every month as part of the divorce settlement. She worked odd jobs in the neighborhood, earning nearly $15,000 a year off the books and $12,000 on the books as a part-time cashier; she also spent countless hours cooking, cleaning, and babysitting. They had once sat down with an insurance agent to see how much insurance they should purchase. After computing the replacement income need, it was concluded that they should take out a larger policy on the mother's life than the father's. An argument ensued, and the insurance was never purchased, but every time Sebastian's father saw that advertisement with the crying baby, he wondered if he was doing the right thing for his family by not buying life insurance.

Now that we have reviewed examples of life insurance decisions, it is time to look into the transaction itself. Focusing on a twenty-year term life insurance policy for one million dollar coverage, we can view this as a straightforward business transaction where the payments and payouts are transparent. The demand side has been discussed above, and now we will explore the supply side—that is, the insurance company's perspective on selling life insurance.

Life insurance companies make their profits by maximizing the difference between how much they charge for insurance and the costs of providing that insurance. Because the industry is competitive, the most successful life insurance companies are those that build accurate models of life expectancy. Specifically, life insurance companies want to build very accurate survival curves that predict the probability that you will be alive one, two, three, or twenty years from now. These probabilities are multiplied by the premiums and payouts to develop a prediction of the typical cash flow of an insurance policy for someone like you. Statistically, this represents the average cash flows over time that would be expected if thousands of people like you signed up for the same policy. Adding up the discounted cash flows gives the insurance company the net present value of the insurance policy. Insurance companies want to have policies with very high positive net present value—or in less technical language, they want to make as much money as possible. The more you pay in premiums and the less likely it is that the insurance company will have to pay out your policy, the more the insurance company earns.

Longer-term policies have higher premiums because the longer you live, the older you get and the more likely it is that you will die. Actuaries have created life tables that track the probability of dying each year in the future as a function of age. These life tables exist for the total population, representing the average of the entire population. Separate life tables also exist for men and women and for different races.

An analogy can be made between a life insurance company and a casino. A casino knows the probability that it will win or lose any given hand or game. Because the odds are in the casino's favor, its business model becomes a numbers game: put simply, the more people there are betting in the casino, the more likely the casino is to win. While some individuals may win, the slight advantage in the casino's favor produces a steady stream of profits. Similarly, an insurance company has estimates of the probability of survival, and its premiums are priced so that on average, it makes a profit. Sometimes someone dies in the first few years, resulting in the insurance company losing money on that policy. Since thousands of people purchase policies, the insurance company profits based on the price difference between the discounted value of the premiums and the discounted value of the total payouts. With casinos and with life insurance, the odds favor the business. In the case of an insurance company, the premiums paid by the people who happily live up to the statistical expectations of the life tables should, on average, more than offset the cost of paying out the policies for those claimants who do not, just as in the case of a casino, where the losses of all of the players should, on average, more than offset payouts to the winners. There is one big difference between casinos and life insurance companies: if you keep purchasing term life insurance, at some point your bet will pay off in the sense that you will die and your beneficiaries will receive a payout. Of course, that payout may turn out to be less than if you had just invested in something else, like tax-free bonds.

PREDICTING DEATH

Insurance companies try to build the most accurate predictive model possible. It is to their advantage to identify all factors that are predictive of survival and include these in their models. The list of factors used in the modeling opens up the questions of what is legal and what is fair.

Insurance companies collect data from applicants and policyholders on a wide range of information, including gender, age, height, weight, family medical history, occupation, smoking and alcohol use, medical history, and current health (identified by a medical exam). Sometimes, they gather information on race, drug use, driving record, credit history, and hobbies. Every factor that is more predictive of dying sooner can result in higher premiums—that is, if the law allows insurance companies to use that variable and a company chooses to do so.

The probability of dying in the next year starts out high for newborns. The United States has one of the highest infant mortality rates of any wealthy country at around six deaths in the first year per every one thousand live births.[10] The probability of dying in the next year declines until an individual is about twelve years old, and then it increases steadily so that on average, a fifty-year-old American has a 0.4 percent probability of dying in the next year, a sixty-five-year-old has a 1.3 percent probability, and an eighty-year-old has about a 5 percent probability.[11] Since older adults have higher probabilities of dying in the next year, if the insurance benefit is kept the same, then the premiums increase with age.

Women live longer than men in nearly every country in the world, with an average life expectancy that is about five years longer.[12] An eighty-year-old woman has about a 4.3 percent probability of dying in the next year, compared to 5.8 percent for a man. So all things being equal, women should have lower life insurance premiums than men.

Race is a sensitive subject in many aspects of American life, including insurance. There are certainly well-established data showing differences in life expectancy as a function of race in America. For example, an eighty-year-old black man has a 7 percent probability of dying in the next year, compared to a 5.8 percent for a white man and 4.7 percent for a Hispanic man.[13]

Family medical history, especially that of your grandparents, parents, and siblings, can also influence your probability of survival. If both your parents died of a genetically linked condition such as coronary artery disease, diabetes, a stroke, or cancer in their early fifties, you will likely have much higher premiums than if they both are alive and kicking at age ninety-five. Family medical history interviews recall the classic joke of when a life insurance applicant said, "I really want to die peacefully in my sleep just like my grandfather . . . not desperately screaming like the passengers in his car."

In addition to requiring you to submit your family medical history and your own medical history, insurance companies often require a physical exam to assess your current health. People with a history of cardiovascular disease, high blood pressure, smoking, or alcohol or drug abuse and those who are obese are likely to pay higher premiums. Smokers must sometimes pay two or more times as much as nonsmokers due to the increased risk of mortality.[14]

People with relatively dangerous occupations, such as logging, fishing, mining, transportation, agriculture, and construction, may pay higher premiums.

Driving records are important to life insurance companies because there were over forty thousand motor vehicle fatalities in the United States in 2016, with the highest fatality rates being for young adults (fifteen to twenty-four years old) and older adults (over seventy-five).[15] The data shows that applicants with poor driving records, such as those with a history of accidents, have higher risks and are likely to pay higher premiums.

Some applicants may be surprised to learn that insurance companies often consider an applicant's lifestyle choices. Risky lifestyles and hobbies such as skydiving, hang gliding, scuba diving, rock climbing, surfing, extreme sports, motor sports, auto racing, and private aviation can also result in higher premiums.

Insurance companies consider this broad mosaic of factors because they hope to make the most informed decisions possible—they want to optimize their models in order to maximize their profits. Companies that build more accurate models can better price their products and should therefore outperform companies with less accurate models. This means that there is a competitive advantage to companies using whatever variables are legally allowed. Variables that customers cannot control, such as age, race, family medical history, and genetic markers, may result in lower or higher rates. It is possible that someone has a set of noncontrollable factors, such as a rare genetic condition, that gives her a very high chance of dying soon. To compensate for this high probability of dying soon, a life insurance company would charge that person very high premiums, possibly pricing her out of the market for insurance.

Risky lifestyle choices such as rock climbing, smoking, hang gliding, and alcohol use are controllable, so applicants could choose to make decisions to lower their rates for those factors. But life insurance is supposed to provide insurance, not dictate how someone lives her life.

When we ask the question, "What controllable and noncontrollable input variables are fair and appropriate to consider in assessing risk?" the textbook free-market answer would generally be that in a competitive market, insurance companies are incented to use any legally allowed variable that enhances their ability to compete. Regulations restrict insurance companies in what information they can and cannot use.[16] One can think of these regulations as reflecting society's judgment of fairness, though other factors, such as the lobbying of special interest groups, also influence legislation. When reviewing regulations, public advocates and watchdog organizations must always be on the lookout for regulatory capture, which is when regulatory agencies that were created to act in the public interest are instead advancing the special concerns of the industry interest groups they are charged with regulating.[17]

In the United States, there is no federal law specifically forbidding life insurance companies from taking into account race, religion, national origin, or gender.[18] This leaves the regulation of life insurance to the states, which each have their own authority over this matter. As it turns out, there is no single set of answers at the state level about what is legal. Many states do not have restrictions on insurers' ability to discriminate on the basis of race, national origin, or religion, while other states impose clear limitations. This suggests that there isn't uniform agreement across America regarding what is legal or, for that matter, fair for insurance companies to consider when pricing insurance. The regulations have clear implications on who bears more of the financial burden. When a group with a higher risk is required to be priced the same as a group with a lower risk, the lower-risk group is overpaying for their level of risk, or in business jargon, the lower-risk group is subsidizing the higher-risk group.

Take age as an example. No state bans the use of age in computing life insurance premiums. If they did, all age groups would pay the same premium for the same insurance. All other factors being equal, this would mean that younger people would be subsidizing older people's life insurance, since younger people would be paying more than is suggested by their mortality risk.

Other noncontrollable variables are important. As we discussed, it is well established that on average, women live longer than men. In fact, at every age from eighteen to ninety-nine, the probability of dying in the next year is higher for men than women. The survival advantage of women increases with age. A sixty-five-year-old man has a 1.6 percent chance of dying in the next year versus 1.0 percent for a woman of the same age, an absolute difference of 0.6 percent. By age eighty, the difference has swelled to 1.5 percent.[19] Most states allow life insurance companies to consider sex in their models, but in Montana it is not allowed. Since sex-based insurance rates are illegal in that state, life insurance companies must use unisex life tables. Consequently, women in Montana are subsidizing the men's life insurance.

Life expectancy data clearly shows that race is a significant predictor of survival, with blacks having lower survival rates than whites or Hispanics. A majority of states do not explicitly ban the use of race in life insurance premium calculations, though a diverse set of states have done so, including California, Georgia, New Jersey, New Mexico, North Carolina, Texas, Washington, and Wisconsin. In contrast, Louisiana law specifically allows life insurance companies to use race in life insurance premium calculations.[20] Some states may not have explicit bans on using race because they assume race is not used as a variable and so regulation is unnecessary. There is reasonably good logic in that assumption. While race-based polices have existed since the 1800s, in 1948 Metropolitan Life Insurance Company began eliminating race-based rates, and by the 1960s most major life insurance companies were using integrated life tables, thus voluntarily ignoring the life expectancy differences between races.[21]

Hispanics and whites have, on average, longer life expectancies than blacks. When insurance companies use integrated life tables, the result is that blacks' life insurance is subsidized by Hispanics and whites, an example of product cross-subsidizing.[22] Hence it is not completely surprising that a 2014 life insurance industry report showed that blacks have higher rates of life insurance than Hispanics or whites (69 percent versus 52 percent).[23] It was thus prudent of Jim, in the unglamorous sense of it being a good statistical bet, to have taken out life insurance on his wife. Supporting that point is the fact that 66 percent of Hispanics said that the expense of life insurance is the main reason they don't have any insurance or don't have a greater level of coverage, compared to 55 percent of blacks. Additionally, 22 percent of blacks stated that they are extremely likely or very likely to purchase life insurance in the next year, compared to 14 percent of Hispanics.[24] It is important to note that one's employer can also play a role in the decision to purchase life insurance. If one's employer is willing to subsidize the cost of life insurance, the policy is more affordable, and more people are likely to purchase it.

There is a risk that cross-subsidizing will fail if there is too much adverse selection—that is, if people who are lower risk react to being overcharged for insurance by deciding to not purchase insurance. Without those lower-risk groups to offset the higher-risk groups, the price for insurance would therefore need to rise. Similarly, it is possible that people who are at high risk may know more than the insurance company regarding their personal risk level and so may be more willing to purchase insurance. For example, imagine someone has had a battery of genetic tests performed that show she has a very high probability of breast cancer. These test results may not be available to the insurer, so if that person purchases a large amount of life insurance, she is doing so from a position of advantage over the insurer.

In this discussion of life insurance, we have focused on the specific situation where a person is taking out insurance on her own life. There are other situations where life insurance is purchased by a third party, such as an employer. Following the September 11 attacks, some employers received compensation before the victim's families were paid for the life insurance policies they held on their employees.[25] An employer's motivation for taking out life insurance may be to manage some of the risks associated with losing a valuable employee, or they may feel the insurance is a "good bet." From the perspective of the employer, the amount of insurance could reflect the potential impact the loss of the employee would have on the company's finances, but this is not always the case. The company could choose to insure for far greater or far less than that amount if it had information that gave it insight into whether insuring a particular employee was a good financial decision.

Another example of third-party involvement in the life insurance market is the viatical market. Viatical companies buy life insurance policies in situations where the policyholder needs money immediately—for example, if someone with a terminal illness cannot afford lifesaving medicine. These companies earn their profits by paying the insured person less than the death benefit for the right to become the beneficiary of the policy when the person dies. The company pays the insurance premiums for the rest of the insured person's life. It is a business transaction in which the company's profits are maximized if the policyholder dies quickly, but the company can lose money if the policyholder survives for a long time.

In life insurance, the valuation of life is only a partial price tag associated with financial need and ability to pay. It is different from many of the other price tags on life in that when someone is purchasing insurance for himself, the individual is pricing himself rather than leaving that responsibility to an external group, such as a jury or an economist. Because this price tag is usually self-generated, it is an area where the individual has control of the value of life decisions. If you have committed murder, you can't determine the punishment you will receive. If you have accidentally run someone over with your car, you don't get to simply write a check for an amount of your own choosing and end the obligation. You don't get to testify in front of Congress about how much your life is worth and why lawmakers should do more to protect you and your family from pollutants, toxic waste, and other dangers. But you do get to decide if you want life insurance, how much you want to purchase, and who the beneficiaries will be. Simply put, when it comes to life insurance, you get to decide the price tag of the replacement need of your life, but you will have to pay high premiums for the privilege of assigning yourself a high value.

Life insurance coverage involves individuals making decisions about coverage amounts, a self-assessment of the price tag of their own replacement value. While life insurance focuses on payments made in the event of death, health insurance, the topic of the next chapter, focuses on payments made in situations where patients require drugs, procedures, or other health care to provide a higher quality of life. Regulators and health insurance companies routinely place price tags on human life as they assess how much money should be spent on new health technology, such as a novel drug or new procedure.

7 To Be Young Again

Terri Schiavo suffered massive brain damage in 1990 following a cardiac arrest.[1] She was diagnosed as being in a permanent vegetative state. After years of unsuccessful therapy, her husband (and legal guardian) petitioned in 1998 to have her feeding tube removed. This decision triggered a legal battle with Terri's parents that was fought through different courts, the appeals process, and appeals to the governor and the president. The final court decision, in 2005, resulted in the removal of her feeding tube. She died within two weeks. The fifteen years that she was in a vegetative state cost hundreds of thousands of dollars in medical and hospice care.[2] All health care systems have finite financial resources. It is necessary and appropriate to ask whether the money that was spent to keep Terri alive could have been better spent to save other people's lives. More generally, this opens up the critical question of what is the best way to allocate the limited amount of money available for health.

The value placed on the quantity and quality of life is one of the most transparent reflections of what society considers fair. How much is spent to extend life or improve health demonstrates our willingness to invest in the future. Society's assessment of fairness is indicated by the considerations that influence that investment decision, such as the person's income, life expectancy, the cost of treatment, or the likelihood of success, as well as how those considerations are weighed. This price tag on health raises personal decisions—such as whether to smoke or not to smoke—and societal decisions—such as whether to privilege wealthier individuals, for-profit concerns, or focus on other concerns.

There is no single price tag placed on human health. The price tag depends on a large variety of considerations, including: Who is paying? What services are being provided? Where is the service being provided? Who is providing the service? More broadly, this price tag depends on how we define health. For the purposes of this discussion, we will use a narrow definition of health as being free from illness or injury.[3]

One of the most critical considerations in determining the value of health, and more generally in determining the value of life, is the question of whose perspective we are considering. Are we discussing a for-profit company that needs to determine which treatments it will or will not pay for? Are we describing what services are covered by a national health insurance scheme in a country with a constitutional obligation to provide essential health services? Are we talking about how much an individual will pay for a treatment to save her life or the life of her child? The answers to these questions result in very different price tags for health and different recommended actions.

The value of health is a consideration not only for regulators and for-profit companies. As individuals, your priorities associated with health are expressed every day. The decisions you make about your health reflect your priorities in how you spend time and money as well as in your perception of health risks.[4] These decisions are real-world indicators of how much you value your health and your life. Do you order a salad for lunch or eat a hamburger and fries instead? Do you smoke? Do you walk, bike, or drive to work? Do you pay for comprehensive health insurance that covers most of your health charges, rely on a catastrophic insurance plan that only begins coverage after your health charges have exceeded a high deductible, or gamble by having no health insurance at all? While these and other decisions will likely improve or damage your health, there are no guarantees when it comes to health.

The fundamental importance of health was stated in the U.S. government's 2010 Global Health Initiative Strategy: "Health is at the heart of human progress. It determines whether parents can work to support their families, children can attend school, women can survive childbirth, and infants can grow and thrive. Where health services are strong and accessible, families and communities flourish. Where health services are inaccessible, weak, or nonexistent, families suffer, adults die prematurely, and communities unravel."[5]

This statement reinforces the point that maintaining and improving health should not be viewed merely as an expense. Health is an investment that reaps large returns, since health is a powerful enabler.[6] Healthier people are more productive and more capable of participating in growing the economy and, more broadly, contributing to society.[7] Health is often unappreciated when present but sorely missed when absent.

Putting a price tag on health can be very challenging and, as with valuing life, controversial. My driving instructor cruelly joked that if we ever ran over a pedestrian, we might save money by "backing up and finishing the job." The September 11th Victim Compensation Fund awards showed that my driving instructor was right in some cases because payouts for injuries can exceed payouts for deaths. Similarly, some civil cases conclude that the compensation for an injury can exceed the compensation for a wrongful death. The justification for this seemingly counterintuitive conclusion is that a lifetime of expensive medical treatments and limitations on someone's ability to work can result in a very high price tag. This logic can easily be criticized. After all, another interpretation is that life itself is insufficiently valued, and if life were given a much higher value, injuries would always be worth less than death.

METRICS AND THE RESPONSIBILITIES OF REGULATORS

Regulatory agencies are tasked with considering impacts to society and not simply looking at the bottom-line considerations that are the focus of for-profit companies' attention. Different regulatory agencies have different perspectives on the value of health, and these perspectives influence how price tags on health are developed and used. Previously, we saw how the Value of a Statistical Life is used by environmental regulators when determining the benefits of lives saved and also of health preserved due to raising air, water and other environmental standards. These higher environmental standards can also reduce the rates of sickness, diseases, and injuries. Cost-benefit analysis for a possible new regulation needs to account for the benefits associated with the lives saved and the diseases, illnesses, and injuries prevented by the new regulation. Reduced health has a price tag associated with the value we place on avoiding suffering, pain, weakness, the inability to perform basic functions that were previously manageable, and the inability to enjoy leisure activities.

For environmental regulators to put a value on the health benefits of a new environmental standard, they need to first understand the relationship between exposure to the pollutant and the risk of a disease. When establishing an acceptable level of a poison, such as arsenic, in water, it is necessary to understand how higher levels of arsenic exposure impact people's health, including what diseases, such as cancer and cardiovascular disease, they are more likely to contract.[8] Similarly, in regulating the pollution produced by coal factories, it is necessary to understand the relationship between the key pollutants, like sulfur dioxide, and the health impacts they cause, such as bronchoconstriction and increased asthma symptoms.[9] After regulators have quantified the relationship between the pollutant and diseases, they then estimate how many people will be impacted by each disease. Finally, a price on the damage to the public's health and on the loss of life is applied.

Health technology regulators use different sets of considerations and criteria than environmental regulators when making decisions. Health technology regulators need to determine how, on a fixed budget, to save the most lives. The types of technologies they examine include drugs, devices, and health procedures such as vaccines and antibiotics, CAT scans and MRIs, and digital health technologies such as smartphone apps that track patient activity and drug compliance. When assessing the decision to invest in a health care intervention, drug, or procedure, health technology regulators take many considerations into account, including the balance of costs and benefits. Are the health benefits of the new technology worth the expense? More generally, health care planners, whether in a government or a health insurance office, need to decide if the health investment is worth the return. Regardless of which method is used for valuing the cost of health, discounting, as we have seen in many other contexts, results in favoring the health of current patients over the health of future patients. Discounting also often results in favoring curative treatments over disease prevention initiatives that can potentially delay future major health issues.

The challenge of placing a price tag on health is very similar to the challenge of placing a price tag on life. When there is an open, competitive market that allows for the trade of a product, we can observe the prices. The amount someone is willing to pay for eggs, orange juice, or gasoline can be easily observed. But good health is not equivalent to a widget traded in an open, competitive market with buyers and sellers. We cannot simply start the year by paying a fixed price to receive good health for the next twelve months. Because good health is not traded openly like a commodity, valuing health requires economists to develop clever methods of assigning price tags to items that do not get bought and sold.

Health economists have designed various metrics to place a value on health, including ones that track health costs and health impacts. Decisions based on these metrics can have far-reaching consequences, determining who receives what health care. As a consequence, these decisions impact whose lives get extended and whose lives end early. In spite of the substantial ramifications of choosing one health economics metrics over another, the decisions regarding these metrics are often left to technical specialists. A clear-eyed review of the commonly used metrics and their corresponding implications is invaluable for the public to understand the ramifications of selecting certain metrics, yet all too often, no such review is done.

The choice of which metric to use depends on the perspective and the priorities of the decision maker, including their own views of what is "fair." In some circumstances, the goal is simply to minimize health costs. In these cases, there is a limited budget, and costs are minimized, with some attention paid to the health impact. Even if the only goal is to minimize costs, there are still critical factors to consider, such as the tradeoff between preventive medicine (which seeks to reduce the chances of disease) and curative medicine (which focuses on treating patients in need of care).

In other circumstances, cost-effectiveness measures are developed that estimate the cost of an outcome, such as the cost per HIV case averted, the cost per cancer case detected, or the cost per hospital readmission. For example, we can readily compare the costs per HIV case averted for different prevention methods, such as needle-exchange programs, condom-distribution programs, and pre-exposure prophylaxis, to see which of these programs methods is the most efficient at preventing the spread of HIV. A cost-effectiveness analysis can help decision makers prioritize these different HIV programs. A limitation with cost-effectiveness measures occurs when you examine different outcomes or compare investments across different diseases. This method would not shed much light on the advantages of investments in HIV prevention versus cancer treatment, cardiovascular disease prevention, or any other health program unrelated to HIV prevention because the outcomes (HIV cases averted, cancer cases treated, cardiovascular diseases prevented) are all different.

To make comparisons with the same outcomes, health economists use cost-utility metrics such as cost per life saved, cost per life year saved, cost per quality-adjusted life year (QALY), or cost per disability-adjusted life year (DALY).[10] Counting life years is simple and transparent. We can agree on when someone is alive or dead. Quality-adjusted life years and disability-adjusted life years are more complex and opaque than life years. Both of these metrics make adjustments that result in a year in the life of an average older person being viewed as less valuable than a year in the life of an average younger person—a result that immediately raises questions about the fairness of the assumptions used in developing these metrics. DALYs often use age-weighting, where years lived as a young adult are weighed more heavily than years lived at other ages.[11] This means that analyses using DALYs do not value all years of one's life equally. Rather, disabilities occurring at age twenty are far more important to a DALY calculation than disabilities occurring at age sixty. Time discounting is also applied to DALY analyses, again deemphasizing the lives of older people. Moreover, the weightings used for quality and disability adjustments are not universal truths; they reflect the priorities of only some people, not all people. The question of fairness reappears when we consider that as a result of quality and disability adjustments, saving the life of a sixty-year-old in perfect health is deemed more important than saving the life of a sixty-year-old with a hip fracture, cancer, or AIDS.[12]

The measurement of cost per life saved does not distinguish between whose lives have been saved. It assumes that saving a newborn baby is just as important as saving a fifteen-year-old or a ninety-year-old. When examining the cost per life year saved, the scales are now tipped in favor of young people. Imagine the choice of providing treatment to either a fifteen-year-old or a ninety-year-old. If the cost of treatment and the probability of treatment success are the same, then the cost per life saved would be the same. But saving the life of a fifteen-year-old means that she is now expected to live many more years. In contrast, saving the life of a ninety-year-old may extend her life by only a few years. The choice of using the metric of the cost per life year saved values the lives of younger people more than the lives of older people.

The metric of the cost per life saved also fails to distinguish between the expected health and productivity of the life saved. Imagine a situation in which two newborns both suffer the same congenital heart condition. The condition requires surgery, rehabilitation, and monitoring that will cost hundreds of thousands of dollars. One newborn also has severe development issues and is not expected to ever achieve the mental capacity of a two-year-old. Should both receive the same health care treatment? Should the expected long-term potential play a role in the decision of how much to spend on saving each newborn's life?

Similarly, consider end-of-life care. Take the example of a patient who is in a permanent vegetative state with a nearly zero percent chance of even a partial recovery. How much money should be spent on keeping this person alive? If this person created a living will, their preferences are stated, but the bill for maintaining their life must be covered by someone, whether that is the health insurance company, the health care provider, the government, or personal savings. If this person failed to create a living will, their legal guardians are left to make the judgment.

On average, we know that ninety-year-olds not only have shorter life expectancies than fifteen-year-olds but also have far greater annual costs for health care. Working-age adults (those aged nineteen to sixty-five) generally spend about 70 percent more for health care than is spent on children eighteen years old or younger, while adults aged sixty-five and older spend more than five times what is spent on children.[13] Within the elderly population, people aged eighty-five years and older consume three times as much health care per person as those aged sixty-five to seventy-four.[14] More generally, a very high percent of U.S. medical expenditures occur as part of end-of-life care. For example, about one-quarter of Medicare expenditures are associated with the last year of life[15].

These facts play heavily into concerns about aging populations around the world and the corresponding rise in health care needs and expenses. They also reinforce the need to invest in preventive care that will reduce future disease burden and expenses.

When discussing the value we place on life, we need to understand how this value depends on the quantity and quality of life. Intuitively, most people value healthy years of life more than unhealthy years. We pay for health insurance, medical procedures, vitamins, and medicines to improve our health and, hopefully, extend our lives, both the healthy and unhealthy years. Of course, there are not merely two states of health, healthy and unhealthy. We can think of health as being a range, from perfect health to death. Between those two extremes are injuries, sickness, and so on. Health economists developed the QALY to account for this idea.[16] One QALY represents one year lived in perfect health. A dead person has zero QALYs. Between death (zero) and perfect health (one) are people living with broken legs, respiratory diseases, AIDS, and other health challenges, where the value used is based on survey responses.[17] The formula used for quality adjustment is subject to criticism, as it does not represent universal truths regarding how people value specific aspects of their health.

When we compare life years, the analysis is rather straightforward. Someone is either dead or alive. Once we introduce the concept of QALYs, we need to determine exactly how to adjust the scales between the extremes of death and perfect health. These scales, known as utility measures, reflect a patient's preference for being in a given state of health. There are many instruments that have been developed to measure QALYs, though one of the most commonly used is the EQ-5D.[18] This measure of quality of life has five dimensions: mobility, pain/discomfort, self-care (washing and dressing oneself), anxiety/depression, and ability to perform usual activities, such as work, study, housework, and leisure.[19] Each dimension has three levels. For example, the three levels of mobility are no problems walking, some problems walking, and confined to bed. Other instruments exist for estimating QALYs that use different dimensions and different ways to measure the dimensions.[20] Not surprisingly, each of these QALY instruments can yield different results, so even if there is agreement to use QALYs as a metric for health economic analysis, an agreement still needs to be reached regarding which measurement instrument will be used. More generally, using QALYs, just like using DALYs, disadvantages older people, as they generally have fewer future years to contribute to a DALY or QALY calculation.

Another issue with using QALYs is that they ignore the fact that people's preferences differ based on their age, gender, lifestyle, priorities, and sources of happiness.[21] A twenty-year-old woman living at home who is busy training for a triathlon has different priorities and preferences than a ninety-year-old frail, bedridden man living in a nursing home. Additionally, QALYs focus on the individual without giving any consideration to the impacts on caregivers, such as family members and members of the community.

Cost-benefit analysis assigns dollar amounts to both the costs and the benefits of a health intervention to identify if it is worth the expense.[22] Both the health care costs and the positive impacts of an intervention, such as preventing diseases, treating illnesses, improving health, and enhancing and prolonging life, are monetized. The advantage of cost-benefit analysis is that it uses a single measure—money—as compared with cost-effectiveness analysis, where the units are cost per outcome. The disadvantage of cost-benefit analysis is that it requires the researcher to monetize health and in doing so put a price tag on the quantity and quality of life.

As seen in many of the examples already given in this book, one method of putting a price tag on life is by linking the price tag to earnings. When cost-benefit analysis is applied at a national level, such as by a health care regulator, the benefits of additional healthy life years are usually estimated as some percentage of the GDP per capita of that country. The logic of linking extended life to the GDP per capita is that in theory, a person who lives longer is able to continue adding to the national economic output.

Developing countries have lower average GDP per capita than wealthy countries. As a result, benefits that are proportional to the national GDP per capita will be lower in developing countries as compared to wealthier countries. If the costs are similar for investing in improving the health of a wealthy country and that of a developing country, then cost-benefit analysis would recommend investing in the health of the wealthier country. More broadly, whenever an outcome is linked to some measure of income or wealth (such as GDP per capita) concerns about inequity will arise since the price tags being placed on lives can be very different across and within countries.

A second method estimates people's willingness to pay for better health. This is performed by doing surveys using the "contingent valuation" approach that was introduced in chapter 2.[23] An example of how this method is implemented involves a respondent being informed about the risks of a specific disease, such as thyroid cancer, along with the treatments required, survival rates, and other key medical information. The surveyor then describes two neighborhoods that are the same in all key features with two exceptions: one neighborhood has a lower risk of thyroid cancer, but it is also more expensive. The respondent is asked to identify which neighborhood they would prefer to live in. The surveyor then varies the price difference between the two neighborhoods and the difference in risk until the respondent has no preference. At the point when the respondent has no preference in the choice of neighborhood, the difference in the costs and the difference in the risk produce an estimate of that individual's willingness to pay to avoid thyroid cancer.

All of the issues associated with survey-based estimates discussed in chapter 2 are also problems in this estimate of willingness to pay. Selection bias stands out as a key issue. The subset of survey respondents is not a random sample of the population but rather represents those willing to answer a survey in the location that the survey was performed. Furthermore, only the subjects who understand the choices being presented, who are willing to answer the hypothetical questions, and whose answers are consistent across questions, sufficiently in line with other respondents, and considered to be "reasonable" by the researchers are used to produce the estimate. Respondents who find the abstract nature of these surveying techniques unclear, find the questions to be unanswerable, or do not provide answers that conform to the researchers expectations are not included in the analysis.

A third method for putting price tags on health involves computing the cost of illness. Cost of illness adds up only the financial costs associated with illness: the costs of treatment and the losses in economic productivity, such as missed work. This method is an overly simplified accounting of health costs. The narrowness of the definition is both its advantage and its disadvantage. The advantage is that the cost of illness can be readily calculated. The disadvantage is that it does not account for emotional damage, pain, suffering, discomfort, or the like and ignores quality of life and other aspects of life outside of earning and spending. For example, cost of illness analysis fails to accurately capture the cost of persistent pain, such as when someone continues to work but with great discomfort and must rest at home every evening and weekend to be able to continue his or her employment. One can think of the cost of illness method as being analogous to when civil trials take into account only financial losses and ignore other impacts.

How might cost effectiveness be considered by national health insurance regulators? When comparing two interventions, a researcher measures the difference in the average QALYs of patients receiving the different treatments. Sometimes, patients are faced with the choice between a shorter average survival time with a higher health-related quality of life and a longer average survival time with a lower health-related quality of life. Imagine a simplified example where we ignore considerations such as cost inflation and discounting. In this example, patients receiving treatment A live on average five more years at a treatment cost of $10,000 per year (see table 2). The total cost would then come out, on average, to $50,000. Imagine in this scenario that the average health state of the patients is 0.5 QALYs higher during these extra five years than if they had no treatment. In this example, patients receiving treatment A would gain an average of 2.5 QALYs, and the cost per QALY would be $50,000 divided by 2.5 QALYs, or $20,000 per QALY gained. Now compare those results to a similar patient population receiving treatment B, a more powerful treatment but one that comes with more side effects. Patients receiving treatment B live on average ten more years, with an average health state of 0.3 QALYs higher than if they had no treatment, meaning that treatment B is associated with an average total gain of 3 QALYs. Treatment B costs $15,000 per year, or an average total treatment cost of $150,000 per patient. Treatment B costs $50,000 per QALY gained ($150,000 divided by 3 QALYs gained).

The choice of metric is critical to the decision. If you base your decision on which option has the overall highest survival rate, then treatment B is

Table 2 Sample Criteria for Comparing Treatments

	Treatment A	*Treatment B*
Treatment cost per year	$10,000	$15,000
Average additional years of survival	5	10
Average additional QALYs per year during survival time	0.5	0.3
Total additional expected cost	$50,000	$150,000
Total expected QALYs gained	2.5	3
Cost per QALY gained	$20,000	$50,000

the better choice. If you base your decision on which option has the lowest cost per life year, then treatment A is the better choice. If you base your decision on which option has the lowest cost per QALY gained, then treatment A is the better choice. Because the choice of metrics is so important in the final decision, the selection of metrics should be both transparent and carefully considered so as to ensure that it accurately reflects society's views of fairness.

The incremental cost per incremental QALY gained is known as the incremental cost effectiveness ratio, or ICER. In this case, the difference between the cost of treatment B and treatment A is, on average, $100,000 ($150,000 for treatment B minus $50,000 for treatment A), and treatment B produces a gain of 0.5 QALYs compared to treatment A. This means that the ICER, the cost per additional QALY gained, is $200,000 when comparing treatment B to treatment A ($100,000 divided by 0.5). National health insurance plans often have a threshold for coverage that is calculated using the incremental cost per incremental QALY gained. This threshold is often linked to the wealth of the country, using a measure such as the GDP per capita.

It is clear that the choice of metrics used for decision-making will greatly impact the resource allocation, resulting in different decisions about which lives receive more money for health care, which receive less money, and ultimately, which lives are more valued and protected. It is important to bring these concepts that influence how health care resources are allocated into a discussion about America's health care system.

AMERICA'S HEALTH SYSTEM

The American market for health is very different from those of other wealthy countries. The various ways that Americans pay for health is more convoluted and far more costly. The distribution of health care in the United States is less equitable, and the American market for health is less cost-effective than those of other wealthy countries. Considerations of cost-effectiveness are at the forefront of the mind of for-profit health insurance companies, health care providers, and pharmaceutical companies, yet the American government lags behind many other countries in doing a systematic analysis of cost-effectiveness for their public health system.

In 2017, America spent nearly 18 percent of its GDP on health care, roughly $3.5 trillion.[24] No other country in the Organisation for Economic Co-operation and Development (OECD), an international organization comprised of thirty-six of the wealthier countries in the world, came close to that figure. Switzerland, the next highest, spent 12.3 percent of its GDP on health, while all other OECD countries spent less than 12 percent.[25] Health is big business nearly everywhere in the world, but especially in the United States. The Fortune 500 company list is filled with health insurance companies, like United HealthCare, Cardinal Health, Anthem, and Aetna; retail pharmacy chains, such as RiteAid and Walgreens; and pharmaceutical companies, like Johnson and Johnson, Pfizer, and Merck.[26] These health companies employ millions of Americans and have a major influence on the national economy.

Besides the high cost of health, another key distinction between the United States and other countries is that universal health coverage is the norm for most wealthy countries and even for some middle-income countries. In 2017, the uninsured rate in America for nonelderly adults was 10.2 percent, while for children it was 5 percent.[27] These are by far the highest rates among nations within the OECD.[28] The fact that there are so many uninsured people in the United States reflects the priorities of American society, where basic health care is not considered a human right.[29] This stands in stark contrast to other wealthy countries, where universal health care coverage is the norm and basic health care coverage is considered to be a fundamental human right.

On average, Americans spend thousands more per person on health than other countries, which raises several questions: Why do Americans spend so much more? Do Americans prioritize health higher than other countries and therefore place higher price tags on their health? Do Americans pay more because these health investments lead to better outcomes, or do they pay more because America's health system is inefficient? Before delving into the details of the data, it is important to recall that there is a broad range of countries within the OECD in terms of population, physical size, wealth, average age, ethnic distribution, and other factors that may relate to life expectancy and the cost of health care.

The national health outcomes data is rather clear that Americans are not getting a very good return on their $3.5 trillion investment in health. The United States has one of the lowest life expectancies of any wealthy country. Of the thirty-six OECD countries, the United States has a lower than average women's life expectancy, men's life expectancy, and total life expectancy.[30] The gap between the United States and other wealthy countries is even starker when measuring infant mortality, the probability of dying in the first year of life.[31] Only three OECD countries have higher infant mortality rates. The United States also has one of the highest maternal mortality ratios, the number of maternal deaths per one thousand live births.[32]

Within the United States, there is an enormous variation in life expectancy, reflecting disparities based on genetics, gender, race, ethnic groups, socioeconomic groups, and geographies.[33] One of the most striking examples is the difference of over fifteen years in the life spans of Asian American women and black males.[34] Blacks have infant mortality rates that are more than twice that of Hispanics and whites and maternal mortality rates that are more than three times that of white women.[35] The disparities in American health care across income strata are enormous. America may be home to some of the finest medical research facilities, most cutting-edge health technologies, and most renowned hospitals in the world, but our public health metrics score vastly below those of most wealthy countries.

Consider our four September 11 victims. Jim and Rick received health insurance through their companies. Jim's family was covered under his comprehensive health insurance plan, which was fully subsidized by his employer, and Rick's fiancé would have been covered under his fireman's insurance when they got married. Sebastian was covered under his father's catastrophic plan, which his parents had selected to manage expenses but which forced them to hope that they never had to make a hospital or ER visit. Anitha was uninsured because her part-time hostess job didn't provide coverage and she couldn't afford insurance premiums. Young and healthy, she knew that if there was ever a medical emergency she would have to pay out of pocket. In the meantime, she skipped her annual checkups to save cash.

These four individuals all had different interactions with America's health care system, reminding us that in the United States, some receive coverage through employers, some are covered by government programs, some buy commercial insurance, and some go uninsured. America's jigsaw puzzle of health care results in greater inefficiencies, higher administrative costs, and larger gaps in coverage than in other wealthy countries. America's health outcomes, such as life expectancy, infant mortality, and maternal mortality, are much worse than in other wealthy countries. These comparatively poor outcomes occur even though Americans pay far more for health than residents of other wealthy countries. Putting these observations together, it is clear that Americans receive a comparatively poor return on health investment than residents of other wealthy countries.

Analyses of the reasons Americans spend so much more on health than other countries have pointed to a number of sources, the largest being outpatient care.[36] Another source of America's overspending on health is the practice of defensive medicine, in which medical tests, procedures, or consultations of doubtful clinical value are ordered to protect the prescribing physician from malpractice lawsuits.[37] The higher costs of health administration and the costs of branded pharmaceuticals are also drivers of America's expensive health care.

The Affordable Care Act, passed in 2010, introduced a number of changes to the American health insurance landscape.[38] The law sought to address concerns over the inequitable distribution of health care by requiring insurance companies to provide all health insurance applicants with new minimum standards and stipulating that insurance companies could not reject or charge more for applicants with preexisting conditions. This provision is very distinct from how life insurance had previously been handled, with states having different laws regarding whether or not an insurance company could consider race or gender when setting the cost of coverage. Before the Affordable Care Act, health insurance companies could reject someone's application if they had an expensive preexisting condition or charge them an exorbitant amount for coverage. The Affordable Care Act also requires that dependent children be covered until they reach the age of twenty-six. The immediate goal of the Affordable Care Act was to reduce the rate of uninsured Americans. By doing so, the chances of having a catastrophic health expense and the rate of impoverishment due to medical issues should be reduced and health outcomes improved.

The Affordable Care Act includes a provision that specifically prohibits the use of cost-effectiveness analysis in comparative effectiveness studies. This limits the ability of the government to optimize health spending by constraining the government's ability to save the most lives or QALYs for a given budget. This restriction also makes it more difficult to contain costs, since regulators are not be able to determine if a more effective treatment is not cost-effective compared to less effective treatment.[39] The act contains other restrictions as well, such as one that prevents Medicare from being able to prioritize resource allocations based on information about a patient's disability, age, or future life expectancy.[40]

Consider cancer care. The costs for preventing, screening, treating, and recovery vary for different types of cancers. The risks of mortality also vary. An analysis of the incremental cost per QALY gained estimated treatments at less than $20,000 for lung cancer, around $100,000 for colorectal cancer, around $400,000 for breast cancer, and nearly $2 million for prostate cancer.[41] A more optimal allocation of resources using the metric of cost per QALY gained would focus on treating lung cancer and colorectal cancer patients given the higher cost-utility. The choice of metric is critical. Choosing a different metric, such as cost per life saved or cost per life year gained, may result in different conclusions.

A patient's personal responsibility is not considered in determining whether or not their treatment should be paid for. For example, a seventy-year-old who smoked two packs a day for decades is far more likely to have lung cancer than one who did not. The decision to treat the cancer has the same threshold for cost per life, cost per life year, or cost per QALY, regardless of the patient's personal choices that may have influenced their current condition. Moreover, that same pattern of personal choices may very well influence the patient's long-term prognosis. A patient with an unhealthy lifestyle may choose to continue their unhealthy patterns even after treatment.

While the limitations in how cost-effectiveness analysis can be applied in the United States are a challenge, Medicare does have a cost-reduction incentive built into Accountable Care Organizations (ACOs). These groups of doctors, hospitals, and other health care providers seek to provide quality care and obtain good patient health outcomes at lower costs. If ACOs can show that they have achieved high-quality service, they earn back some of the saved costs.

Other countries allow their regulatory agencies more power to make decisions related to health care based on cost effectiveness and empower their governments to negotiate for better prices. Australia's Pharmaceutical Benefits Scheme is an example of this type of negotiation leverage. It purchases pharmaceuticals for the country at negotiated rates and then makes the drugs available at affordable prices to Australians.

The United Kingdom's National Institute for Health and Care Excellence (NICE) considers health economics in their guideline recommendations. NICE's Guideline Development Group is required to consider both clinical impact and cost effectiveness. If the scientific evidence indicates that an intervention or health service provides significant health benefits below the cost-effectiveness threshold, then that service is recommended. Both the costs and the health impacts are discounted, and sensitivity analysis is performed to examine the uncertainty of the economic analysis results.[42]

Thailand's Health Intervention and Technology Assessment Program (HITAP) performs a similar function. HITAP not only assesses health technologies but also supports Thailand's price-negotiation process. HITAP's structured analysis of health technologies, such as medications and procedures, provides inputs to policy decisions. Key factors in HITAP's process include safety, efficacy and effectiveness (health benefits), value for money (cost effectiveness), social considerations (such as the prevention of catastrophic diseases or the potential for lifesaving interventions), ethical considerations (such as the impact on the most vulnerable sections of society or the treatment of rare diseases), and institutional and political considerations.[43]

Regulatory agencies such as HITAP and NICE and those in other countries build value-evaluation frameworks that reflect their respective countries' priorities. Some societies are more focused on equity or the cost effectiveness of health care and emphasize that in their health care planning. Others place greater emphasis on ethical considerations. Still others place more weight on aspects of personal responsibility, giving less consideration to the role of the public health sector.

Whether a health technology assessment is performed by the United Kingdom, Thailand, or some other country, cost-utility is a consideration. Countries often have a ceiling for the maximum cost-utility allowed when approving a drug or procedure that is usually linked to a measure of the country's income or wealth, such as GDP per capita. This reflects the country's ability to pay. A developing country that has only $1,000 per capita in income every year would have a difficult time financing payments for expensive treatments that are over $100,000 per person per year except for the rarest of diseases. If the country commits to paying for those rare diseases, then how can that government justify not paying for other diseases with treatments costing only $50,000 per person per year? This issue of affordability cannot be ignored in any discussion of the willingness to pay.

Despite the need for some guidance on thresholds, exceptions can be made based on nonfinancial factors, such as social and ethical considerations. Consequently, both in the United Kingdom and Thailand, there are instances where some types of care are approved even if the threshold is exceeded. Both the rich and the poor would like to enjoy good health, but poorer people and less affluent governments often cannot afford many important treatments.

Many countries have committed to providing universal health coverage, where everyone in the country is entitled to receive a basic package of essential health services.[44] Countries providing universal health coverage include Japan, Singapore, Australia, Switzerland, and the United Kingdom.[45] The services included in these packages vary from country to country but usually consist of a mix of preventive and curative care. Similarly, the Affordable Care Act requires that health plans offer an essential health benefits package that includes services within a specific set of defined categories.[46]

HEALTH INSURANCE

Government-provided health care programs such as Medicare have financial constraints due to limited budgets and capacity constraints due to a limited number of service providers, and since they are providing a public service based on tax revenues, they must consider how to distribute their resources fairly.

For-profit health insurance companies, like other for-profit enterprises, have a narrower set of constraints and motivations. They seek to maximize their revenue and minimizing their costs while staying in line with regulatory requirements. Equity considerations, such as the Affordable Care Act's regulatory requirements that health insurance companies can't deny coverage or charge more for people with preexisting conditions, and quality standards add restrictions to for-profit companies that impact their goal of maximizing profitability.

For-profit health insurance companies maximize revenue by trying to increase both the number of customers and the amount that each customer pays. Minimizing costs can be achieved by paying as little as possible for the health care expenses of the lives they are covering, but this tendency is buffered by the quality requirements included in the Affordable Care Act. These companies can minimize health care expenses by introducing efficiency strategies as well as by taking less elegant approaches, including implementing administrative barriers that make it more difficult for their customers to use health services, denying coverage for expensive treatments, and before the Affordable Care Act, denying coverage to people with specific preexisting conditions.

Not-for-profit health insurance companies find themselves in a similar situation as government health care regulators. They have a limited budget and need to ensure financial viability while trying to save the most lives or life years. It is a cost-utility situation, where they have take into account fiscal constraints and other considerations, such as equity.

Health insurance companies perform data analyses and build cost-simulation models to help maximize their profits. Budgetary impact models examine the expected patient costs for different treatment options where the costs reflect outpatient and inpatient care, equipment, and prescription drugs. The results of these analyses inform companies on how to prioritize different therapies and treatments.

The mechanisms that insurance companies use to pay for services are also changing. Traditionally, these companies would have a fee-for-service model, where the health care provider was paid for the service they provided, or a capitation model, where the provider was paid a fixed price per patient. Both models had incentive issues. The former incentivized health care providers to maximize the number of services they performed, whether or not they were necessary. The latter incentivized providers to accept a maximum number of patients and then provide minimal service. Quality standards exist to try to control the potential negative consequences of these incentives. Insurance companies seeking to contain costs are trying to implement risk-sharing agreements with providers and pharmaceutical companies. Regardless of the structure of the payment plan and the legal requirements on what care must be provided, the incentives of the patient, provider, and insurer are not all aligned.

Insurance is generally a way to manage risk. In the case of health, paying for health insurance guarantees that you will pay some amount for health care, but it also reduces the maximum amount you may have to pay. The choice of purchasing or not purchasing health insurance can be considered a bet. Younger people in good health might feel confident that the money they save not paying for insurance is a good bet. If they do not get into an accident, contract a serious disease, or have some other major medical need, then they win the bet. Often, however, this bet turns out poorly. Roughly half of all bankruptcies in the United States are medically related, and uninsured people are more likely to fall into medical bankruptcy than those with insurance.[47]

The Affordable Care Act has helped reduce the number of uninsured in the United States from over 40 million nonelderly (under sixty-five years old) in 2013 to 27.4 million in 2017.[48] Yet the number of uninsured in the United States is still substantial, only about 25 percent less than the entire population of Canada. The future implementation of the Affordable Care Act will continue to be affected by changes in the political climate, economic conditions, and evidence associated with the financial and health impacts of new policies.

More than 80 percent of uninsured Americans belong to families where someone is employed, and over half of the uninsured were in families with incomes less than twice the poverty level. These families have limited incomes and need to make critical decisions about how to spend their money. Some of these uninsured are eligible for subsidized health insurance, while others would need to pay the full price. Either way, the cost of health insurance must be weighed against paying for other priorities, like rent, food, electricity, and other necessities. Not purchasing health insurance allows families to spend their limited funds on other necessities, but it leaves them susceptible to catastrophic health expenses and further impoverishment.

OUT OF POCKET: FOR OURSELVES AND OUR FAMILIES

In the movie *Vacation*, Chevy Chase asks how much a car repair will cost, and the mechanic responds, "How much you got?" Anyone who has paid out of pocket for health care understands this situation.

Unfettered capitalism leads to a small percent of the population accumulating much of the wealth while a substantial percent of the population has little or nothing. In terms of health, a pure free-market with no regulatory constraints to enforce some measures of fairness will result in the wealthiest members of society receiving world-class health care while those who cannot afford it are left to die. In this world, the price tags placed on health are limited by the ability to pay, with no upper bound on the care provided for those with very deep pockets and little or no care for those with no money. America's Medicaid system ensures that there is some support for the poorest, but the organ transplant system presents a window into how money can purchase health and even life.

Out-of-pocket payments for health care services are rarely transparent in the United States, and only some health care customers are aware that these prices can be negotiable. The variation in costs is dramatic. For example, in 2011, the hospital prices for lower-limb MRIs were twelve times higher in the Bronx than in Baltimore. Even more dramatically, the prices could vary by up to a factor of nine within Miami alone.[49] Even for the same health service provided by the same physician, the costs could vary substantially depending on whether the patient had insurance and if they did, on the specific insurance carrier. The lack of pricing transparency is so common in America that when health service prices are clearly listed, we are often taken aback.

But bargain shopping or negotiating prices is not at the top of your mind when you are in need of health care. In a health emergency, the first thought is to get care. In some countries, the prices are fixed. In other countries, like the United Kingdom, the health care is covered by a national health care system and is usually free at the point of service. In the United States, health is a thriving business, with out-of-pocket expenses often being a major source of revenue for many for-profit entities.

When considering how much health is valued, there are two critical questions: How much would you pay to improve your health or the health of a sick family member? How much would you pay to gain ten or twenty more years of healthy life for yourself, your parents, or your children? These questions get to the root issue with the for-profit model of health care. Free-market evangelists often like to lump health care into the bucket of services that they believe will benefit from less regulation, less governance, and less government control. They are making the mistake of ignoring a crucial feature of health: inelastic demand. Unlike with widgets, cheeseburgers, or new smartphones, the demand for lifesaving health care does not decrease when the price goes up. If there is a lifesaving drug that can cure your illness, your parent's cancer, or your child's rare disease, you will pay whatever it costs to get that drug. Doubling or tripling the cost of the lifesaving drug or treatment will not cause the demand to drop. A market-based approach to health care is often at odds with the idea that basic health care is a human right.

Preventive medicine, such as immunizations and screenings, is one aspect of health care that does often exhibit elastic demand, meaning that as the costs of these services increase, people may use fewer of them. Health care that could prevent a long-term, often expensive condition may be sacrificed due to short-term cash flow problems. This is unfortunate not only because of the healthy life years that are lost but also from an economic point of view, since preventive medicine is often more cost effective than curative care.

Money cannot guarantee good health, but it can buy better health care service. Consider the case of organ transplants, where the demand is much greater than the supply of healthy, compatible kidneys, livers, hearts, and other vital, transplantable organs. It is important to develop a mechanism for fairly distributing these life-extending organs, yet for-profit motivations easily creep into these lifesaving procedures. Transplant tourism is a major business, with kidney, liver, heart, and lung transplants all being advertised online at prices often well over $100,000. Countries such as India, Pakistan, and China are net organ exporters, while citizens of wealthier countries such as Australia, Canada, Japan, and the United States are net organ transplant recipients.[50]

Health and the extension of life are clearly for sale when it comes to the organ market. A new organ may be available for those who can afford transplant tourism, while others without sufficient means may be resigned to an early death.

How can organ recipients be fairly prioritized? Is one person's life worth more than another's? Should a younger person receive a transplant before an older person? How should the expected number of future healthy life years impact the prioritization or the perceived importance of the individual? Should the president of a corporation get priority over a former sports star, a high school janitor, or a migrant farm worker? How should society prioritize the needs of a ninety-year-old Nobel Prize winner with late-stage dementia versus those of a developmentally challenged fifteen-year-old student, both of whom need the same organ? Should a sixty-year-old who smokes two packs a day, drinks whiskey for breakfast, and never exercises have the same priority as a sixty-year-old vegan marathon runner who has never smoked?

Lastly, what should society have done with Terri Schiavo, who lived in a permanent vegetative state for fifteen years? Could the money spent to keep her alive have been better used to save other people's lives, and if so, whose lives should have been saved? The answers to these questions go far beyond cost-benefit analysis and invoke many other considerations, including human rights, equity, and justice.

Health insurance places price tags on health and, correspondingly, on a patient's higher quality of life. The next chapter focuses on fertility decisions. Fertility decisions are more fundamental in that they concern the decision of whether or not to create new human life and if so, how many. This decision of whether to have children and how to allocate resources to children involve both monetary price tags and nonmonetary considerations.

8 Can We Afford a Little One?

Jenny is a twenty-three-year-old graduate student living with her boyfriend. She was on the pill, but the method failed. Now that she is pregnant, she needs to consider her new life options. She could decide to deliver the baby and then put it up for adoption. She would bear the challenges of pregnancy but would not be responsible for the child after birth—and would not be a parent. Or she could deliver the baby and raise the child herself. This would mean being responsible for the child, with all of the time, effort, and costs associated with being a parent, as well as being able to receive the benefits of parenthood. This may impact her plans to finish graduate school and would affect many other decisions for the rest of her life. Raising the child would have substantial financial implications for Jenny for decades, starting with prenatal care and potentially extending throughout her entire life. A third option would be to have the pregnancy terminated. Jenny wrestles with the choices, unsure of what step she should take.

Fertility decisions have profound implications for individuals, families, communities, and societies. Rather than discussing all decisions related to fertility, this chapter will focus attention on the topic of abortions, including abortion rights, sex-selective abortions, and disability-selective abortions, since this is where the concept of equity and price tags play a clear and prominent role.

Abortion rights relate to the relative value placed on the life of a pregnant woman versus her fetus, while sex-selective and disability-selective abortion decisions provide insight into how some prospective parents value different potential lives. These examples also reflect a recurring theme throughout the book, that certain lives that are less valued are less protected.

COSTS AND BENEFITS OF CHILDREN

Only an extraordinarily detail-oriented couple (maybe a pair of data scientists, economists, or statisticians) would use a spreadsheet to compute the expected financial costs and expected financial benefits of having a child. Few grandparents celebrate family get-togethers by showing the positive income statement associated with having a large family. But couples do have discussions about having children and the costs associated with raising them. Our firefighter Rick and his fiancé were clear that they wanted to have at least two children, and they were confident that his fireman's salary could cover the costs. Sebastian's parents hadn't been planning to have children just yet, but they were thrilled when they learned that Amelia was pregnant. They knew that their parents had raised them on far less than they were earning and assumed that if the money got tight, their extended family would lend a hand. After the birth of their second daughter, Jim and his wife were not sure if they wanted to have a third child, so they decided to freeze some of his wife's eggs when she was approaching her fortieth birthday.

Formal financial analysis about raising children does not occur explicitly in many relationships, yet couples that make a conscious decision to have children certainly think about the expected expenses. Viewing the decision of whether or not to have children as merely a financial calculation, similar to the cost-benefit analysis performed by companies, is narrow-minded and removed from the reality of deciding to become a parent. There are countless other considerations to take into account, including the desire to give love, to reciprocate the gift of life to another, and to bring joy to grandparents. The desire to have sex and the resulting production of children is the engine that keeps the human species from going extinct. With these qualifications aside, it is useful to step away from the emotional and evolutionary motivations of having children to consider just the financial aspects of parenting.

While some researchers have added up expenses to develop an estimate of the total costs of raising a child, this number varies dramatically depending on exactly how the child will be raised. Specific choices parents make regarding how to raise their children and what to support financially will greatly influence how much it costs. Later, the role of the child in caring for the parents influences the financial benefits. As a parent, one can have expectations of the support a child might provide, but there is no guarantee that these benefits will materialize.

It has been estimated that it costs a middle-income American family roughly $250,000 to raise a child to age eighteen, though this amount can have a very large range.[1] This estimate does not include costs parents may incur after their children reach age eighteen, such as paying for college tuition, covering wedding expenses, helping buy a car or a home, and other financial support.

Key cost elements in raising a child include food, clothing, health care, education, incremental housing costs, and entertainment. Health care costs include pregnancy care, delivery care, and later the health care of the child. Educational choices include deciding what schools the child will attend (public or private), if the child needs tutoring, and whether to pay for extra educational opportunities. Do the parents pay for college? Public college or private college? What about graduate school, medical school, or law school? Do the parents give the child a hand with buying her first house? Do the parents pay for a wedding or buy a generous wedding gift? Do the parents provide money for the grandchildren? Children of couples with lesser means will usually incur fewer costs as many of the options above are limited.

Parents may receive government support and employee benefits immediately to defray some of the child-rearing costs. Some parents will receive financial benefits from their children later on. Some children offer their parents financial support in their old age. Some provide their parents long-term care or help them by driving, cleaning, cooking, or performing other tasks that the parent would otherwise have to pay someone else to do. Beyond financial exchanges, children can give emotional support, love, and companionship to their parents. The emotional benefits of having a loving relationship with your children are impossible to monetize with exactitude.

Similarly, civil trial judgments do not include emotional benefits in the valuation of a wrongful death but rather focus on economic impacts.

In many families, having children is a negative net present value decision, using the definition of net present value discussed in chapter 4. The fact that billions of humans have continued to have children points to the obvious fallacy in simply considering children to be a financial investment. Evolution did not proceed based on an analysis of discounted cash flows. In earlier times, however, children may have been more likely to have produced a higher return on investment for parents than today.

One can imagine a situation where we could track the expenses of raising a child and the revenue that the child brings into the family by adding up his or her financial costs and contributions over time. Before the child reaches adulthood, the expenses are incurred on a daily basis, while the financial contributions are usually minimal, since employment opportunities are limited for minors in America.[2]

In the United States, the level of child labor has subsided greatly since the early twentieth century, though it is still common in many parts of the world today.[3] About one hundred years ago, many American children worked in mines or factories, sold newspapers, delivered messages, or polished shoes rather than attending school. At that time, an American child could legitimately have been viewed as a potential source of revenue since, at a very young age, the child could be earning an income and bringing that money back to the family. Although the income these children earned was less than that of an adult, from the point of view of the parents, a young child could have been cash-flow positive.

This dynamic changed in America during the twentieth century. Child labor rates declined due to the creation of mandatory, free public education, declining poverty levels, and the introduction of federal laws that restricted child labor. This shift reflected a broader change in American society and, throughout many parts of the world, a transition from viewing children as property of the parents to children being considered protected members of society with special rights[4]

From the perspective of price tags, children in the United States represent a major financial investment by parents of often hundreds of thousands of dollars, where the costs occur earlier in time and the potential financial benefits, if there are any at all, occur years later. More critically, the financial equation of having children can vary greatly based on the expected costs of the children and the future expected financial benefits, a concept that we will revisit later in the chapter in the discussion of abortion.

BABY MARKET

While raising a child has substantial financial implications, thousands of people each year choose to incur substantial costs for medical and surgical infertility treatments.[5] Those having trouble conceiving may undergo in-vitro fertilization, a procedure that can easily cost tens of thousands of dollars.[6] For women who either cannot carry a baby to term or chose not to, there is the thriving business of surrogates, also known as gestational carriers. The biological mother's eggs are extracted, fertilized, and then inserted into a surrogate mother to carry for the term of the pregnancy at a cost of about $90,000 to $130,000.[7] Biological mothers relying on gestational carriers may also need fertility treatment, resulting in even higher costs. Surrogacy has taken on an international flavor, with some couples opting to hire lower-cost surrogate mothers in India rather than use surrogates in the United States.[8]

Adoption is another option open to those who want to become parents. Adoption requires an investment of often tens of thousands of dollars to cover the legal and administrative fees, an expense that is above and beyond the normal costs of raising a child. Adoption of an unrelated child specifically means that the parents are nurturing (as well as incurring expenses for) someone with whom they lack a genetic linkage. Darwinism may struggle to explain the motivations behind adoption, but it cannot be denied that this is an emotionally fulfilling option for many parents. Adoption links to the broader concept of empathy and the relative value of lives, topics that will be examined later in the book.

Foster care is another alternative for those wishing to be responsible for children. Foster care is different from adoption in that foster care is temporary (compared to the permanence of adoption), foster parents lack parental legal rights, and foster parents receive stipends to cover the expenses of the child (whereas adoptive parents absorb these expenses). In 2017, there were nearly half a million children in foster care in the United States.[9]

Whether through fertility treatments, surrogate mothers, foster care, or adoption, many adults are willing to incur large expenses for the opportunity to be parents, with all of the responsibilities, costs, and benefits that being a parent entails.

ABORTION

There is no such thing as a woman being a little pregnant. A pregnancy is either planned or unplanned. Unplanned pregnancies happen often. They happen to women who are married and to women who are single. Unplanned pregnancies happen to teenagers and to women in their forties. Often, they happen because couples do not use contraception, use contraception incorrectly, or use a contraceptive that fails to work. While some contraceptive methods, such as implants, intrauterine devices, and sterilization, have low failure rates (less than one pregnancy per one hundred women in a year), other methods, such as sponges, condoms, spermicide, and withdrawal, fail at relatively high rates (more than eighteen pregnancies per one hundred women in a year).[10]

There are few more contentious topics in America than abortion. The topic of abortion can divide families and turn friends into enemies. Passionate supporters on both sides of the debate often use abortion as a litmus test for politicians and judges. Discussions about abortion stimulate very challenging questions, including: When does life begin? Is a fetus a person? Does a fetus have rights? What is the balance between individual autonomy and society's rules and norms? Can a woman be forced to nurture life against her will? Many of those questions cut across areas of religion, philosophy, law, and ethics.

This chapter will not attempt to answer these questions. Rather, we will use induced abortion as an issue to examine two critical questions: What is the value placed on a fetus? What are some of the ramifications of placing a higher value on the life of one fetus over another fetus, specifically when considering the sex or genetic make-up of the fetus?

Induced abortions are when a pregnancy is terminated intentionally, either through a surgical procedure or with medication, in contrast to the roughly 15 to 20 percent of recognized pregnancies that end in spontaneous abortions, also called miscarriages.[11] Whether a pregnancy was planned or unplanned, there are many possible reasons why a woman may want to have an induced abortion, including: her life or health is at risk, she does not want to carry the pregnancy to full term due to some attribute of the fetus, or she never wanted to be pregnant in the first place.

Abortion rights vary around the world. National laws range from absolutely restrictive, where abortions are illegal under any circumstances (including rape, incest, and possible death of the mother), to extremely liberal, where abortions are allowed without restrictions during the early stages of pregnancy. Between these two most extreme scenarios of abortion rights, there are gradations of abortion legality. Some countries allow abortions to save the life or preserve the health of the pregnant woman and/or on socioeconomic grounds. More than 60 percent of the global population lives in countries where induced abortion is permitted during the early stages of pregnancy either without restrictions or for a relatively wide range of reasons.[12]

Rights and values go hand in hand. Induced abortions represent a balance of rights between the pregnant woman and the fetus. An induced abortion also reflects the relative value society places on the pregnant woman's life versus the fetus. When society protects someone's life, it shows that society values that life. Contrarily, when society fails to protect someone's right to live, it means that it values that life less or not at all. When a society allows for abortions to protect the life of the pregnant woman, it implies that the society values the life and rights of the pregnant woman more than the rights of the fetus. More generally, increasing levels of abortion rights for the mother correspond to decreasing levels of the relative rights of the fetus.

Abortion rights have changed over time within the United States, and to this day, these rights are actively debated by the public and in the courts. In the late 1800s, nearly all states had laws that made abortion or attempted abortion at any stage in a pregnancy illegal. By the early 1960s, forty-four states allowed abortions only if the pregnancy endangered the woman's life. Five states allowed abortions if the woman's life or physical health were in jeopardy.[13] Pennsylvania did not allow abortions under any circumstances. Abortion rights moved rapidly in the next decade so that by 1972, thirteen states had laws that permitted abortions "if the pregnant woman's life or physical or mental health were endangered, if the fetus would be born with a severe physical or mental defect, or if the pregnancy had resulted from rape or incest."[14]

By this time, the pregnant woman's life and health were not the only allowable factors that would permit an abortion. The circumstances of the pregnancy as well as the expected physical and mental outlook of the fetus were also allowed as considerations. In *Roe v. Wade* (1973), the Supreme Court ruled that a pregnant woman has a constitutional right to an abortion until the fetus is viable. Viable was defined as being potentially able to live outside the womb with artificial aid. States can implement laws that restrict a woman's right to an abortion after the fetus has advanced enough to be deemed viable to only situations where an abortion is needed to preserve her life or her mental or physical health.

The Supreme Court ruled that the legality of abortion is a fundamental right included within the guarantee of personal privacy, with Nixon appointee Harry Blackmun authoring the decision: "This right of privacy . . . is broad enough to encompass a woman's decision whether or not to terminate her pregnancy."[15]

The Supreme Court stated that regulations limiting abortions must be justified by a "compelling state interest." This point is important in that it reminds us that abortions are also about the balance between individual autonomy (the right of a pregnant woman to have control of her body) versus society's norms and rules. Phrased more crudely, the requirement of a "compelling state interest" opens the door to the question of whether a woman's reproductive organs are privately owned or whether they are collectively owned and managed by society with rules governing what she can and cannot do with her own body.

There are many key questions surrounding the *Roe v. Wade* decision. One of the most basic ones is whether the fetus has rights. The Bill of Rights discusses rights for "people." Human rights are for humans. Is it fair to characterize a fetus as either a person or a human? In *Roe v. Wade,* the court's view was that a fetus is not "a person within the meaning of the Fourteenth Amendment" and so is not subject to the Equal Protection Clause of that amendment. Those wishing to avoid being thrust fully into this debate often describe a fetus as having the "potential for human life."

The court's ruling regarding the importance of the viability of the fetus can be interpreted as a jump in the relative value of the fetus versus the pregnant woman's life. A fetus that is not viable can be terminated at the pregnant woman's will. U.S. law provides more rights to fetuses that are determined to be viable. Once determined to be viable, the relative value of the fetus to society increases so that an abortion can be performed legally only under a limited, state-defined set of circumstances. At the time of the *Roe v. Wade* decision, it was recognized that the gestational age associated with viability was arbitrary and subject to change based on scientific advances.

In general, the shorter the gestation period and the lighter the baby, the less likely it is to survive. In wealthy countries, a majority of infants born at twenty-five or more weeks' gestation and with a birth weight of six hundred or more grams survive.[16] Additionally, at least 50 percent of babies twenty-three to twenty-four weeks old survive when born in developed countries.[17] The youngest preterm baby to survive and grow to be a healthy adult had a gestational age of only twenty-one weeks old.[18]

Because of the historical link between the United States and the United Kingdom, it is worthwhile to consider British abortion laws. The Abortion Act 1967 made abortion legal in the United Kingdom up to twenty-eight weeks' gestation. In 1990, the period of gestation was reduced to twenty-four weeks, although there was still the option of a later-term abortion in a limited number of situations, including extreme fetal abnormality and to save the life or preserve the health of the pregnant woman. This shortening of the time frame may have reflected improvements in medical care of preterm babies.

The gestation period is an important consideration in pregnancy discussions. In the United States, across all political persuasions, support for abortion rights wanes as the fetus ages. In a 2018 poll, 13 percent of respondents agreed that "abortion should generally be legal" in the last three months of a pregnancy. This is significantly lower than the 28 percent that agreed that second-trimester abortions should be legal and the 60 percent who believed that first-trimester abortions should be legal.[19] This changing perception of the appropriateness of abortion likely reflects people's intuition regarding the viability of the fetus.

Perceptions about abortion rights as a function of gestational stage reflect the shifting relative value that society places on a fetus as the fetus ages. One way to explore this is by examining the relative value of the fetus versus the pregnant woman's life. When a pregnant woman can choose to have an abortion for any reason with no restrictions, then the fetus has an insignificant relative value compared to the life of the pregnant woman. Legal restrictions on abortions represent situations where the fetus has some rights, meaning that the relative value of the fetus is more than zero. The fetus has at least equal rights as the pregnant woman in situations where abortion is not permitted under any circumstances. In these situations, abortions are considered murder, equivalent to if the child had been born and then killed. When abortion is illegal even if the fetus threatens the pregnant women's life, it can be implied that the women is being denied her fundamental right to preserve her own life. In this case, one can interpret that the fetus is actually being accorded more rights than the pregnant women.

Imagine that the right of a pregnant woman to have an abortion was measured on a scale of 0 to 100 percent. Situations where abortions are illegal regardless of the risk to the woman's life would be 0 percent. In countries where abortions are legal under certain circumstances, the percent would range from greater than 0 to 100, depending on the rights of the pregnant woman and the stage of the pregnancy. A measure of 100 percent would correspond to situations where the pregnant woman can have an abortion for any reason. This 100 percent rights situation exists in some parts of the United States until the fetus is considered viable. After that stage, the percent declines, as the abortion often has to be justified based on specific concerns, such as saving the pregnant woman's life or health. The percentage declines sharply as the fetus approaches a gestation age of nine months. The percent is close to 0 near the moment of delivery. Consider as an extreme example that a woman cannot decide to abort the fetus an hour before delivery.

There is a wide range of state-level laws related to abortion, many passed in the last few years. As of October 2019, sex-selective abortions are illegal in nine states. Two states (Missouri and North Dakota) prohibit abortions of fetuses with genetic anomalies, and two states (Arizona and Missouri) have made abortions based on race selection illegal.[20]

The more legal rights that a fetus is accorded, the higher the relative value of the fetus as measured by society's laws. Those wishing to enshrine a fetus with rights have found state laws on aggravated crimes to be an entry point. Aggravated assault is usually differentiated from simple assault by factors including the use of a weapon, the status of the victim, the intent of the perpetrator, and the degree of injury caused.[21] Some states have passed aggravated assault legislation that increases the penalties for crimes where the victim is a pregnant woman. Known as fetal homicide laws, they exist in thirty-eight states and vary widely in terms of language and intention.[22] In California, murder is defined as the premeditated unlawful killing with malicious intent of a human being or a fetus.[23] In Rhode Island, the definition of manslaughter includes the willful killing of a viable fetus by any injury to a pregnant woman.[24] Some people have interpreted the additional sentencing for fetal homicide to mean that in those states, the right of the fetus to live is being recognized. That point remains contentious, with state and federal legal decisions coming down on different sides of the issue. More broadly, legal challenges to *Roe v. Wade* continue on different levels of the court system, where the decision on the constitutionality of abortions may be changed at any time by a shift of one or two votes, as it nearly did in the Supreme Court decision *Webster v. Reproductive Health Services* (1989).[25]

Science continues to advance so that a fetus can survive at earlier gestational stages and increasingly lower birth weights. If science reaches the point at which a sperm and an egg can be combined outside of the human body, fertilized, and the resulting embryo nurtured in an artificial womb to the development stage of a newborn, then there will no longer be a shift from a fetus not being viable to being viable. If a woman's womb is never required to produce a baby, then wouldn't a fetus always be viable? Artificial wombs would make it very difficult to argue the case that a fetus, at any stage of gestation, has no rights. If technology reaches the stage where a woman's womb is not necessary for fetal development, would the debate over the balance between a woman's control over her own body versus society's norms and rules also be eliminated? Would artificial wombs eliminate the possibility of a woman potentially being required by law to nurture a life in her own body against her will? If nine months after in vitro fertilization, a healthy baby could be delivered from an artificial womb, then when exactly did the fetus, that never saw the inside of a woman's womb, become a person? When exactly did human life begin?

It is not at all clear whether technology could ever reach this stage. But if artificial wombs were an option, then there would need to be a fundamental rethinking of what it means to be a living person. This book does not seek to answer these important philosophical questions, but it is critical to raise them for consideration in this era of rapidly advancing medical technology.

Disability-Selective Abortions

Disability-selective abortion options, such as for fetuses identified with Down Syndrome, anencephaly, or Tay-Sachs disease, allow parents to weigh the expected values of time and money against the challenges and costs of raising a child with congenital abnormalities. This is an emotional decision that is influenced by religion, ethics, personal values, and economics. The information from these screening is usually available in the first and second trimester.

Again, parents do not generally create spreadsheets to analyze the expected financial flows over the next few decades associated with choosing between allowing a fetus with congenital abnormalities to come to term and be delivered or aborting the fetus and trying to get pregnant again. That said, it would be a major omission to not recognize that financial considerations often play a role for many prospective parents in the decision of whether or not to abort a fetus with congenital abnormalities. Prospective parents may estimate that a child with congenital abnormalities could incur, on average, more costs related to areas such as healthcare and education. In terms of expected revenue, those same prospective parents may estimate that an adult child with congenital abnormalities could earn, on average, less than a typical adult child and hence potentially provide them with less support in their old age. Thinking from a purely financial point of view, some parents may see a fetus with congenital abnormalities as having a lower net present value, or price tag, than a typical fetus.

This lower price tag may be reflected in the fact that fetuses with congenital abnormalities are frequently aborted. In America, the majority of fetuses with Down syndrome are aborted, a rate that is significantly higher than that for fetuses that do not have identified congenital abnormalities.[26] Many support the right of a woman to make this choice, while others believe that disability-selective abortions are immoral.

Some fear that disability-selective abortions open the door to selecting for other genetic factors. It is not difficult to imagine a world where a detailed genetic map is created for every fetus. This map could be used to predict hair color, longevity, and height. More detailed analysis could predict the probability of specific diseases, including cancers and cardiovascular diseases, or perhaps even some measures related to intelligence.

Values of life could be placed on fetuses based on a vast number of genetic factors, with parents selecting the fetus that they believe has the maximum value. Some fertility clinics already perform a variation of this service when they allow prospective mothers to select for certain traits in their donors. While designer babies are still a ways off, the Repository for Germinal Choice, a sperm bank that accepted only Nobel Prize winners in science and other scientists as donors, resulted in more than two hundred children being born.[27] Meanwhile, technologies like Clustered Regularly Interspaced Short Palindromic Repeats (CRISPR), allow scientists to change a single nucleotide or to insert or delete entire genes at the embryonic stage, thus permanently altering the germ line and potentially eliminating diseases like sickle cell anemia and cystic fibrosis.[28] In December 2018, He Jiankui announced that he had used CRISPR technology to genetically edit the DNA of human embryos during in vitro fertilization.[29] Arguments about abortion rights and an individual's right to privacy get mixed up with debates about eugenics whenever parents seek to select what they believe will be a more perfect child based on genetic testing.

A brave new world exists with preconception and postconception screening for more than just sex. The entire scope of anything with genetic linkages is potentially open for selection. Ethical issues come marching along as technology advances and should be rigorously explored and discussed to ensure that science doesn't race off too far ahead of ethics and moral considerations.

Sex Selection

Mention the phrase "sex selection," and one immediately thinks of countries like China and India, yet sex selection is not confined within one or two national borders. It creates regional ripple effects throughout Asia, Europe, and even parts of America, where some prospective parents are selecting boys rather than girls.

Sex selection is driven by the motive of son preference and is highlighted by situations of declining fertility.[30] Son preference refers to circumstances where parents place a higher value on having a son than on having a daughter. It has many roots. Many societies are historically male-dominated, with property rights, inheritance laws, and dowry systems all designed to favor men. In East Asian cultures, Confucian hierarchy explicitly places women in a subservient position to men.[31] Parents may need a son to ensure that family fortunes do not get absorbed by the state or passed on to another family. Birthright refers to the eldest son receiving a special share of the inheritance. In the Bible, a hungry Esau transferred his birthright to his younger twin brother, Jacob, for a meal.

One consistent theme across all methods of valuing life is that whenever one life is valued more than another, the lower-valued life is less protected. In the case of son preference, the lives of girls are lower-valued and thus less protected than the higher-valued lives of boys. Here, the word *value* can refer to both nonmonetary considerations and monetary price tags. For the purposes of this discussion, we will focus more on the monetary price tags.

There is no single explanation for son preference. In many cultures, there were, and in some still are, financial advantages in having a boy rather than a girl. In some traditional male-dominated cultures, a girl is expected to marry young and forgo her education. The marriage may require a dowry, which involves the parents of the young girl having to transfer money and/or property to the husband at the time of the marriage. The girl is often expected to move in with her husband's family, raise children, and help care for her husband's parents. From a parent's point of view, the net present value of a son in this type of society would often be noticeably more positive than that of a daughter. Simply put, in some cultures, having a daughter was, and sometimes still is, not as good of a financial investment for the parents as having a son. Prospective parents are not busy developing spreadsheets with net present value calculations to contrast the expected financial value of a son versus a daughter, but the fact remains that in some cultures, there has been, and still may be, a true financial difference from the point of view of the parent.

Son preference has existed for millennia. What is new in the past few decades is the decline in fertility that has resulted in much smaller family sizes. Total fertility rates in China and India exceeded five children per woman in the 1950s, but China's fertility rate dropped below three in the 1970s. India's fertility rates have been below that level for over a decade. Today, China has a total fertility rate of around 1.6, and India has a rate of around 2.3.[32] Families with five or six children were very likely to have at least one son. As family sizes dropped, the situation changed. If families will have only one or two children, there's a good chance they will not have a son unless they do something to tip the odds.

Where sex selection takes place, there are "missing girls," the difference between the actual number of girls born and the number that would be expected if there were no female infanticide or sex-selective abortions.[33] There are historical examples of newborn and young girls being selectively killed, but this practice isn't confined to history.[34] Chinese girls still experience excessive mortality despite Mao's poetic statement that "women hold up half the sky."[35] The most common reason for "missing girls" is prenatal selection, not female infanticide. Ultrasound is used to identify the sex of the fetus. The decision of whether or not to abort then follows. In India, about 87 percent of the "missing girls" are due to prenatal selection, while 13 percent are missing due to so-called postnatal selection, such as infanticide and reduced medical care for newborn girls.[36]

Demography can easily determine if prenatal sex selection is occurring. Count the ratio of newborn boys to newborn girls in a given population. If no sex selection is performed, there will be about 105 boys born for every 100 girls. The ratio of boys to girls jumps up when parents preferentially select boys.

The countries that have the most extreme sex ratios at birth include the Asian countries of China, India, and Vietnam and the Eastern European countries of Armenia, Azerbaijan, and Georgia, although sex selection is not limited to these examples.[37] Combined, these countries represent roughly 40 percent of the world's population. In 2017, four countries had sex ratios at birth of 110 boys per 100 girls or higher: China, Armenia, Azerbaijan, and India.[38] By 2030, there are projected to be over 40 million excess men of prime reproductive age (ages fifteen to forty-nine) in China and over 30 million in India.[39] That is more than the entire population of the metropolitan areas of Beijing, Shanghai, and Delhi combined. Sex selection rates vary wildly within India and China. Punjab, in northern India, has a sex ratio at birth of at least 120 boys per 100 girls, while some other parts of India have normal ratios.[40] In China, the region of Tibet has normal sex ratios at birth, while regions including Xaanxi, Henan, Hubei, and Fujian all have abnormal sex ratios.[41]

Sex selection, as with other medical technology, often begins with the elites, who have the best access to and ability to afford the latest technology.

In South Korea, sex selection started in Seoul. Sex selection in Azerbaijan began in the capital, Baku. In India, children born to high school graduates have a higher male to female ratio at birth than those born to nongraduates. Wealthy urban dwellers are the first to have access to ultrasound services. Consequently, in countries where sex selection occurs, those populations were the first to see rising male to female ratios at births as female fetuses were selectively aborted. Over time, ultrasound technology spreads to poorer and rural populations, and sex selective abortions can spread with it.[42]

Birth parity, the number of children a woman has already delivered, is a predictor of sex ratio at birth in many countries. In son-preference cultures, parents feel the "birth squeeze" tightening after each child. After having one or two girls, parents influenced by son preference will experience greater pressure to have a son. In Armenia, the ratio of boys to girls among first and second children is normal, but it explodes to over 150 boys per 100 girls for later births.[43] Similar trends are seen in Vietnam, Hong Kong, and other countries where the male to female ratio increases with parity.[44] Sex selection is also apparent in America, where American-born children of Chinese, Korean, and Indian parents have elevated male to female ratios at birth for the second and third child when the first or first two children are girls.[45] These ratios are linked to sex-specific stopping, a concept that will be explained in the following section, and may also be related to the fact that Asian Americans have abortion rates that are more than twice that of whites.[46]

Countries where sex selection occurs can also eliminate it. Sex selection was rampant in South Korea in the early 1990s, but by 2007 the sex ratio at birth was back in the normal range.[47] This trend was driven by reducing the motive—son preference—as well as tightening regulations on ultrasound technology use.[48]

Reducing son preference helps eliminate sex selection, but ramping up legal threats doesn't always work. Sex selection is illegal in China and India, where there are strongly worded laws and penalties prohibiting it. However, while fierce on paper, these measures lack teeth in practice.[49] Abortions are legal in both China and India, and despite legislation to restrict sex selection, the selective abortion of female fetuses remains rampant. As previously mentioned, as of October 2019, sex-selective abortions are illegal in nine U.S. states.[50]

SOFTER SEX SELECTION

Before ultrasound, people used the soft and hard methods of sex selection. The hard method involved horrible practices like killing newborns or denying them medical treatment. The soft method was to keep having children until you finally got the boy or girl you always wanted. This is called "sex-specific stopping," because once parents have their desired number and sex of children, they begin using family planning methods. In many countries, a couple with two girls is more likely to continue to try having children than a couple who already has a boy and a girl.[51]

In societies with son preference, sex-specific stopping means that the sex ratio of the last child is heavily skewed toward boys. In India, for example, the sex ratio at birth is around 110 boys per 100 girls, but the sex ratio at last birth is close to 150 boys per 100 girls.[52]

Spillover Effects

The ramifications of sex selection and the underlying son preference, with boys' lives being valued more than girls' lives, are far-reaching. The current excessive number of males in China alone will leave tens of millions of men unable to find a mate. Millions of unpaired, testosterone-elevated men can lead to societal problems, including rising delinquency, increased crime, and possibly political instability. Senior officials in both India and China have expressed concerns about potential political instability associated with the sex imbalances.[53]

The lack of available potential brides could drive increases in sex trafficking and prostitution. Forced marriages, negotiated by families, may flourish as families try to get money for their daughters. Cross-border marriages, as men from countries with an excess of single men seek brides in nearby countries, will rise. This means that one country's gender imbalance impacts the neighboring countries. A national issue of not having enough women can become a regional issue. Vietnam has struggled with its own lack of women due to sex selection, but the country has nonetheless seen a massive influx of Taiwanese and mainland Chinese men on marriage tourism visits, shopping for wives.[54] This means that the dating and marriage pools for Vietnamese men get even more shallow as the men must compete against both local men and foreigners for the limited number of Vietnamese women. This imbalance in the supply of available women should eventually result in the relative value of having a girl rising, but cultural traditions of son preference would likely persist in some populations.

Looking Forward

Technology, in the form of ultrasounds combined with selective abortions, has made sex selection less personal and more medicalized. Sex-selection technology continues advancing. Today, we can separate out male and female sperm, although the process isn't 100 percent accurate. With sperm sorting, parents can select male or female sperm to be used for artificial insemination. There are also preimplantation diagnostics, which involve screening fertilized embryos for desired sex as well as for more than one hundred genetic conditions prior to implantation.

Sperm sorting and preimplantation diagnostics are currently expensive and limited to the wealthier populations in a handful of countries, just as ultrasound technology was a few decades ago. They will probably grow more popular and more affordable over time. In the meantime, fertility tourism trips may head to the United States, where these services are offered at some fertility clinics.

One key advantage for parents and pro-choice advocates is that these services circumvent the discussions of sex-selective abortion, since the sex of the fetus is selected before implantation. Nonetheless, these methods still enable parents to weigh the relative value of having a boy versus a girl and then tilt nature's randomness in one direction.

The Future of Sex Selection

Some of the distortions in sex ratios at birth will reverse to normal due to shifts in the same expected cash flows that motivate some sex selection. Women have already achieved similar property and inheritance rights as men in most countries. Women's rising educational opportunities are creating a changing gender dynamic, one where women are more empowered to have greater economic opportunities and choices in life. Girls now achieve similar levels of primary and secondary education as boys in many countries.[55] This rise in women's education is associated with declining marriage rates and later marriages for those who choose to marry. The global good of improving women's education has resulted in a comparative increase in the economic strength and empowerment of women. Not coincidentally, these improved opportunities for women are associated with lower fertility rates, as there is a strong negative correlation between the average number of years of education and the total number of children women have.[56]

Women tend to be caregivers to the elderly more often than men. Son preference should decline as women's economic opportunities increase and the need for caregivers rises with the aging population. Women's increasing political roles throughout the world will enhance parents' understanding of the potential power of having a girl. More broadly, in populations that currently practice sex selection, it is reasonable to expect that as women become more politically and socially empowered, better educated, and more able to earn better salaries, the financial advantages of having a boy versus a girl will diminish. While there will continue to be population pockets that adhere to dowry systems, Confucian hierarchy rules, and other forms of son preference, these may become a progressively smaller percentage of the total population in countries practicing sex selection.

One single decision to select for a boy may seem innocuous. But millions of individuals making this same choice can lead to a collective disaster. It is an example of the "tragedy of the commons," where each person does what is in their own interests, causing the broader society to suffer.

This brings back the age-old debates about the balance between individual rights and collective benefit. What sacrifices must an individual make as a member of a society? This topic will likely be debated until the end of history and is well beyond the scope of this book.

For our purposes, it is critical to understand not only the factors that impact Jenny's decision about her pregnancy but also the factors that influence the hundreds of thousands of pregnancies that occur every single day and some of the consequences of these pregnancy decisions.[57]

9 Broken Calculators

In October 1987, eighteen-month-old Jessica McClure fell into a well in the backyard of her aunt's Texas home. The rescue effort attracted national media coverage. Donations flooded in to help rescue Jessica and pay for her medical care after the harrowing ordeal. Most of that money was not needed. It was put into a trust fund, believed to be worth nearly $1 million, which "Baby" Jessica gained access to on her twenty-fifth birthday. She is now in her thirties, married, and has two children of her own. Also in 1987, an estimated thirteen million children under the age of five died; many of these deaths were preventable.[1] Unlike Jessica, these millions of children received a miniscule fraction of the media's attention, and the prospect of saving them attracted little private money.

Jessica was an identified life and was facing an impending identifiable death unless something was done to save her. She was a specific person who had a name and a family, and she was trapped in a tragic situation. The danger she faced, along with her photograph, was conveyed to the public via television screens. Viewers could easily imagine Jessica's life if she were to be saved and the horrible feelings of loss her family would experience if she were to die this unnecessary death. Those viewers gave money to save Baby Jessica because they had the noble goal of wanting to help save this identified life, a life with which they could readily emphasize.

By contrast, few of us know personal details about the millions of children dying unnecessarily across the globe. The media doesn't flood us with information about each child's life history, family, dreams, and suffering. Also, we don't know which specific children that are at risk would be saved if we helped them. These millions of lives are bundled together as statistics that we can discuss in terms of probabilities of mortality and expected number of total deaths. These numbers are reported in scientific journals, analyzed by academics and development organizations, and discussed in international conferences. A calculation could be performed to compare the outcomes of hypothetical situations in which the money that was raised for Baby Jessica's rescue (and trust fund) was instead spent on vaccinating children or improving water supplies in developing countries. Jessica was an identified child that was certain to die if she was not rescued. The many children that might have been saved had the same rescue (and trust fund) money been used for vaccinations or improved water supplies are not individually identified and are unknown to the public.

The media attention and subsequent money raised was directed toward Baby Jessica's certain impending death and not a set of unknown children at risk. The certainty of her impending death also played a role in the public's response, since humans tend to place more weight on outcomes that are certain rather than uncertain, a phenomenon known as the "certainty effect."[2]

The contrast between the public's response to Baby Jessica and to the millions of children dying that same year is an example of an identified victim effect, referred to here as identification bias. People are often more concerned with risks that are concentrated on a specific individual or set of individuals rather than risks that are spread out across a large population.[3] Or, as expressed by Mother Theresa, "If I look at the mass, I will never act. If I look at the one, I will."[4,5]

When discussing estimates for the Value of a Statistical Life, economists emphasize that these are not identified lives. These economic estimates have no meaning when recast in the point of view of a specific person that you know—a colleague, a friend, a parent. Similarly, in discussing how we value health, the discussion breaks down when the question becomes personal. While health economists can compute the necessary cure rate of a new cancer drug to justify its use from a cost-benefit point of view, this analysis is irrelevant to the question of how much you would spend to preserve your own health or the health of one of your loved ones.

Identification bias is one of the more powerful biases that impact our assessments of the value of life. There are countless examples of how moving from statistics to individual lives increases the perceived value of life, often prompting actions that might otherwise not be taken. In 2010, the world watched as thirty-three Chilean miners were trapped 2,300 feet below ground following a cave-in. A rescue operation, costing roughly $20 million, succeeded in bringing all the miners out alive after they had been underground for more than two months. Television and Internet coverage ensured that millions around the world immediately heard about the successful rescue. The costs of the rescue mission were borne by the mining company, the Chilean government, and individual donors. During those same sixty-nine days that the miners were trapped underground, hundreds, if not thousands, of miners around the world died doing their jobs.[6] Americans were not aware of most of those other mining deaths. These other miners received little news coverage, their personal stories were not shared, and the amount of money expended to save their lives was likely substantially less than that made available to save the thirty-three Chileans.

As of October 2019, the Syrian civil war has resulted in more than half of the country's population being either killed or displaced.[7] There are now over five million Syrian refugees in neighboring countries, including Turkey, Lebanon, Iraq, Egypt, and Jordan. In spite of those huge numbers and the breadth of this humanitarian crisis, the phrase "Syrian refugee" brings to the minds of many Americans a single image: the picture of the drowned body of three-year-old Aylan Kurdi, lying face down on a beach in Turkey.[8] The photograph generated a spike in American interest in the Syrian civil war and the Syrian refugee crisis as it personalized the tragedy, adding a specific individual human story to the statistics.

Organizations that are trying to raise funding are well aware of this identification bias. Citing statistics about the number of lives that can be saved by donations is limited in its effectiveness. Showing a picture of a starving or crying child, offering the chance to sponsor that child, and even giving donors the opportunity to communicate directly with the child whose life they are saving is often far more powerful than merely listing facts and data.[9]

EMPATHY

Identification bias is one factor that impacts assessments of the value of life. Identification bias impacts empathy, our ability to understand and be concerned with the feelings of others. Empathy can impact preconceived notions, and it affects how we value lives. As discussed in Paul Bloom's book *Against Empathy,* empathy sometimes results in us valuing life more fairly and other times in us valuing lives less fairly.[10] Empathy is not a static value. It changes depending on our own physical, mental, and financial circumstances, our moods, our recent experiences, and changes in our relationships.

Empathy is fundamental to normal human behavior, and it underlies our social fabric by providing much of the glue that allows our societies to function and our species to survive. Empathy is natural and necessary within a family. Given the inability of babies to care for themselves, empathy for newborns is a biological necessity. Without the interest or willingness to care for our progeny, our species would have died out quickly. Evolution is dependent on which genes are transferred to future generations.[11] This circle of concern reaches beyond immediate dependents to our extended families. It also spreads to larger groups, such as tribes, as well as to those who are not directly related but have similar cultures, ethnicities, religions, nationalities, special interests, and other characteristics we use to identify and categorize humans. Empathy may depend on age, where we may have more concern about the feelings of the very young, the very old, or people our own age.[12]

The greater our empathy for someone, the more we value their life. This value can be expressed in the time that we spend trying to improve that person's life, the concern that we express for that life, or in situations involving money, the price tag we place on that life.

The opposite of empathy is apathy, a lack of concern. A consequence of apathy is that the lives of those with whom we feel less connected are often comparatively less valued. This may include those with whom we lack closely shared genetics, familiar connections, cultures, ethnicities, religions, nationalities, special interests, or other characteristics.

Citizenship is one of the most powerful forms of self-identify and can dramatically influence how we value an individual's life. During peacetime, shared citizenship can raise the concern for one person's life while the lives of those from other countries are left undervalued and sometimes underprotected. Recall ACME, the fictional coal-fired power plant near the Canadian border discussed in chapter 4, which exposed people to more risk when Canadian lives were ignored in the cost-benefit analysis.

During wartime, the considerations of how life is valued undergo a radical shift. In times of war, it is no longer a crime for a soldier to kill a human who happens to be his or her country's enemy. It is a justifiable homicide, one that is considered moral, and is often glorified, in the eyes of the soldier's country. Armed conflicts between nations, states, or groups result in dramatically lower values being placed on the lives of the enemy. The goal of war is to defeat the enemy, and killing enemy soldiers is not only morally and socially acceptable but also often worthy of medals and public celebrations. The enemy is often dehumanized, and the threat it poses exaggerated or even simply fabricated to help justify the war and the corresponding killing. This dehumanization is specifically carried out to reduce our empathy for the enemy—the less they are seen as fellow humans, the less guilt we will feel when our soldiers kill them. Lost American lives are justifiably mourned, while the deaths of enemy citizens, let alone enemy soldiers, are largely ignored by the American media and public.

Few question the idea that killing someone in self-defense is morally defensible. Justifiable homicide is the killing of a person in a situation where you are faced with an imminent threat to your life. Beyond self-defense, justifiable homicide also covers situations where a homicide would prevent greater harm to innocents. Self-defense arguments have been used by politicians since time immemorial to justify war, since these arguments allow war to be seen as a situation where taking another's life is morally, socially, and legally acceptable. This is true in American history, where the trope of America as a reluctant warrior is based on efforts to portray nearly all of our national conflicts as necessary for self-defense or for the protection of human rights.

Nationalist fervor can be quickly whipped into a bloodthirsty frenzy through effective propaganda that dehumanizes the enemy and is often infused with messages of the country's need for self-defense. Americans rallied in support of the Mexican-American War (1846–48) with the battle cry "Remember the Alamo," with little regard for the Mexicans killed. The American justification was that the war was necessary for self-defense following skirmishes between American and Mexican soldiers across the Rio Grande. Mexicans have a very different perspective of these events, one that pays more attention to the history of the land north of the Rio Grande and America's persistent efforts to expand its territory.

Half a century later, American support for the Spanish-American War (1898) was drummed up by newspapers with the rallying cry "Remember the *Maine*," in reference to the USS *Maine*, which sank in Havana Harbor following an explosion. While the cause of the explosion was never conclusively determined, in the eyes of the newspapers and the public, the loss of hundreds of Americans sailors needed to be avenged. Roughly two months later, America was at war with Spain.

World War II saw the United States distribute a massive amount of propaganda that dehumanized the Japanese, presenting them as animalistic savages. At the same time, this propaganda was designed to instill fear in Americans and convey to them that the enemy was powerful and needed to be defeated. This representation of the Japanese as subhumans who presented an existential threat to America provided moral cover not just for the devastation of Japanese soldiers but also for the civilian slaughter wrought by the United States during the firebombing of Tokyo and by the dropping of atomic bombs on Hiroshima and Nagasaki.[13]

The killing of enemy soldiers is an expected outcome of war and is considered part of the duty of a soldier fighting to defend America. The life of an enemy soldier has little value in wartime and from the American perspective potentially could be considered to have negative value, since the destruction of that life brings the American side closer to victory. The slaughter of enemy civilians, rather than soldiers, speaks to the power of a state of war to diminish the value of human life. Today, World War II is viewed in the eyes of many Americans as a just war, one in which our Greatest Generation served the world.[14] The justification for the war was predicated not only on the Japanese attack on Pearl Harbor but also on the inhuman brutality of the war's aggressors.

Nazi Germany's propaganda machine portrayed Jewish people as a threat to Germany while simultaneously dehumanizing them. Representing Aryans as superior to other humans and Jews as subhuman facilitated the Holocaust and the mass destruction of human lives. Beyond the treatment of those in concentration camps, prisoners of war held by the Germans and Japanese were often worked or starved to death. Germany readily bombed civilian areas, and this action was reciprocated by the Allies, who famously bombed Dresden, killing tens of thousands of German civilians.[15] The Japanese conquest of China went far beyond military engagements, extending to attacks on civilians, such as the Rape of Nanjing, a heinous massacre that left hundreds of thousands of civilians slaughtered, an event the Japanese still do not fully acknowledge.[16]

The sacrifices made by the United States during the war are justifiably lauded, and the approximately 420,000 American soldiers who died during the war are honored by our country. Yet there is minimal mention in American history books of the far greater casualties suffered by America's allies: the Soviet Union lost roughly ten million soldiers and an additional fourteen million citizens, and China lost about three to four million soldiers.[17] The millions of German and Japanese soldiers and civilians killed during the war also receive scant attention from the American media and public, since the lives of our enemies are less valued.

Following the incredible inhumanity and destruction of World War II, it was deemed necessary and appropriate to try war criminals for their actions as well as to codify the rules of war. The Nuremberg trials, which begun in 1945, sought to punish Nazi war criminals. These military tribunals required there to be clear definitions of what actions constituted war crimes and what actions were acceptable in times of war. The Nuremberg principles established definitions for war crimes, crimes against humanity, and crimes against peace, such as waging a war of aggression. While the principles that were established were clear, the hypocrisy was also transparent. The point about the hypocrisy was best explained by World War II Air Force General Curtis LeMay, commander of the 1945 Tokyo firebombing operation, when he stated, "I suppose if I had lost the war, I would have been tried as a war criminal. Fortunately, we were on the winning side."[18]

Just a few decades later, on August 7, 1964, the Gulf of Tonkin Resolution was passed by the United States Congress in response to incidents in the Gulf of Tonkin involving the North Vietnamese navy and the American navy that had occurred that week. Ships from these two navies engaged on August 2, but what set Congress in motion was an alleged second attack by the North Vietnamese on American ships on August 4. This second attack later proved to be an American fabrication. The resolution enabled the intensification of the conflict. Bolstered by the argument of self-defense and the fear of a domino effect of communist countries in the region, Congress and the American people became more comfortable with the escalation of forces. The Vietnam War ended with nearly sixty thousand American soldiers killed and sparked a MIA/POW campaign that continues to this day. The touching memorial in Washington, D.C., symbolizes the nation's grief. What is rarely ever mentioned are the one million or more Vietnamese deaths associated with the war.[19] These Vietnamese lives are simply not valued by Americans as much as the lives of the American soldiers.

The Persian Gulf War (1990-91) was prefaced by a massive propaganda campaign that sought to create the impression that Saddam Hussein and his forces represented an existential threat that could be contained only by America's military might. Reports of Iraq's powerful "million man army" were designed to inspire fear in the American people and support the deployment of over five hundred thousand troops to the region.[20] President George H. W. Bush referred to the Iraqi leader in the same context as Hitler and pronounced his name similar to that of Satan. The demonization of the enemy and the fiction of Iraq being an existential threat to the United States served to effectively build support for the imminent killing of Iraqis and deaths of Americans. Many Americans worried about American soldiers being put in harm's way by this conflict, but the actual ground fighting was over in a matter of days as the reality of Iraq's comparative weakness was readily apparent. Today, the war is often viewed by Americans as a just one in which the United States gathered an international coalition, defended the Kuwaitis' human rights, and defeated the brutal dictator Saddam Hussein. The few hundred Americans killed in the war are still remembered by the American public, yet little attention was ever paid to the tens of thousands of Iraqis that died in the conflict, many of them civilians.

The arguments for self-defense were again raised before President George W. Bush led the 2003 invasion of Iraq. At first, the administration tried to link the Iraqis to the September 11 attacks, a connection that would have made invading Iraq easier to justify. When that failed, they moved on to promoting the claim that Iraq was stockpiling weapons of mass destruction that posed an imminent, existential threat to the United States. This became solidified in the justification for preemptive strikes within the Bush Doctrine. The drumbeat for urgent preemptive strikes was loudest in General Colin Powell's now infamous presentation to the United Nations, a presentation that was meant to convince the world that America's upcoming attack on Iraq was justifiable and not one of aggression. The fact that Iraq had neither the intention nor the capacity to attack the United States with weapons of mass destruction was obvious to many at the time and is even more transparent today. At the time, however, America's nationalistic furor against Iraq rose to a fever pitch. The invasion and subsequent occupation of Iraq resulted in the loss of nearly five thousand American soldiers, tens of thousands of Americans wounded, and trillions of dollars in costs.[21] Iraq suffered far more, with roughly half a million deaths attributable to the war and occupation, which lasted from 2003 to 2011; many of the dead were civilians.[22] The Iraqi causalities are rarely mentioned in the American media, a reflection of the fact that those Iraqi lives are not valued by Americans as much as the lives of the Americans that were lost.

Today, drone strikes are increasingly used by America's military as a means of killing. From America's point of view, these drone strikes have the advantage of not risking American lives. From the point of view of the countries where the attacks are taking place, these drones represent an illegal incursion into their territory. These drone strikes have killed Americans and non-Americans outside of the United States border. Some question whether our government has the right to assassinate its own citizens without due process.[23] Others argue that these drone strikes are legal but insist that drone strikes against United States citizens cannot occur on American soil. Few politicians question America's legal right to assassinate foreigners and whether doing so violates international law. This lack of political debate reflects the fact that in the eyes of Americans, foreign lives are simply not as protected or valuable as American lives. Moreover, few politicians express concern that a substantial percent of people killed by these drone strikes are innocent bystanders.[24,25] These innocent bystanders are considered by political analysts to be collateral damage in America's stated goal of self-protection.

This nationalistic perspective and the limited concern for killing foreign civilians is buoyed by America's confidence in being the dominant global military power. Imagine that a foreign country floated drones over American soil, occasionally blasting missiles that resulted in killing peaceful American civilians. That foreign country would soon feel the wrath of America's powerful military.[26]

Few would argue against the idea that a government has a greater obligation to support its citizens than to support foreign nationals. This is not merely a reflection of our national self-identify but also a reflection of cash flow. Taxes are raised from citizens, who expect that these revenues will be mostly spent on them. National constitutions often state the rights of their own citizens but do not discuss the rights of foreigners. No country could function economically if it sought to provide services and protections to all global citizens irrespective of their nationality or place of residence. This internal focus toward citizens is necessary for a government to survive.

Another insight into how nationalism impacts the relative value of life can be gained from examining how countries conduct prisoner exchanges. If all countries valued the lives of all prisoners equally, then one would normally expect equal prisoner exchanges. The reality is that prisoner exchanges are rarely equal but rather reflect both the relative value of the prisoners and the political climate. Consider the release of American Sgt. Bowe Bergdahl in exchange for five Taliban detainees being held at Guantánamo.[27] Soon after his return to the United States, Sgt. Bergdahl was charged with desertion, raising many people's concerns over why the American government chose to make such a lopsided trade.[28] This exchange pales in comparison to the one made by the Israeli government to obtain one of their soldiers, Gilad Shalit. Shalit had been captured by Palestinians in a cross-border raid and held captive for five years. Through the efforts of support groups and activist organizations, Shalit's ongoing captivity remained a focus of the Israeli public and global media. In exchange for his release, the Israeli government released 1,027 prisoners, nearly 300 of whom had been serving life sentences for planning and/or perpetrating terror attacks.[29] This massive asymmetry in the prisoner swap was viewed by some as a negotiating coup by the Palestinians and by others as a necessary political action by the Israeli government. Looking through the lens of valuing life, one can draw a very different conclusion—that the Israeli government placed an extremely high price on the life of Shalit as compared to the lives of their prisoners.

Our bonding as Americans creates a connection among us that is not limited to conflict situations. It is a connection that is created through laws, socialization, and the messaging we receive throughout our lives. It is reinforced in our schools, by our media, and though behaviors like reciting the Pledge of Allegiance and singing our national anthem. The result of these nationalistic feelings is that we usually care more about the lives of Americans than the lives of citizens of other countries.

Sometimes, a trigger for these feelings is fear. Consider the 2014 Ebola outbreak. The outbreak started in the first quarter of 2014 and claimed over one thousand lives by the end of August 2014.[30] Over eleven thousand people died before the outbreak was finally contained, with most of the deaths in Guinea, Sierra Leone, and Liberia.[31] The first Ebola case treated in the United States occurred in August 2014, when Dr. Kent Brantly was flown in from Liberia, where he had contracted the disease. The next month, the first Ebola case was identified in the United States. The American government stepped up its response to this deadly epidemic only in September 2014, when the virus had hit American shores, at which point it made major commitments of troops and other aid. The delay between the identification of the spread of Ebola and major action by the American government is understandable. Ebola was neither front-page news nor a major concern for many Americans until there was widespread fear about possible contagion across the United States.[32] Additionally, it was much easier for Americans to empathize with the plight of Dr. Brantly and other Americans than to empathize with a crisis unfolding on a different continent in countries that are not prominent on American tourist maps.[33]

This is understandable. It is not the American government's constitutional responsibility to care for the health of the entire world. Nonetheless, the striking change in the response of both the government and the public to the Ebola crisis following the first domestic cases of the virus is a reflection of how fear for our lives and empathy for our neighbors, rather than altruism, often influences our behavior.

OTHER IN-GROUPS

Empathy stretches beyond nationalism to other in-groups, religion being a powerful example. Many wars have been fought over religious differences from antiquity to today. These battles may pit different religions—such as Christianity, Islam, Judaism, Hinduism, or Mormonism—against each other. Examples of interreligious wars include the Crusades and the civil wars in Sudan and Nigeria. Other religious wars are waged within different sects of the same religious group, such as the Thirty Years' War, in which Catholics fought Protestants, and the armed conflicts between Shia and Sunni Muslims.

Religious battles are an extreme example of asymmetric empathy, where the lives of those of the same religion are highly valued and those of a different religion—labeled as the "enemy"—are given less, zero, or even negative value. Religions can be a source of guidance for behavior and morality, yet they have also been a trigger for conflict. Religious wars stand in stark contrast to the following quote, attributed to Mahatma Gandhi: "There are many causes I would die for. There is not a single cause I would kill for."

Race is another in-group that can influence empathy and impact assessments of the value of someone's life. Pervasive racism is an insidious problem: we expect it from others, yet few of us will actually acknowledge being racist. It is rare to meet Americans who openly state that they believe their race is superior or who express that they have more confidence in or concern about people of their own race. Most Americans, if asked to serve on a jury, would insist that they could consider the merits of the case and not be swayed by the race of the defendant and victim. Despite our self-assessments about being race-blind, race is a factor in both criminal and civil cases, as we saw in chapter 3. Blacks are more likely than whites to receive harsher criminal penalties for similar crimes. For crimes such as vehicular manslaughter, the punishments are less severe when the victim is black.

PERSONAL EXPERIENCES

Empathy is often linked to personal experience. If you have ever traveled to a specific country or have a positive relationship with someone from that region or culture, then you are more likely to be empathetic toward that country's people. The influence that personal experience has on empathy is dramatic, and more broadly, familiarity often breeds appreciation, understanding, respect, and empathy.

Americans were shocked after the attacks in Paris, France, in November 2015 that killed 130 people.[34] Outpourings of empathy and calls for solidarity and support with the Parisians flooded social media, news outlets, and political statements. A major terrorist attack the day before in Beirut, Lebanon, that left nearly 90 dead had gone mostly unnoticed by the American media and public. The contrast between these responses was stark, leaving little doubt that the American public expressed far more concern over the Paris attacks than the attack in Beirut. Why the higher level of empathy for the French as compared with the Lebanese? Partially, this may reflect the fact that many more Americans have direct and indirect experiences with France than with Lebanon. France is one of the five most-visited foreign countries for Americans, while Lebanon is not in the top thirty.[35] Besides those Americans who have traveled to France, many more have relatives and friends who have been there. In addition to travel, roughly ten million Americans have French ancestry, more than those who identify as having Lebanese ancestry.[36] France, a wealthy, politically stable country, had not seen a terrorist attack on this scale nor has been invaded by a foreign country since World War II. Lebanon, a middle-income country, has experienced external and civil wars over the past few decades. Americans' higher levels of empathy for the Parisian attacks reflects our fears that a similar attack could easily happen in America, while the Beirut attack may seem more remote and therefore less shocking to many Americans.

A similar comparison can be drawn between the reactions to two different natural disasters in Asia: the 2004 tsunami in South and Southeast Asia and the 2008 cyclone in Myanmar. The 2004 tsunami left over 200,000 dead, with the largest number of deaths in Indonesia, Sri Lanka, India, and Thailand. International outpourings of support resulted in a total of $14 billion being raised to assist these damaged regions. Less than four years later, nearly 150,000 people were killed as a result of a cyclone in Myanmar. The international response was far more muted, and aid pledges were substantially lower than they had been in the wake of the tsunami. Part of this diminished empathy and response is related to the fact that far fewer Americans and Europeans have direct or indirect experiences with Burmese culture as compared to the cultures of the countries impacted by the tsunami.[37]

Consider the cases of James Brady, Christopher Reeve, and John Walsh. For each of these men, a personal experience was responsible for a change in their priorities and how they allocated their time in life. James Brady was the White House press secretary under Ronald Reagan. He was a conservative Republican. He is known for the Brady Bill, the most important piece of gun control legislation to be passed in the 1990s. His support for gun control legislation came after he was disabled by a gunshot wound during the Reagan assassination attempt. Christopher Reeve was best known for being the actor who played Superman until he was injured in a horse riding accident in 1995. He used his fame to bring attention to spinal cord injuries, such as by hosting the 1996 Paralympics in Atlanta and creating the Christopher and Dana Reeve Foundation. John Walsh was working as a hotelier in Florida when his six-year-old son, Adam, was kidnapped and murdered in 1981. John and his wife founded the Adam Walsh Child Resource Center, and their outreach efforts led to the Missing Children Act of 1982, the Missing Children's Assistance Act of 1984, and the Adam Walsh Child Protection and Safety Act of 2006. Walsh also became host of the crime TV show *America's Most Wanted,* which ran from 1988 to 2011.

The point of these stories is that each began with a person who either was personally affected by a near fatality or had a loved one who was affected by a fatality. Had James Brady not been shot and Christopher Reeve not been paralyzed, they would not have dedicated the rest of their lives to their respective causes. Had Adam Walsh never disappeared at a

Sears department store, his father would not have become a passionate advocate for missing children.

While personal experiences and personal connections impact empathy, there are practical, known limitations on our circles of socialization. These figures, called Dunbar's numbers, are approximate, yet they represent the rough limit of the number of people with whom one can maintain a given depth of relationships.[38] The number of acquaintances can be large, often ranging from five hundred to fifteen hundred. The number of people that one considers casual friends (including relatives) ranges for most between one hundred to two hundred people. Within that group, there are roughly fifty close friends who one might see often but who are not people one confides in for the most personal issues. Within that group of fifty, there is a support circle that may be one third the size that one turns to for sympathy and support, and lastly one's close support group of the five or so people one relies on the most. These numbers are not absolute, but they represent tendencies in terms of the size of relationship circles.

The size of a casual friend circle, roughly one hundred to two hundred people, is consistent with the size of other social circles, including the average group within modern hunter-gatherer societies and the average military company. Social networks such as Facebook, Twitter, and LinkedIn have enabled humans to expand their circle of acquaintances. This comes with the potential to simultaneously broaden our circle of empathy. Greater direct interaction with people of other cultures, backgrounds, and ethnicities opens the opportunity to increase understanding and appreciation for others. As this happens, the relative value of these people's lives increases from your perspective. They are no longer strangers to whom you have no connection. Rather, they are people you have heard of, written to, and possibly spoken with or shared information with. Unfortunately, this idea that the Internet would create a greater sense of global community has not generally occurred. Often, the Internet replicates the real-world phenomenon of people socially self-segregating so that online they listen to an echo chamber of ideas similar to their own.

Empathy is reflected in our responses to crises and our expressions of support or remorse. Our levels of empathy are often influenced by cultural perceptions of self-sufficiency as well as biases regarding age, sex, and class. Many people are less empathetic to the plight of a healthy looking man in his midtwenties begging for food than that of an emaciated woman with a newborn baby doing the same. Young children are less able to safely care for themselves physically, mentally, and financially, and so we naturally empathize with them more than with those we expect to be self-sufficient. The old rescue phrase "women and children first" is more than a cliché. Historical records from the *Titanic* show that sex and age were major factors in predicting who went onto the lifeboats and who died.[39] Only 20 percent of the male passengers survived compared with 74 percent of the female passengers and 50 percent of the child passengers. Social standing was also a major factor in survival: 62 percent of the first-class passengers survived, compared with 41 percent of the standard-class passengers and only 25 percent of the third-class passengers.[40]

COGNITIVE ERRORS

Imagine a world where we were not influenced by identification bias or the "certainty effect" and where we had equal empathy for all humans irrespective of their family lineage, nationality, religion, ethnicity, sex, and race. In that scenario, we would still make decisions that would result in valuing some lives more than others. This stems from the fact that the human mind is not a perfect decision-making instrument that computes accurate probabilities and outcomes objectively and then uses that information to make rational, data-driven decisions. Rather, we suffer from numerous cognitive errors that influence our decision-making as our brains try to take shortcuts in analyzing information. These cognitive errors can cause us to make irrational decisions that can influence our perceived value of a life.

Since much of the data on cognitive errors derives from surveys that ask a nonrandom sample of the population hypothetical questions, the results should be considered with caution. In spite of these methodological limitations, we will assume that there is some correspondence between people's stated preferences and their actual preferences. That said, there is information from many nonsurvey data sources, such as market-trading behavior, that shows that humans are not perfect risk calculators.

Humans are typically more likely to take risks when it comes to losses. A certain loss is seen as being much worse than an uncertain loss of the same average value. Imagine two scenarios, one in which fifty people will definitely die and another in which there is a fifty percent chance that no one will die and a fifty percent chance that one hundred people die. More people will prefer the second option to the first. The results change when the wording is adjusted so that the scenarios refer to people's lives being saved rather than people dying. In that case, more people will prefer the option that guarantees that fifty people will be saved.[41] The fact that humans suffer from this "framing effect," where our preferences change based on whether we are looking at lives being saved or lives being lost, reminds us to be cautious about overinterpreting preference surveys. Moreover, it is reminiscent of any survey involving understanding how much customers value something, since the amount of money customers are willing to pay for a given good is often quite different from the amount of money they are willing to accept to give that good up.[42]

Another instance where cognitive errors occur is in proportional dominance, where we put more weight on the probability of an event than on the payout itself. In a survey that probed support for a new airport safety regulation, respondents were asked whether they would support the regulation if it saved 150 lives where the risk is not specified as compared to a regulation that saved a certain percentage of 150 lives that were at risk. Logically, all of us should agree that saving 150 lives is better than saving fewer than 150 lives, yet the results of this survey found that respondents came to the opposite conclusion: respondents valued saving 98 percent, 95 percent, 90 percent, and even 85 percent of 150 lives that were at risk over saving all 150 lives.[43] An interpretation of these results is that many people are more interested in supporting a measure that appears successful (saving 95 percent of lives at risk) than one that saves more lives but with no success rate specified.

Scope insensitivity is a type of cognitive error where, absent a reference group, people are insensitive to large numbers. If saving one life has a specific value, then saving two lives should logically have twice that amount, and saving one hundred thousand lives should have one hundred thousand times that value. Yet our mental calculations are often different. Frequently, the explanation for scope insensitivity is that people's willingness to pay for a cause is based on emotion, which results in a fixed price tag, regardless of the number of people affected by an intervention.[44] In a similar fashion, it is sometimes seen in civil court cases that the punitive damages amount is not well correlated with the impact of the infraction.[45] This is because the punitive damages may be more impacted by the emotional connection the jurors have to the case.

Another type of cognitive error is the availability heuristic, a mental shortcut in which you determine how common a problem is based on how many examples you can come up with quickly rather than with the objective facts.[46] The impression of many Americans that there is an upward trend in violence is an example of the availability heuristic, in this case driven by a distorted sampling of media coverage. News organizations seek to maximize their viewership by focusing on bombastic stories that grab attention. These stories are often violent in nature, leaving many to draw the false conclusion that America is becoming a more violent and dangerous place to live. In spite of the news that focuses on murders, terrorism, and wars, America has, on average, become a much safer place to live over the past few decades.[47] The average rates of assault, rape, murder, and other violent crimes are all far lower than they were decades ago. The wartime deaths produced in World War II have not been replicated in later wars, and civil life has become noticeably less violent. These historical trends of declining violence are clear yet many find them to be counterintuitive. While this does not mean that these trends will necessarily continue in the future, it does leave us somewhat comforted in the face of seemingly perpetual national and personal security concerns.

TROLLEY PROBLEM

Some of the factors that affect our decision-making ability, including cognitive errors and empathy biases, can be examined within the famous hypothetical example of the trolley problem, which we will describe here as a runaway train.[48] In the scenario, there is a runaway train that can be steered only from one track to another. The train is headed down a track with five men on it. The second track has only person on it. Anyone on the track that the train takes will be killed. This situation represents the choice between saving one person and saving five. In making either choice, the driver has affected the death or deaths of those on the tracks. Given no information about the people other than their number, most people will say that they prefer to save five people at the cost of killing the one.

For many people, the equation changes when we start to assign these people with identities. Empathy can have more influence on our decision-making process once we have more details about the people on the tracks. What if the five people on track one are very old men and the one person on track two is a child? Would it still be rational to save the lives of the five old men over the life of the single child if the combined life expectancy of the men is less than that of the child? What if the five on track one are convicted murderers and the person on track two is the prison guard?

And of course, there are the variants where familiarity plays a role: What if the five are strangers and the one is a friend? What if the five are strangers and the one is your child? What if the five are friends and the one is your child? As expected, surveys have shown that people are more likely to save the life of the one person on track two if that person is a relative or a romantic partner.[49]

In a wartime situation, these kinds of decisions take many twists and turns. If the five are soldiers and the one is a civilian, some would argue for saving the civilian. The logic behind this decision is that the soldiers are expected to risk their lives, but the civilian is not. What if the person making the choice is also a soldier and fights for the same country as the five, whereas the civilian is a citizen of the enemy country? These choices are challenging, whereas others are simple: What if they are all soldiers, but the five are enemies and the one is a friend?

The point of this exercise is not to demonstrate that there is some underlying moral principle that everyone will agree with. Clearly this is not the case. Rather, the point is that every question pulls at your ethical beliefs and makes you question what would be a clear choice under anonymity: when all of the people on the tracks are anonymous, a rational person would choose to save five over one. However, with more information, the decision can change. You may choose the one because the one is your child, but everyone is someone's child.

Finally, how does the decision change when that one person on the track is you?

10 What's Next?

Price tags are placed on our lives from the day we are born to the day we die. Philosophers may develop elegant concepts about how life should be valued and what is a fair distribution of resources, but these concepts collide daily with the real world of price tags. This real world of price tags is derived from business analysts making cost-benefit calculations on auto safety, regulators determining acceptable levels of water contaminants, health insurers determining what drugs to cover, and jurors awarding damages. If these real-world price tags conclude that your life is not worth much, then your life will be more exposed to risk, while the lives of those deemed more valuable will be better protected.

Regardless of how price tags are arrived at, and by whom, they regularly impact our lives and are not always fair. They affect our health, our rights, our safety, our finances, and our longevity. Given that there is a substantial amount of unfairness in price tags, we need to understand how these valuations and the values that stand behind them affect our lives, confront inequities whenever possible, and minimize their negative consequences.

This book began with a deceptively simple question: How much is a human life worth? The question's complexity resides in the fact that how we arrive at a price tag on human life says a great deal about our priorities. The price tags, and the methods used to develop them, are a reflection of our values as a society. They are infused with influences from economics, ethics, religion, human rights, and law.

Ideally, there would be a simple answer of how to value a human life that most people could agree on. Yet there is no such answer. The philosopher Isiah Berlin stated that humans have a "deep and incurable metaphysical need" to search for timeless truth that does not exist. Instead, we need to accept that there are many competing truths and a "plurality of values."[1] The task of valuing life has many competing truths and no simple answer. Readers may find it frustrating that we cannot conclude with one key bullet point or a single take-home message about how human life is valued, but topics as complicated as this often cannot be boiled down to one pithy solution that satisfies nearly all interested parties.

Some take the philosophical perspective that human life is priceless.[2] Individuals who take this stance conclude that the question of how much a human life is worth is meaningless or unanswerable. However intellectually satisfying, this perspective ignores the reality that human life is constantly being monetized and that this should therefore be done in an equitable way.

This book has taken the pragmatic approach of focusing on the real-world methods of how life is valued and the implications and limitations of these methods. The prices depend on who is doing the valuation, the methods they are using, the purpose for the valuation, and quite often, whose life is being valued.

Valuing all lives the same has some intuitive logic. It is a simple answer. It resonates with many people's stated perspective, and it is in line with the perspective that if life must be valued, then no one should receive preferential treatment. This notion of valuing lives equally is not a throwback to an idealistic, egalitarian philosophy but rather one that resonates among many people. Consider billionaires Mark Zuckerberg and his wife, Priscilla Chan. Their open letter to their newborn daughter stated, "We believe all lives have equal value, and that includes the many more people who will live in future generations than live today."[3] This sentiment is mirrored in the philosophy of the Bill and Melinda Gates Foundation: "We see equal value in all lives."[4]

As noble and eloquent as these statements of equality are, they are at odds with the real world and their authors' circumstances. The fact that lives are routinely valued differently has been demonstrated throughout this book. A consequence of this inequality is that all lives are not protected equally. On a personal level, the Zuckerbergs and the Gates are certainly not going to spend as much of their fortune to save the life of an unknown person in a different country as they would to save one of their parents, one of their children, or themselves.

The September 11th Victim Compensation Fund awards were meant to be similar to the awards from a civil trial. These awards, ranging from $250,000 to over $7 million, were mostly driven by economic considerations, though Special Master Kenneth Feinberg tried to limit the inequities. He placed both lower and upper limitations on award amounts. Families of victims were guaranteed a minimal compensation. The top end of the compensation was capped so families of victims who were earning millions did not receive taxpayer-funded checks worth tens of millions of dollars. Mr. Feinberg later concluded that all lives should have been valued the same, which would have resulted in the families of our fictional characters Rick, Jim, Anitha, and Sebastian all being equally compensated. This method would have been easier to administer, less controversial, and more acceptable to the public.

Recall that civil courts base their awards on a number of factors, including economic losses. The lives of those best compensated are valued most in a civil trial. Recall, too, that juries sometimes come to the inhumane conclusion that a victim's family is not entitled to compensation when the victim's accidental death results in the family saving money. Mr. Feinberg provided a minimum value for the loss of life in the September 11th Victim Compensation Fund. This minimum value signified that regardless of someone's income, human life itself has some intrinsic value, so that the loss of any human life, regardless of income, still merits compensation. This concept of a minimum value seems reasonable and fair since it prevents the inhumane conclusion that can reduce the loss of some human lives to below the level of chattel. More generally, the inequities of racial and gender pay gaps are built into the inputs whenever income is used in valuing someone's life. A result of this is that, on average, the lives of women and minorities are valued less than those of white men unless race- and gender-based adjustments are made to award amounts.

Justice is supposed to be blind, yet the criminal justice system routinely values some lives more than others. All murderers are not punished equally. The death penalty is more likely to be applied when murder victims are white and the murderer is black. Vehicular manslaughter sentencing affirms that all lives are not valued nor protected equally, since shorter sentences are handed out to the drivers when the victim is black or male and when the victim is unemployed. The lives of agents and representatives of the state, such as police officers, are valued highly, but the violent actions that some of them take are far less likely to be punished by the government. Prosecution and sentencing inequalities need to be addressed to achieve a fairer society.

Regulatory agencies routinely place price tags on human lives. These prices vary across agencies, but within a given agency, current lives are all priced equally (at least as of the date this was written). In the past, the EPA valued the lives of the elderly less than the young, but the public protested, and the EPA retreated to using equal values. Health-economics statistics, such as quality-adjusted life years, value the lives of young people more than those of older people. Because regulators use discounting in their analyses, they value current lives more than future lives; the higher the discount rate, the greater the disparity between current and future lives. Methods that test the sensitivity of the outcomes to these assumptions exist and must always be used.

Companies always put different price tags on people's lives. Employee compensation varies by education, skill set, experience, industry, union membership, race, sex, and sometimes the risk of the job. Some of these factors can be justified based on how much value the employee adds to the company's bottom line. After all, it is reasonable that a CEO is paid more than a line worker. But how much more? It is difficult to justify American CEOs receiving three hundred times more than an average worker when this ratio is not seen in other wealthy countries or in America's past. More equitable approaches to compensation have been achieved in other wealthy countries and can be achieved in America, too.

Companies use a different set of price tags for people's lives when making other business decisions. They routinely run cost-benefit analyses to determine how much they should invest in improving product safety to avoid preventable deaths and injuries. The costs used in these calculations include estimates of what the company might lose in a civil trial, which means that poorer people's lives are valued less and are consequently less protected.

When it comes to preserving health and life, there are limits to the coverage provided by any private or public insurance. No health system could survive financially without limitations on what care will be guaranteed. Individuals must pay out of pocket when costs are not covered by health insurance. What this means is that the wealthy can afford better health care and are more likely to receive health benefits. This is most evident in America, where health care is a major for-profit industry and where tens of millions still lack health insurance. This is in stark contrast with other wealthy countries, where basic health care is a guaranteed right.[5] These gaps in basic health care and health insurance are inconsistent with the 1948 Universal Declaration of Human Rights, a document America codrafted and signed, which includes the statement that all people have a right to basic health and social services.[6] The concept of equity supports the principle that all humans have the right to basic health care, yet for many Americans, the price tag for preserving their own health is too high and is in daily competition with the needs of providing food and shelter for themselves and their families. Steps must be taken to reduce the price tag for basic health care for all.

Price tags are placed even before birth. Parents regularly consider the value of life as they plan for and raise their young ones. Many parents weigh not only the costs of raising children but also the benefits those children can provide. Sex-selective abortions usually reflect son preference. In some cultures, this preference is rooted in the belief that having a son can be a better financial investment than having a daughter. Disability-selective abortions occur when prospective parents choose to abort the fetus rather than incur the challenges and expenses of raising a child with congenital disorders. The ramifications of parents making abortion decisions based partially on the financial prospects of the fetus are harrowing and far-reaching. We must engage ethics, science, and politics to understand the long-term consequences to the human race of the worlds of gene editing, selective fertilization, selective abortions, and selective infanticide all coinciding and then establish a just set of moral and legal boundaries.

While some declare life priceless, and many assert that all lives should be equally valued, we live in a world that constantly assumes the opposite. This reflects another widely held belief, that some lives should be valued more than others. Valuing some lives more than others seems logical and natural to many of us. Given the choice of saving the life of a convicted serial murderer or the life of a heroic policeman, most would choose to save the policeman. On a more personal level, empathy drives us to value the lives of those closest to us more than the lives of those we do not know. If you had to choose between saving the life of a stranger or the life of your child, you would save your child. More generally, we often have a higher level of empathy for those with whom we share a similar culture, religion, ethnicity, nationality, language, or personal experiences. Given the many conflicting viewpoints on how to value life, what should we do? Beyond all the disparate opinions about what should and shouldn't be done when valuing life, the reality is that price tags are being applied on a daily basis, and thus we must decide how their values should be determined.

ECONOMISTS' DILEMMA

Many excellent economists have tackled the daunting task of putting a price tag on life. These economists view this as a necessary exercise to generate key inputs for cost-benefit analyses. This attempt at monetizing life flies in the face of those who maintain that life is priceless and cannot be valued. It also confronts the challenge that there is no open, free market for buying and selling human life. Economists must make assumptions, and while the math underneath their estimates may sometimes be complex, the key assumptions built into these estimates are straightforward and, unfortunately, riddled with limitations and often flaws.

Methods that rely on surveys that pose hypothetical questions with little basis in reality will always produce questionable results. The fact that these surveys are given to an unrepresentative sample of the population adds more issues. The additional step of excluding responses that do not fit within the bounds of what has been predefined as acceptable compounds those flaws. Clearly, these methods are highly suspect both theoretically and practically. But they exist and are being used to develop key inputs that influence decision-making in our lives. Unlike philosophical debates, these methods and their outcomes can be readily examined and tweaked to produce different, potentially fairer, outcomes. To diminish the issues with these surveys, the sample biases should be corrected to reflect the broader population, restrictions should not be placed on responses, and an extremely large value should be used to represent the opinion of those who say the value of life is priceless.

Methods that rely on people's real-world decisions seem to have a stronger basis in reflecting how society values life, yet these methods also have major theoretical and practical issues. They examine how much more someone requires to be paid in order to work a risky job or how much one is willing to spend on safety measures that reduce the risks of their mortality. These methods assume that people are aware of the implications of their decisions and that they have other options. The inferred Value of a Statistical Life is biased because the subjects often lack options, the leverage needed to negotiate, or the knowledge of the risks involved. Still this measure is an algorithm with real-world consequences in spite of its readily apparent theoretical and practical limitations.

With all of these limitations on how to estimate the value of life, we are left with a limited number of choices. This book has shown that price tags are being continuously placed on our lives. If we care about equity, we need to ensure that the science behind these estimates is not oversold and that fairness is always a consideration when cost-benefit analysis is performed.

One option is to not rely on cost-benefit analysis for government decisions. As radical as this sounds, recall that for centuries the American government made policy decisions without attempting to incorporate a monetary value of life. In some areas, such as national defense, our government continues to ignore cost-benefit analysis and other efforts to monetize life. Often, there is little consideration given to how many lives will be saved or need to be saved to justify military or security expenses. Ignoring cost-benefit analysis is not a compelling option for the many parts of our government that need to protect human lives while also ensuring that they don't damage the national economy with excessive restrictions.

A more comprehensive approach would be to include cost-benefit analysis as one of a number of considerations in regulatory planning. This is similar to the approach taken by national health agencies such as the United Kingdom's NICE and Thailand's HITAP. They incorporate not only economic considerations but also ethics, politics, and fairness.

This more comprehensive approach was exemplified in the for-profit world when Merck committed to donating the Mectizan needed to control river blindness in Africa.[7] This model for corporate social responsibility, later emulated by other companies, has improved the health of millions of people and provided positive benefits to both employee morale and public sentiment for Merck.[8] However, ignoring cost-benefit analysis is not generally an option for companies. They need to make business decisions and need to understand the potential financial consequences of their actions. Broadening the considerations used in cost-benefit analysis can sometimes lead companies to go beyond the standard calculus and open themselves up to making sweeping impacts on society and on their own financial prospects, as in the case of effective corporate social responsibility.

PRESERVING JUSTICE

Estimates of the value of human life are riddled with injustices. This is seen in all of the contexts in which valuations of life are determined, including civil judgments, criminal sentencing, employee compensation, selective abortions, and population planning. Injustices have existed and will continue to exist in this world. We should seek to minimize injustices wherever possible. This can only be done if we challenge injustices wherever they appear, especially when lives are unfairly valued.

Given the limitations of the science, we need to continuously challenge the notion that economists have determined true values for life and question the methods that are used to develop these estimates. In acknowledging that putting price tags on life is necessary for doing some calculations, we need to recognize that the methods behind developing these price tags are not unimpeachably scientifically objective but rather are highly subjective. This is not meant to denigrate the skill of the economists working in these areas but is rather a matter-of-fact statement about the limits in quantifying something as abstract as human life. The uncertainty and limitations in the estimates of valuing human life need to be reflected in any analysis.

We need to insist that whatever price tag is used to value life is high enough to sufficiently protect human life. We need to insist that inequitable wage gaps, such as racial and gender pay gaps, be eliminated since they impact valuations of life. We need to insist that when income is used in valuing life, steps must be taken to ensure that the lives of the poorest, the retired, the unemployed, and those volunteering their time are protected and not left susceptible to the whims of governments, organizations, and corporations.

No situation should exist where a court determines that someone's death does not merit damages since their death "saved money." No situation should exist where the death of one billionaire is deemed to be worth more than the deaths of a hundred people who earned much less. No situation should exist where a company or government unnecessarily risks people's lives to save a few dollars. No situation should exist where unequal valuing of human life leads to the denial of basic human rights.

All lives are precious, but they are not priceless. Rather, they are priced all the time. Often the price tags are unfair. We need to ensure that when lives are priced, that they are priced fairly so that human rights and human lives are always protected.

Notes

CHAPTER 1. YOUR MONEY OR YOUR LIFE?

1. This book focuses specifically on the value humans place on human life. This concept could be extended to examine more broadly the value humans place on all sentient lives, all animal lives, or all living things. It is reasonable to anticipate that future generations may criticize the species focus of this book.

2. Lexico.com, s.v. "price tag," accessed September 29, 2019, www.oxforddictionaries.com/us/definition/american_english/price-tag.

3. Lexico.com, s.v. "value," accessed September 29, 2019, www.oxforddictionaries.com/us/definition/american_english/value.

4. Arthur D. Little International, "Public Finance Balance of Smoking in the Czech Republic, Report to: Philip Morris CR," November 28, 2000, www.tobaccofreekids.org/assets/content/what_we_do/industry_watch/philip_morris_czech/pmczechstudy.pdf; Greg Gardner, Alisa Priddle, and Brent Snavely, "GM Could Settle DOJ Criminal Investigation This Summer," *Detroit Free Press,* May 23, 2015, www.freep.com/story/money/2015/05/22/general-motors-justice-department-ignition-switch-deaths/27820247; Sanjoy Hazarika, "Bhopal Payments by Union Carbide Set at $470 Million," *New York Times,* February 15, 1989, www.nytimes.com/1989/02/15/business/bhopal-payments-by-union-carbide-set-at-470-million.html.

5. September 11th Victim Compensation Fund, "Frequently Asked Questions," last updated September 6, 2019, www.vcf.gov/faq.html#gen1.

6. Katharine Q. Seelye and John Tierney, "E.P.A. Drops Age-Based Cost Studies," *New York Times,* May 8, 2003, www.nytimes.com/2003/05/08/us/epa-drops-age-based-cost-studies.html.

CHAPTER 2. WHEN THE TOWERS FELL

1. Vice President Dick Cheney, interview by Tim Russert, *Meet the Press,* March 16, 2003, www.nbcnews.com/id/3080244/ns/meet_the_press/t/transcript-sept/#.XZIFpUZKiUk. This interview took place three days before the invasion of Iraq began on March 19, 2003. The impending costs of the war, in terms of human lives and dollars, were not discussed adequately and were often minimized. In a Pentagon news conference held on October 2, 2003, U.S. Secretary of Defense Donald Rumsfeld stated, "The bulk of the funds for Iraq's reconstruction will come from Iraqis." ProCon.org, "Will the Revenue from Iraqi Oil Production Pay for Reconstruction?," last updated January 23, 2009, http://usiraq.procon.org/view.answers.php?questionID=000946.

2. Linda J. Bilmes and Joseph E. Stiglitz, *The Three Trillion Dollar War: The True Cost of the Iraq Conflict* (New York: W. W. Norton, 2008).

3. Based on Dow Jones Industrial Average closing values extracted from Google Finance, www.google.com/finance.

4. United States Department of Labor, Bureau of Labor and Statistics, "Labor Force Statistics from the Current Population Survey," accessed September 30, 2019, http://data.bls.gov/timeseries/LNS14000000.

5. Air Transportation Safety and System Stabilization Act, United States Government Publishing Office, September 22, 2001, www.gpo.gov/fdsys/pkg/PLAW-107publ42/html/PLAW-107publ42.htm.

6. September 11th Victim Compensation Fund, "Frequently Asked Questions," last updated September 6, 2019, www.vcf.gov/faq.html#gen1.

7. Kenneth R. Feinberg, *Who Gets What?* (New York: PublicAffairs, 2012), 42.

8. Fred Andrews, "Finding the Price of Fairness," *New York Times,* August 2, 2012, www.nytimes.com/2012/08/05/business/kenneth-feinbergs-new-look-at-fairnesss-price-review.html.

9. Approximately half of the victims were parents (an estimated 1,459 people out of 2,996 immediate victims). Andrea Elliot, "Growing Up Grieving, with Constant Reminders of 9/11," *New York Times,* September 11, 2004, www.nytimes.com/2004/09/11/nyregion/11kids.html.

10. Kenneth R. Feinberg, *What Is Life Worth?* (New York: PublicAffairs, 2005), 202.

11. "American Flight 77 Victims at a Glance," *USA Today,* September 25, 2011. http://usatoday30.usatoday.com/news/nation/2001/09/12/victim-capsule-flight77.htm.

12. Julia Talanova, "Cantor Fitzgerald, American Airlines Settle 9/11 lawsuit for $135 Million," *CNN News*, December 17, 2013, www.cnn.com/2013/12/17/us/new-york-cantor-fitzgerald-american-settlement.

13. Feinberg, *What Is Life Worth?*, 70.

14. Feinberg, *What Is Life Worth?*, 42.

15. Feinberg, *What Is Life Worth?*, 51.

16. Gretchen Livingston, "Stay-at-Home Moms and Dads Account for About One-in-Five U.S. Parents," Pew Research Center, September 24, 2018, www.pewresearch.org/fact-tank/2018/09/24/stay-at-home-moms-and-dads-account-for-about-one-in-five-u-s-parents.

17. National Alliance for Caregiving and AARP, *Caregiving in the U.S. 2009* (Washington, DC: National Alliance for Caregiving, 2009), www.caregiving.org/pdf/research/Caregiving_in_the_US_2009_full_report.pdf.

18. Computed based on Feinberg, *What Is Life Worth?*, 195.

19. U.S. Department of Education, *Status and Trends in the Education of Racial and Ethnic Groups*, July 2010, http://nces.ed.gov/pubs2010/2010015.pdf.

20. There is a large literature on the topic of the gender wage gap. A simple overview can be found in Natalia Kolesnikova and Yang Liu, "Gender Wage Gap May Be Much Smaller Than Most Think," *Regional Economist* 19, no. 4 (October 2011): 14–15, www.stlouisfed.org/~/media/Files/PDFs/publications/pub_assets/pdf/re/2011/d/gender_wage_gap.

21. September 11th Victim Compensation Fund, "Frequently Asked Questions."

22. Computed based on Feinberg, *What Is Life Worth?*, 195, 202.

23. Feinberg, *What Is Life Worth?*, 202.

24. Kenneth Feinberg, "What Have We Learned about Compensating Victims of Terrorism?" *Rand Review* 28, no. 2 (Summer 2004): 33–34, www.rand.org/pubs/periodicals/rand-review/issues/summer2004/33.html.

25. Feinberg, *What Is Life Worth?*, 185.

26. Patrick Mackin, Richard Parodi, and David Purcell, "Chapter 12: Review of Survivor Benefits," in *Eleventh Quadrennial Review of Military Compensation*, June 2012, https://militarypay.defense.gov/Portals/3/Documents/Reports/11th_QRMC_Supporting_Research_Papers_(932pp)_Linked.pdf.

27. A number of researchers have contributed to the field of estimating the Value of a Statistical Life, including Kip Viscusi and James Hammitt. Some publications in this space include Thomas J. Kniesner, W. Kip Viscusi, Christopher Woock, and James P. Ziliak, "The Value of a Statistical Life: Evidence from Panel Data," *Review of Economics and Statistics* 94, no. 1 (2012): 74–87; Joseph E. Aldy and W. Kip Viscusi, "Adjusting the Value of a Statistical Life for Age and Cohort Effects," *Review of Economics and Statistics* 90 (2008): 573–81; James Hammitt, "Extrapolating the Value per Statistical Life between Populations: Theoretical Implications," *Journal of Benefit-Cost Analysis* 8, no. 2 (2017): 215–25; and

James Hammitt and Lisa Robinson, "The Income Elasticity of the Value per Statistical Life: Transferring Estimates between High and Low Income Populations," *Journal of Benefit-Cost Analysis* 2, no. 1 (2011): 1–29.

28. Bert Metz, Ogunlade Davidson, Rob Swart, and Jiahua Pan, eds., *Climate Change 2001: Mitigation; Contribution of Working Group III to the Third Assessment Report of the Intergovernmental Panel on Climate Change* (Cambridge: Cambridge University Press, 2001), section 7.4.4.2.

29. World Bank Database, "GDP per Capita (Current US$)," accessed September 30, 2019, http://data.worldbank.org/indicator/NY.GDP.PCAP.CD.

30. Karin Stenberg, Henrik Axelson, Peter Sheehan, Ian Anderson,A. Metin Gülmezoglu,Marleen Temmerman, Elizabeth Mason,et al., "Advancing Social and Economic Development by Investing in Women's and Children's Health: A New Global Investment Framework," *The Lancet* 383, no. 9925 (2014): 1333–54; Peter Sheehan, Kim Sweeny, Bruce Rasmussen, Annababette Wils, Howard S. Friedman, Jacqueline Mahon, George C. Patton, et al., "Building the Foundations for Sustainable Development: A Case for Global Investment in the Capabilities of Adolescents," *The Lancet* 390, no. 10104 (2017): 1792–806. In these papers, the noneconomic values were referred to as the "social benefit," to be contrasted with the "economic benefit."

31. Katharine Q. Seelye and John Tierney, "E.P.A. Drops Age-Based Cost Studies," *New York Times,* May 8, 2003, www.nytimes.com/2003/05/08/us/epa-drops-age-based-cost-studies.html.

32. W. Kip Viscusi, *Pricing Lives* (Princeton, NJ: Princeton University Press, 2018), 20.

33. Binyamin Appelbaum, "As US Agencies Put More Value on a Life, Businesses Fret," *New York Times,* February 16, 2011, www.nytimes.com/2011/02/17/business/economy/17regulation.html; Viscusi, *Pricing Lives,* 35–36. Values used for other U.S. agencies in the past few years are summarized in Viscusi, *Pricing Lives.*

34. The present value of future earnings will be discussed further in chapter 5, which looks at when the National Highway Traffic Safety Administration in the 1970s advised using future earnings as an estimate for the value of life when performing cost-benefit analysis on auto safety regulations.

35. Viscusi, *Pricing Lives.* 33.

36. Discussed in detail in Cass Sunstein, *Valuing Life: Humanizing the Regulatory State* (Chicago: University of Chicago Press, 2014).

37. Daniel Kahneman and Amos Tversky, "Choices, Values, and Frames," *American Psychologist* 39, no. 4 (April 1984): 342–47.

38. J. K. Horowitz and K. E. McConnell, "A Review of WTA/WTP Studies," *Journal of Environmental Economics and Management* 44 (2002): 426–47.

39. Janusz Mrozek and Laura Taylor, "What Determines the Value of Life? A Meta-Analysis," *Journal of Policy Analysis and Management* 21, no. 2 (Spring 2002): 253–70.

40. Frank Ackerman and Lisa Heinzerling, *Priceless: On Knowing The Price Of Everything and the Value Of Nothing* (New York: New Press, 2005), 61–90.

41. John D. Leeth and John Ruser, "Compensating Wage Differentials for Fatal and Non-Fatal Risk by Gender and Race," *Journal of Risk and Uncertainty* 27, no. 3 (December 2003): 257–77.

42. Viscusi, *Pricing Lives*. 28–29; W. K. Viscusi and C. Masterman, "Anchoring Biases in International Estimates of the Value of a Statistical Life," *Journal of Risk and Uncertainty* 54, no. 2 (2017): 103–28.

43. Viscusi, *Pricing Lives*. 39–40; Viscusi and Masterman, "Anchoring Biases."

44. U.S. Department of Homeland Security, "About DHS," last updated July 5, 2019, www.dhs.gov/about-dhs.

45. While the interpretation of this phrase depends on the reference, it generally refers to the idea that when you use incorrect or unreliable inputs in a calculation, the output will, by definition, be incorrect or unreliable.

46. Amanda Ripley, "WTC Victims: What's A Life Worth?," *Time*, February 6 2002, http://content.time.com/time/nation/article/0,8599,198866-3,00.html.

47. Federal Bureau of Investigation, "Crime in the United States 2001," accessed September 30, 2019, https://ucr.fbi.gov/crime-in-the-u.s/2001.

48. James Oliphant, "Why Boston Bombing Victims Get Millions When Wounded Soldiers Only Get Thousands," *National Journal*, August 3, 2013, http://qz.com/111285/why-boston-bombing-victims-get-millions-when-wounded-soldiers-only-get-thousands.

CHAPTER 3. JUSTICE IS NOT BLIND

1. Massimo Calabresi, "Why a Medical Examiner Called Eric Garner's Death a 'Homicide,'" *Time*, December 4, 2014, http://time.com/3618279/eric-garner-chokehold-crime-staten-island-daniel-pantaleo.

2. Rene Stutzman, "Trayvon Martin's Parents Settle Wrongful-Death Claim," *Orlando Sentinel*, April 5, 2013, http://articles.orlandosentinel.com/2013-04-05/news/os-trayvon-martin-settlement-20130405_1_trayvon-martin-benjamin-crump-george-zimmerman.

3. Deborah R. Hensler, "Money Talks: Searching for Justice through Compensation for Personal Injury and Death," *DePaul Law Review* 53, no. 2 (2013): 417–56, http://via.library.depaul.edu/law-review/vol53/iss2/9.

4. Andrew Jay McClurg, "Dead Sorrow: A Story about Loss and a New Theory of Wrongful Death Damages," *Boston University Law Review* 85 (2005): 1–51.

5. In some states that recognize the tort of negligent or intentional infliction of emotional harm, a person within the scope of harm (usually a close family member who) who witnesses the act causing the death may have grounds for recovery.

6. Nolo Law for All, "Damages in a Wrongful Death Lawsuit," accessed September 30, 2019, www.nolo.com/legal-encyclopedia/wrongful-death-claims-overview-30141-2.html.

7. Hensler, "Money Talks," 417–56. Note that some entities, including most government agencies, are not subject to punitive damages (U.S. Equal Employment Opportunity Commission, "Enforcement Guidance: Compensatory and Punitive Damages Available under § 102 of the Civil Rights Act of 1991," July 14, 1992, www.eeoc.gov/policy/docs/damages.html). Punitive damages did not appear in the September 11th Victim Compensation Fund.

8. Exxon Shipping Co. et al. v. Baker et al., 554 U.S. 471 (2008), www.law.cornell.edu/supct/html/07-219.ZS.html; BMW of North America, Inc., v. Gore, 517 U.S. 559 (1996), www.law.cornell.edu/supct/html/94-896.ZO.html.

9. Adam Davidson, "Working Stiffs," *Harper's Magazine* 303, no. 1815 (August 2001): 48–54, https://adamdavidson.com/harpers-magazine-working-stiffs.

10. Baker v. Bolton. 1 Campbell 493, 170 Eng. Rep. 1033, 1033 (K.B. 1808).

11. Peter Handford, "Lord Campbell and the Fatal Accidents Act," *Law Quarterly Review* 420 (2013): http://ssrn.com/abstract=2333018.

12. Stuart M. Speiser and Stuart S. Malawer, "American Tragedy: Damages for Mental Anguish of Bereaved Relatives in Wrongful Death Actions," *Tulane Law Review* 51, no. 1 (1976): 1–32.

13. Ibid.

14. Leonard Decof, "Damages in Actions for Wrongful Death of Children," *Notre Dame Law Review* 47, no. 2 (1971): 197–229.

15. Ibid.

16. Michael L. Brookshire and Frank L. Slesnick, "Self-Consumption in Wrongful Death Cases: Decedent or Family Income?," *Journal of Forensic Economics* 21, no. 1 (December 2009): 35–53.

17. David Paul Horowitz, "The Value of Life," *New York State Bar Association Journal* 85, no. 9 (2013): 14–16.

18. Thurston v. The State of New York, New York State Court of Claims, claim number 117361 (2013), http://vertumnus.courts.state.ny.us/claims/wp-html/2013-031-019.htm

19. Meredith A. Wegener, "Purposeful Uniformity: Wrongful Death Damages for Unmarried, Childless Adults," *South Texas Law Review* 51, no. 339 (2009): 339–67.

20. Michael L. Brookshire and Frank L. Slesnick, "Self-Consumption in Wrongful Death Cases: Decedent or Family Income?," *Journal of Forensic Economics* 21, no. 1 (December 2009): 35–53.

21. Davidson, "Working Stiffs," 48–54.

22. C.J. Sullivan, "$3.25M Settlement in Sean Bell Shooting an Eerie Birthday Gift," *New York Post*, July 28, 2010, http://nypost.com/2010/07/28/3-25m-settlement-in-sean-bell-shooting-an-eerie-birthday-gift.

23. Three of the five police officers involved in the shooting were indicted by a grand jury. The officers submitted to a bench trial (trial by judge) rather than a jury trial. Justice Arthur J. Cooperman acquitted the detectives on all counts.

24. Frank Donnelly, "Misdemeanor Cases over Alleged Untaxed Cigarettes Preceded Fatal Police Incident with Eric Garner," *Staten Island Live,* July 18, 2014, www.silive.com/northshore/index.ssf/2014/07/eric_garner_who_died_in_police.html.

25. Faith Karimi, Kim Berryman, and Dana Ford, "Who Was Freddie Gray, Whose Death Has Reignited Protests Against Police?," *CNN,* May 2, 2015, www.cnn.com/2015/05/01/us/freddie-gray-who-is-he.

26. John Bacon, "Freddie Gray Settlement 'Obscene,' Police Union Chief Says," *USA TODAY,* September 9, 2015, www.usatoday.com/story/news/nation/2015/09/09/baltimore-panel-approves-freddie-gray-settlement/71928226.

27. B. Drummond Ayres, Jr., "Jury Decides Simpson Must Pay $25 Million in Punitive Award," *New York Times,* February 11, 1997, www.nytimes.com/1997/02/11/us/jury-decides-simpson-must-pay-25-million-in-punitive-award.html.

28. The Innocence Project, "Compensating The Wrongly Convicted," December 11, 2018, www.innocenceproject.org/compensating-wrongly-convicted; Editorial Board, "Paying for Years Lost Behind Bars," *New York Times,* May 18, 2016, www.nytimes.com/2016/05/18/opinion/paying-for-years-lost-behind-bars.html.

29. The Innocence Project, "Compensation Statutes: A National Overview," 2017, www.innocenceproject.org/wp-content/uploads/2017/09/Adeles_Compensation-Chart_Version-2017.pdf.

30. A. G. Sulzberger and Tim Stelloh, "Bell Case Underlines Limits of Wrongful-Death Payouts," *New York Times,* July 28, 2010, www.nytimes.com/2010/07/29/nyregion/29bell.html.

31. Eliot McLaughin, "He Spent 39 Years in Prison for a Double Murder He Didn't Commit. Now, He's Getting $21 Million," *CNN,* February 25, 2019, www.cnn.com/2019/02/24/us/craig-coley-simi-valley-21-million-wrongful-conviction/index.html.

32. Jonathan M. Katz, "2 Men Awarded $750,000 for Wrongful Convictions in 1983 Murder," *New York Times,* September 2, 2015, www.nytimes.com/2015/09/03/us/2-men-awarded-750000-for-wrongful-convictions-in-1983-murder.html.

33. Kenneth R. Feinberg, *What Is Life Worth?* (New York: PublicAffairs, 2005), 202

34. United States Courts, "Criminal Cases," United States Courts, www.uscourts.gov/about-federal-courts/types-cases/criminal-cases.

35. World Bank, "Intentional Homicides (per 100,000 People)," accessed September 30, 2019, http://data.worldbank.org/indicator/VC.IHR.PSRC.P5.

36. Federal Bureau of Investigation, "Crime in the United States 2011: Expanded Homicide Data Table 8," accessed September 30, 2019, www.fbi.gov

/about-us/cjis/ucr/crime-in-the-u.s/2011/crime-in-the-u.s.-2011/tables/expanded-homicide-data-table-8.

37. Centers for Disease Control and Prevention, "QuickStats: Suicide and Homicide Rates,* by Age Group—United States, 2009," July 20, 2012, accessed September 30, 2019, www.cdc.gov/mmwr/preview/mmwrhtml/mm6128a8.htm; Federal Bureau of Investigation, "Expanded Homicide Data Table 1: Murder Victims by Race and Sex, 2010," accessed September 30, 2019, www.fbi.gov/about-us/cjis/ucr/crime-in-the-u.s/2010/crime-in-the-u.s.-2010/tables/10shrtbl01.xls.

38. Jillian Boyce and Adam Cotter, "Homicide in Canada, 2012,"Canadian Centre for Justice Statistics, December 19, 2013, www.statcan.gc.ca/pub/85-002-x/2013001/article/11882-eng.htm; OECD, "Better Life Index," accessed September 30, 2019, www.oecdbetterlifeindex.org/topics/safety.

39. Nate Silver, "Black Americans Are Killed at 12 Times the Rate of People in Other Developed Countries," *FiveThirtyEight*, June 18, 2015, http://fivethirtyeight.com/datalab/black-americans-are-killed-at-12-times-the-rate-of-people-in-other-developed-countries.

40. Computed from Federal Bureau of Investigation, "Expanded Homicide Data Table 1."

41. Federal Bureau of Investigation, "Expanded Homicide Data Table 10: Murder Circumstances by Relationship, 2010," accessed September 30, 2019, www.fbi.gov/about-us/cjis/ucr/crime-in-the-u.s/2010/crime-in-the-u.s.-2010/tables/10shrtbl10.xls.

42. B. Page, "Bible Says It's Okay to Beat Your Slave, As Long As They Don't Die? Exodus 21:20–21?," Revelation.co, June 9, 2013, www.revelation.co/2013/06/09/bible-says-its-okay-to-beat-your-slave-as-long-as-they-dont-die-exodus-2120-21.

43. Murder, 18 U.S. Code § 1111, www.law.cornell.edu/uscode/text/18/1111.

44. Cornell Law School, "Manslaughter," Legal Information Institute, accessed October 21, 2019, www.law.cornell.edu/wex/manslaughter.

45. Murder or Manslaughter of Foreign Officials, Official Guests, or Internationally Protected Persons, 18 U.S. Code § 1116, www.law.cornell.edu/uscode/text/18/1116.

46. John Blume, Theodore Eisenberg, and Martin T. Wells. "Explaining Death Row's Population and Racial Composition," *Journal of Empirical Legal Studies* 1, no. 1 (2004): 165–207; Death Penalty Information Center, "States with and without the Death Penalty," accessed October 21, 2019, https://deathpenaltyinfo.org/state-and-federal-info/state-by-state.

47. J.L. Lauritsen, R.J. Sampson, and J.H. Laub, "The Link between Offending and Victimization among Adolescents," *Criminology* 29, no. (1991): 265–92.

48. T. Bynum, G. Cordner, and J. Greene, "Victim and Offense Characteristics: Impact on Police Investigative Decision-Making," *Criminology* 20, no. 3 (1982): 301–18.

49. Shila R. Hawk and Dean A. Dabney, "Are All Cases Treated Equal? Using Goffman's Frame Analysis to Understand How Homicide Detectives Orient to Their Work," *British Journal of Criminology* 54 (2014): 1129–47.

50. Ibid.

51. Jason Rydberg and Jesenia M. Pizarro, "Victim Lifestyle as a Correlate of Homicide Clearance," *Homicide Studies* 18, no. 4 (2014): 342–62.

52. Jan Ransom and Ashley Southall, "'Race-Biased Dragnet': DNA from 360 Black Men Was Collected to Solve Vetrano Murder, Defense Lawyers Say," *New York Times*, March 31, 2019, www.nytimes.com/2019/03/31/nyregion/karina-vetrano-trial.html.

53. Much of the content from this paragraph on Karina Vetrano is a synthesis of a confidential discussion with a member of New York City's police force.

54. Edward L. Glaeser and Bruce Sacerdote, "Sentencing in Homicide Cases and the Role of Vengeance," *Journal of Legal Studies* 32 (2003): 363–82.

55. Death Penalty Information Center, "Abolitionist and Retentionist Countries," last updated December 31, 2017, www.deathpenaltyinfo.org/abolitionist-and-retentionist-countries.

56. *Death Sentences and Executions 2017* (London: Amnesty International, 2018), www.amnesty.org/download/Documents/ACT5079552018ENGLISH.PDF.

57. Peter A. Collins, Robert C. Boruchowitz, Matthew J. Hickman, and Mark A. Larranaga, *An Analysis of the Economic Costs of Seeking the Death Penalty in Washington* (Seattle: Seattle University School of Law 2015), http://digitalcommons.law.seattleu.edu/faculty/616; Paul V. Townsend, *Performance Audit: Fiscal Costs of the Death Penalty, 2014* (Carson City, NV: State of Nevada, 2014), www.leg.state.nv.us/audit/Full/BE2014/Costs%20of%20Death%20Penalty,%20LA14-25,%20Full.pdf; Arthur L. Alarcón and Paula M. Mitchell, "Costs of Capital Punishment in California: Will Voters Choose Reform this November?," special issue, *Loyola Law Review* 46, no. 0 (2012).

58. Death Penalty Information Center, "Death Penalty for Offenses Other Than Murder," accessed October 21, 2019, https://deathpenaltyinfo.org/facts-and-research/crimes-punishable-by-death/death-penalty-for-offenses-other-than-murder.

59. Karen F. Parker, Mari A. DeWees, and Michael L. Radelet, "Race, the Death Penalty, and Wrongful Convictions," *Criminal Justice* 18, no. 49 (2003): 48–54; Hugo Adam Bedau, "Racism, Wrongful Convictions, and the Death Penalty," *Tennessee Law Review* 76, no. 615 (2009): 615–24; Samuel Sommers and Phoebe Ellsworth, "White Juror Bias: An Investigation of Prejudice Against Black Defendants in the American Courtroom," *Psychology, Public Policy and Law* 7, no. 1 (2001): 201–29, www.ase.tufts.edu/psychology/sommerslab/documents/raceRealSommersEllsworth2001.pdf.

60. John Blume, Theodore Eisenberg, and Martin T. Wells, "Explaining Death Row's Population and Racial Composition," *Journal of Empirical Legal Studies*

1, no. 1 (2004): 165–207, http://scholarship.law.cornell.edu/cgi/viewcontent.cgi?article=1240&context=facpub.

61. Scott Phillips, "Racial Disparities in the Capital of Capital Punishment," *Houston Law Review* 45 (208): 807–40.

62. Death Penalty Information Center, "Number of Executions by State and Region since 1976," accessed October 21, 2019, www.deathpenaltyinfo.org/number-executions-state-and-region-1976.

63. Death Penalty Information Center, "Executions by Country," accessed October 21, 2019, www.deathpenaltyinfo.org/executions-county#overall.

64. Phillips, "Racial Disparities."

65. Marian R. Williams and Jefferson E. Holcomb, "The Interactive Effects of Victim Race and Gender on Death Sentence Disparity Findings," *Homicide Studies* 8, no. 4 (2004): 350–76.

66. Lane Kirkland Gillespie, Thomas A. Loughran, Dwayne M. Smith, Sondra J. Fogel, and Beth Bjerregaard, "Exploring the Role of Victim Sex, Victim Conduct, and Victim-Defendant Relationship in Capital Punishment Sentencing," *Homicide Studies* 18, no. 2 (2014): 175–95, http://dx.doi.org/10.1177/1088767913485747.

67. Samuel R. Gross, Maurice Possley, and Klara Stephens, *Race and Wrongful Convictions in the United States* (Irvine, CA: National Registry of Exonerations, March 7, 2017), www.law.umich.edu/special/exoneration/Documents/Race_and_Wrongful_Convictions.pdf.

68. Cal. Pen. Code § 187–199, https://leginfo.legislature.ca.gov/faces/codes_displayText.xhtml?lawCode=PEN&division=&title=8.&part=1.&chapter=1.&article; Veronica Rose, "Killing a Police Officer," OLR Research Report, May 23, 2000, www.cga.ct.gov/2000/rpt/2000-R-0564.htm.

69. *Washington Post*, "Fatal Force," accessed September 30, 2019, www.washingtonpost.com/graphics/2018/national/police-shootings-2018. The total number of people killed each year by police in the line of duty reported by the *Washington Post* (992 shot and killed by police in 2018) is more than twice the average (around 400 people) reported by the FBI. See Federal Bureau of Investigation, "Expanded Homicide Data Table 14: Justifiable Homicide by Weapon, Law Enforcement, 2008–2012," accessed September 30, 2019, www.fbi.gov/about-us/cjis/ucr/crime-in-the-u.s/2012/crime-in-the-u.s.-2012/offenses-known-to-law-enforcement/expanded-homicide/expanded_homicide_data_table_14_justifiable_homicide_by_weapon_law_enforcement_2008-2012.xls.

70. Human Rights Watch, "Local Criminal Prosecution," accessed September 30, 2019, www.hrw.org/legacy/reports98/police/uspo31.htm.

71. Mapping Police Violence, "Unarmed Victims," accessed September 30, 2019, http://mappingpoliceviolence.org/unarmed.

72. Human Rights Watch, "Local Criminal Prosecution," accessed September 30, 2019, www.hrw.org/legacy/reports98/police/uspo31.htm.

73. Calabresi, "Why a Medical Examiner Called Eric Garner's Death a 'Homicide.'"

74. United States Census Bureau, "Income, Poverty and Health Insurance Coverage in the United States: 2014," release number CB15–157, September 16, 2015, www.census.gov/newsroom/press-releases/2015/cb15-157.html; Rakesh Kochhar and Richard Fry, "Wealth Inequality Has Widened along Racial, Ethnic Lines since End of Great Recession," Pew Research Center, December 12, 2014, www.pewresearch.org/fact-tank/2014/12/12/racial-wealth-gaps-great-recession.

CHAPTER 4. A LITTLE MORE ARSENIC IN YOUR WATER

1. The discussion in this chapter focuses on federal regulations. State and local regulations are often not subject to cost-benefit analysis. A complete list of federal agencies may be found on the website of the Federal Register, www.federalregister.gov/agencies.

2. Paperwork Reduction Act, Public Law 96–511, 96th Congress (1980) www.congress.gov/bill/96th-congress/house-bill/6410; Exec. Order No. 13563, 76 Fed. Reg. 3821 (January 18, 2011) www.gpo.gov/fdsys/pkg/FR-2011-01-21/pdf/2011-1385.pdf.

3. Exec. Order No. 12291, 46 Fed. Reg. 13193 (February 17, 1981) www.archives.gov/federal-register/codification/executive-order/12291.html; Exec. Order No. 12866, 58 Fed. Reg. 190 (September 30, 1993) www.reginfo.gov/public/jsp/Utilities/EO_12866.pdf; Exec. Order No. 13563.

4. Flood Control Act of 1939, Public Law 76–396, 76th Congress (1939) www.legisworks.org/congress/76/publaw-396.pdf.

5. For an overview, see Anthony Boardman, David Greenberg, Aidan Vining, and David Weimer, *Cost-Benefit Analysis Concepts and Practice,* 4th ed., Pearson Series in Economics (Upper Saddle River, NJ: Prentice Hall, 2010).

6. Winston Harrington, Richard Morgenstern, and Peter Nelson, "How Accurate Are Regulatory Cost Estimates?" *Resources for the Future,* March 5, 2010, https://grist.files.wordpress.com/2010/10/harringtonmorgensternnelson_regulatory_estimates.pdf; Winston Harrington, "Grading Estimates of the Benefits and Costs of Federal Regulation: A Review of Reviews" (discussion paper 06-39, Resources for the Future, Washington, DC, 2006), https://ideas.repec.org/p/rff/dpaper/dp-06-39.html; Winston Harrington, Richard D. Morgenstern, and Peter Nelson, "On the Accuracy of Regulatory Cost Estimates," *Journal of Policy Analysis and Management* 19, no. 2 (2000): 297–322, https://onlinelibrary.wiley.com/doi/abs/10.1002/%28SICI%291520-6688%28200021%2919%3A2%3C297%3A%3AAID-PAM7%3E3.0.CO%3B2-X.

7. Noel Brinkerhoff, "Many of Largest U.S. Corporations Paid More for Lobbying Than for Federal Income Taxes," Allgov.com, January 27, 2012, www.allgov.com/Top_Stories/ViewNews/Many_of_Largest_US_Corporations_Paid_More_for_Lobbying_than_for_Federal_Income_Taxes_120127.

8. Alex Blumberg, "Forget Stocks or Bonds, Invest in a Lobbyist," National Public Radio, January 6, 2012, www.npr.org/sections/money/2012/01/06/144737864/forget-stocks-or-bonds-invest-in-a-lobbyist.

9. Cass Sunstein, *Valuing Life* (Chicago: University of Chicago Press, 2014), 74.

10. Lisa Heinzerling, "The Rights of Statistical People," *Harvard Environmental Law Review* 189, no. 24 (2000): 203–6, http://scholarship.law.georgetown.edu/cgi/viewcontent.cgi?article=1322&context=facpub.

11. "Economic Analysis of Federal Regulations under Executive Order 12866," (Report of Interagency Group Chaired by a Member of the Council of Economic Advisors, January 11, 1996), part III.B.5(a), https://georgewbush-whitehouse.archives.gov/omb/inforeg/riaguide.html .

12. W. Kip Viscusi, *Pricing Lives* (Princeton: Princeton University Press, 2018), 35–36.

13. Frank Ackerman and Lisa Heinzerling, "If It Exists, It's Getting Bigger: Revising the Value of a Statistical Life," (Global Development and Environment Institute Working Paper No. 01-06, Tufts University, Medford, MA, October 2001), http://frankackerman.com/publications/costbenefit/Value_Statistical_Life.pdf.

14. Sunstein, *Valuing Life,* 52.

15. Katharine Q. Seelye and John Tierney, "E.P.A. Drops Age-Based Cost Studies," *New York Times,* May 8, 2003, www.nytimes.com/2003/05/08/us/epa-drops-age-based-cost-studies.html; Frank Ackerman and Lisa Heinzerling, *Priceless: On Knowing the Price of Everything and the Value of Nothing* (New York: New Press, 2005), 61–90; Bert Metz, Ogunlade Davidson, Rob Swart, and Jiahua Pan, *Climate Change 2001: Mitigation* (Cambridge: Cambridge University Press, 2001), section 7.4.4.2.

16. Clean Air Task Force, "The Toll from Coal: An Updated Assessment of Death and Disease from America's Dirtiest Energy Source," September 2010, www.catf.us/resources/publications/files/The_Toll_from_Coal.pdf; Abt Associates, "Technical Support Document for the Powerplant Impact Estimator Software Tool," July 2010, www.catf.us/resources/publications/files/Abt-Technical_Support_Document_for_the_Powerplant_Impact_Estimator_Software_Tool.pdf.

17. Cass R. Sunstein, *The Cost-Benefit Revolution* (Cambridge, MA: MIT Press, 2018), 74, 80, 142, 170.

18. This could be probed by stratifying survey results by age to see if values are changing by age group, but this method would be convolved with many other factors, including the ability to pay.

19. For more details on discounting and compounding, I suggest reading Boardman et al., *Cost-Benefit Analysis Concepts and Practices.*

20. Boardman et al., *Cost-Benefit Analysis Concepts and Practices,* 247.

21. There is substantial discussion of what is the appropriate discount rate to use. Different discount rates that have been used include the marginal rate of return on private-sector investments, the marginal social rate of time preference, and the government's real long-term borrowing rate.

22. When the assumed growth in the value of life is set equal to the discount rate, the net discount rate is zero even though the discount rate applied is nonzero.

23. Some studies have tried to show that people apply discount rates to future lives (see, e.g., Maureen L. Cropper, Sema K. Aydede, and Paul R. Portney, "Rates of Time Preference for Saving Lives," *American Economic Review* 82, no. 2 [May 1992]: 469–72). These studies suffer from the same sample bias issues as all surveys of this nature and from the fact that the rates observed depended on how far into the future projections were made.

24. A summary of the concerns is identified in the section on intergenerational accounting in "Economic Analysis of Federal Regulations under Executive Order 12866," part III.B.5(a).

25. T. Tan-Torres Edejer, R. Baltussen, T. Adam, R. Hutubessy, A. Acharya, D. B. Evans, and C. J. L. Murray, eds., "WHO Guide to Cost-Effectiveness Analysis," (Geneva: World Health Organization, 2003), 70, www.who.int/choice /publications/p_2003_generalised_cea.pdf.

26. Stephanie Riegg Cellini and James Edwin Kee, "Cost-Effectiveness and Cost-Benefit Analysis," in *Handbook of Practical Program Evaluation,* 3rd ed., ed. Joseph S. Wholey, Harry P. Hatry, and Kathryn E. Newcomer (San Francisco: Jossey-Bass, 2010), 493–530.

27. Clean Air Task Force, "Toll from Coal."

28. Adam Liptak and Coral Davenport, "Supreme Court Blocks Obama's Limits on Power Plants," *New York Times,* June 29, 2015, www.nytimes.com/2015/06/30 /us/supreme-court-blocks-obamas-limits-on-power-plants.html.

29. Michigan et al. v. Environmental Protection Agency et al., 135 S. Ct. 2699 (2015), www.supremecourt.gov/opinions/14pdf/14-46_bqmc.pdf.

30. For more discussion on the topic of regulatory capture, see Ernesto Dal Bó, "Regulatory Capture: A Review," *Oxford Review of Economic Policy* 22 no. 2 (2006): 203–25, http://faculty.haas.berkeley.edu/dalbo/Regulatory_Capture_ Published.pdf.

31. Laurie Garrett, "EPA Misled Public on 9/11 Pollution / White House Ordered False Assurances on Air Quality, Report Says," *Newsday,* August 23, 2003, www.sfgate.com/news/article/EPA-misled-public-on-9-11-pollution-White-House-2560252.php.

32. Jennifer Lee, "White House Sway Is Seen in E.P.A. Response to 9/11," *New York Times,* August 9, 2003, www.nytimes.com/2003/08/09/nyregion/white-house-sway-is-seen-in-epa-response-to-9-11.html

33. The public can provide comment under the Administrative Procedures Act, Public Law 79–404, 79th Congress (1946).

34. Exec. Order No. 13563.

35. Dwight D. Eisenhower, "Military-Industrial Complex Speech," 1961, https://avalon.law.yale.edu/20th_century/eisenhower001.asp.

CHAPTER 5. MAXIMIZING PROFITS AT WHOSE EXPENSE?

1. E. S. Grush and C. S. Saunby, "Fatalities Associated with Crash Induced Fuel Leakage and Fires," 1973, http://lawprofessors.typepad.com/tortsprof/files/FordMemo.pdf. This document is also referred to as the Ford Pinto Memo.

2. Gary T. Schwartz, "The Myth of the Ford Pinto Case," *Rutgers Law Review* 43, no. 1013 (1991): 1013–68, www.pointoflaw.com/articles/The_Myth_of_the_Ford_Pinto_Case.pdf.

3. The author has personal experience working as a statistician supporting mock trials.

4. William H. Shaw and Vincent Barry, *Moral Issues in Business,* 8th ed. (Belmont, CA: Wadsworth Publishing, 2001), 83–86.

5. Mark Dowie, "Pinto Madness," *Mother Jones,* September/October 1977, www.motherjones.com/politics/1977/09/pinto-madness.

6. Grimshaw v. Ford Motor Co., 119 Cal. 3d 757 (1981), http://online.ceb.com/calcases/CA3/119CA3d757.htm. It is noteworthy that adjusting the $2.5 million in compensatory damages awarded in this landmark case by the cost of living adjustments over the past three decades results in a price tag that is similar to the values used by regulators today. This computation uses the Social Security administration's cost of living adjustments (www.ssa.gov/oact/cola/colaseries.html) based on the award amount in 1978 and reaffirmed in 1981 for the 2010 Value of a Statistical Life.

7. History, "This Day in History: July 13 1978; Henry Ford II Fires Lee Iacocca," January 27, 2010, www.history.com/this-day-in-history/henry-ford-ii-fires-lee-iacocca.

8. Greg Gardner, Alisa Priddle, and Brent Snavely, "GM Could Settle DOJ Criminal Investigation This Summer," *Detroit Free Press,* May 23, 2015, www.freep.com/story/money/2015/05/22/general-motors-justice-department-ignition-switch-deaths/27820247.

9. Bill Vlasic and Matt Apuzzo, "Toyota Is Fined $1.2 Billion for Concealing Safety Defects," *New York Times,* March 19, 2014, www.nytimes.com/2014/03/20/business/toyota-reaches-1-2-billion-settlement-in-criminal-inquiry.html.

10. "A Scandal in the Motor Industry: Dirty Secrets," *The Economist,* September 26, 2015, www.economist.com/news/leaders/21666226-volkswagens-falsification-pollution-tests-opens-door-very-different-car.

11. Ralph Nader, *Breaking Though Power* (San Francisco: City Lights Books, 2016), 61.

12. Subodh Varma, "Arbitrary? 92% of All Injuries Termed Minor," *The Times of India,* June 20, 2010, http://timesofindia.indiatimes.com/india/Arbitrary-92-of-all-injuries-termed-minor/articleshow/6069528.cms.

13. Sanjoy Hazarika, "Bhopal Payments by Union Carbide Set at $470 Million," *New York Times,* February 15, 1989, www.nytimes.com/1989/02/15/business/bhopal-payments-by-union-carbide-set-at-470-million.html.

14. The ratio of the U.S. GDP to the Indian GDP per capita in 1989 was 20.9 (nominal) and 64.9 (purchase power parity). World Bank, "GDP per Capita (Current US$)," accessed September 30, 2019, http://data.worldbank.org/indicator/NY.GDP.PCAP.CD; World Bank, "GDP per Capita, PPP (Current International $)," accessed September 30, 2019, http://data.worldbank.org/indicator/NY.GDP.PCAP.PP.CD.

15. "Compensation Fund for Bangladesh Factory Victims Reaches US$30m Target," *Channel News Asia,* June 9, 2015, www.channelnewsasia.com/news/asiapacific/compensation-fund-for/1902092.html.

16. Arthur D. Little International, "Public Finance Balance of Smoking in the Czech Republic, Report to: Philip Morris CR," November 28, 2000, www.no-smoke.org/pdf/pmczechstudy.pdf.

17. A. Raynauld and J. Vidal, "Smoker's Burden on Society: Myth and Reality in Canada," *Canadian Public Policy* 18, no. 3 (1992): 300–317; G. Stoddart, R. LaBelle, M. Barer, and R. Evans, "Tobacco Taxes and Health Care Costs: Do Canadian Smokers Pay Their Way?," *Journal of Health Economics* 5, no. 1 (1986): 63–80; J. Prabhat and F.J. Chaloupka, *Curbing the Epidemic: Governments and the Economics of Tobacco Control,* (Washington, DC: World Bank, 1999).

18. "Smoking Can Help Czech Economy, Philip Morris-Little Report Says," *WallStreetJournal,*July16,2001,www.wsj.com/articles/SB995230746855683470.

19. "Philip Morris Issues Apology for Czech Study on Smoking," *New York Times,* July 27, 2001, www.nytimes.com/2001/07/27/business/philip-morris-issues-apology-for-czech-study-on-smoking.html.

20. Samuel H. Williamson and Louis P. Cain, "Slavery in 2011 Dollars," MeasuringWorth, 2019, www.measuringworth.com/slavery.php.

21. Slavery Convention, September 25, 1926, 60 L.N.T.S. 254, www.ohchr.org/Documents/ProfessionalInterest/slavery.pdf; Supplementary Convention on the Abolition of Slavery, the Slave Trade, and Institutions and Practices Similar to Slavery, September 7, 1956, 266 U.N.T.S. 3, www.ohchr.org/Documents/ProfessionalInterest/slaverytrade.pdf; *The Global Slavery Index 2014* (Australia: Hope for Children Organization, 2014) https://reporterbrasil.org.br/wp-content/uploads/2014/11/GlobalSlavery_2014_LR-FINAL.pdf.

22. *Global Slavery Index 2014*; Adam Withnall, "Isis Releases 'Abhorrent' Sex Slaves Pamphlet with 27 Tips for Militants on Taking, Punishing and Raping

Female Captives," *Independent,* December 10, 2014, www.independent.co.uk/news/world/middle-east/isis-releases-abhorrent-sex-slaves-pamphlet-with-27-tips-for-militants-on-taking-punishing-and-raping-female-captives-9915913.html.

23. Doug Bolton, "Isis 'Price List' for Child Slaves Confirmed as Genuine by UN Official Zainab Bangura," *Independent,* August 4, 2015, www.independent.co.uk/news/world/middle-east/isis-price-list-for-child-slaves-confirmed-as-genuine-by-un-official-zainab-bangura-10437348.html.

24. Eric Foner, *Give Me Liberty* (New York: W.W. Norton, 2004).

25. United Nations Office on Drugs and Crime, "Factsheet on Human Trafficking," accessed September 30, 2019, www.unodc.org/documents/human-trafficking/UNVTF_fs_HT_EN.pdf.

26. U.S. General Accounting Office, "Alien Smuggling: Management and Operational Improvements Needed to Address Growing Problem," (Washington, DC: U.S. Government Printing Office, 2000), www.gao.gov/assets/230/229061.pdf.

27. "Walk Tall: Why It Pays to Be a Lanky Teenager," *The Economist,* April 25 2002, www.economist.com/node/1099333.

28. Carol Peckham, "Medscape Radiologist Compensation Report 2015," Medscape, April 21, 2015, www.medscape.com/features/slideshow/compensation/2015/radiology. For the purpose of this calculation, I have used a forty-hour workweek and four weeks of vacation.

29. Milton Friedman, *Capitalism and Freedom* (Chicago: University Of Chicago Press, 2002).

30. Thomas Friedman, *The World Is Flat* (New York: Farrar, Straus, and Giroux, 2005).

31. Elizabeth Olson, "Welcome to Your First Year as a Lawyer. Your Salary Is $160,000," *New York Times,* April 16, 2015, www.nytimes.com/2015/04/17/business/dealbook/welcome-to-your-first-year-as-a-lawyer-your-salary-is-160000-a-year.html; Association of American Medical Colleges, "Starting Salaries for Physicians," accessed January 10, 2019, https://www.aamc.org/services/first/first_factsheets/399572/compensation.html.

32. New York City Fire Department, "Firefighter Benefits and Salaries," accessed September 30, 2019, www1.nyc.gov/site/fdny/jobs/career-paths/firefighter-salary-guide.page.

33. Howard Steven Friedman, *Measure of a Nation* (New York: Prometheus Books, 2012).

34. Using $7.25 an hour, forty hours a week, fifty weeks per year results in a salary of $14,500, compared with the 2017 GDP per capita of the United States, which was approximately $59,531. See World Bank, GDP per Capita (Current US$); Organisation for Economic Co-operation and Development, "Focus on Minimum Wages after the Crisis: Making Them Pay," May 2015, www.oecd.org/social/Focus-on-Minimum-Wages-after-the-crisis-2015.pdf.

35. Bureau of Labor and Statistics, "United States Department of Labor," accessed September 30, 2019, www.bls.gov/emp/chart-unemployment-earnings-education.htm.

36. "Is Your Degree Worth It? It Depends What You Study, Not Where," *The Economist,* March 12, 2015, www.economist.com/news/united-states/21646220-it-depends-what-you-study-not-where.

37. United Nations International Civil Service Commission, "Danger Pay," accessed September 30, 2019, https://icsc.un.org/Home/DangerPay.

38. Hanna Rosin, "The Gender Wage Gap Lie," *Slate Magazine,* August 30, 2013, www.slate.com/articles/double_x/doublex/2013/08/gender_pay_gap_the_familiar_line_that_women_make_77_cents_to_every_man_s.html.

39. Francine D. Blau and Lawrence M. Kahn, "The Gender Pay Gap: Have Women Gone as Far as They Can?," *Academy of Managed Perspectives* 21, no. 1 (2007): 7–23, http://web.stanford.edu/group/scspi/_media/pdf/key_issues/gender_research.pdf.

40. Joanne Lipman, "Let's Expose the Gender Pay Gap," *New York Times,* August 13, 2015, www.nytimes.com/2015/08/13/opinion/lets-expose-the-gender-pay-gap.html.

41. Deborah Ashton, "Does Race or Gender Matter More to Your Paycheck?," *Harvard Business Review,* November 4, 2016, https://hbr.org/2014/06/does-race-or-gender-matter-more-to-your-paycheck.

42. Susan Aud, Mary Ann Fox, Angelina Kewal Ramani, *Status and Trends in the Education of Racial and Ethnic Groups,* (Washington, DC: U.S. Department of Education, July 2010), http://nces.ed.gov/pubs2010/2010015.pdf.

43. The "informal sector" generally refers to the part of an economy that is neither taxed nor monitored by any form of government. A discussion of some definitions of "informal economy" can be found in Friedrich Schneider, "Size and Measurement of the Informal Economy in 110 Countries around the World," (paper presented at a Workshop of Australian National Tax Centre, Canberra, Australia, July 17, 2002), www.amnet.co.il/attachments/informal_economy110.pdf.

44. Prison Policy Initiative, "Section III: The Prison Economy," accessed September 30, 2019, www.prisonpolicy.org/blog/2017/04/10/wages; Peter Wagner, *The Prison Index: Taking the Pulse of the Crime Control Industry* (Northampton MA: Western Prison Project and the Prison Policy Initiative, 2003).

45. Chuck Collins, *Economic Apartheid in America: A Primer on Economic Inequality and Security* (New York: New Press, 2000), 111.

46. Lawrence Mishel and Jessica Schieder, "CEO Compensation Surged in 2017 Report," *Economic Policy Institute,* August 16, 2018, www.epi.org/publication/ceo-compensation-surged-in-2017.

47. Gretchen Gavett, "CEOs Get Paid Too Much, According to Pretty Much Everyone in the World," *Harvard Business Review,* September 23, 2014, https://hbr.org/2014/09/ceos-get-paid-too-much-according-to-pretty-much-everyone-in-the-world.

CHAPTER 6. I WANT TO DIE THE WAY GRANDPA DID

1. *2014 Life Insurance and Annuity Industry Outlook: Transforming for Growth; Getting Back on Track,* Deloitte Center for Financial Services, 2014, www2.deloitte.com/content/dam/Deloitte/global/Documents/Financial-Services/dttl-fsi-us-Life-Insurance-Outlook-2014-01.pdf.

2. World Bank, "GDP (Current US$)," accessed September 30, 2019, http://data.worldbank.org/indicator/NY.GDP.MKTP.CD.

3. *ACLI 2017 Fact Book* (Washington, DC: American Council of Life Insurers, 2017), chapter 7, www.acli.com/-/media/ACLI/Files/Fact-Books-Public/FB17CH7.ashx?.

4. Computed based on population estimates of Americans. United States Census Bureau, data tables, accessed September 30, 2019, www.census.gov/popclock/data_tables.php?component=growth.

5. Jennifer Rudden, "Total Number of Life Insurance Policies in Force in the United States from 2008 to 2017 (In Millions)," Statistica, last edited July 17, 2019, www.statista.com/statistics/207651/us-life-insurance-policies-in-force.

6. Term life insurance provides insurance for a fixed period of time. If you die during that time period, the insurance company will pay the coverage amount to your beneficiaries. If you survive the time period, the insurance company will pay nothing. This can be contrasted with permanent life insurance policies that, by definition, do not expire. With a permanent policy, the customer pays the insurance company for the promise that it will pay the beneficiaries a certain amount when the policyholder dies. A helpful summary of life insurance options may be found at Khan Academy,www.khanacademy.org/economics-finance-domain/core-finance/investment-vehicles-tutorial/life-insurance/v/term-life-insurance-and-death-probability.

7. *ACLI 2017 Fact Book,* chapter 7.

8. Ashley Durham, "2015 Insurance Barometer Study," (LL Global, 2015), www.orgcorp.com/wp-content/uploads/2015-Insurance-Barometer.pdf.

9. First Symetra National Life Insurance Company of New York, "Uniformed Firefighters Association of Greater New York: Summary Plan Description," Uniformed Firefighters Association, revised October 1, 2017, www.ufanyc.org/pdf/ufa_life_insurance_doc.pdf.

10. Centers for Disease Control and Prevention, "Infant Mortality," page last reviewed March 27, 2019, www.cdc.gov/reproductivehealth/MaternalInfantHealth/InfantMortality.htm; Marian F. MacDorman, T. J. Mathews, Ashna D. Mohangoo, and Jennifer Zeitlin, "International Comparisons of Infant Mortality and Related Factors: United States and Europe, 2010," *National Vital Statistics Reports* 63, no. 5 (2014), www.cdc.gov/nchs/data/nvsr/nvsr63/nvsr63_05.pdf.

11. Elizabeth Arias, Melonie Heron, and Jiaquan Xu, "United States Life Tables, 2013," *National Vital Statistics Reports* 66, no. 3 (2017), www.cdc.gov/nchs/data/nvsr/nvsr66/nvsr66_03.pdf.

12. World Health Organization, "Life Expectancy by Country," last updated April 6, 2018, http://apps.who.int/gho/data/node.main.688?lang=en.

13. Arias, Heron, and Xu, "United States Life Tables, 2013."

14. "Life Insurance: Smoker vs. Non-Smoker," ProFam.com, accessed September 30, 2019, www.profam.com/smoker-vs-non-smoker.asp.

15. Jiaquan Xu, Sherry L. Murphy, Kenneth D. Kochanek, Brigham Bastian, and Elizabeth Arias, "Deaths: Final Data for 2016," *National Vital Statistics Reports* 67, no. 5 (2018), www.cdc.gov/nchs/data/nvsr/nvsr67/nvsr67_05.pdf.

16. For an overview of the logic behind regulations imposed on insurance companies, see Ronen Avraham, Kyle D. Logue, and Daniel Benjamin Schwarcz, "Explaining Variation in Insurance Anti-Discrimination Laws," *Law & Economics Working Papers* 82 (2013), http://repository.law.umich.edu/law_econ_current/82.

17. Will Kenton, "Definition of 'Regulatory Capture,'" Investopedia, last updated March 28, 2019, www.investopedia.com/terms/r/regulatory-capture.asp.

18. Ronen Avraham, Kyle D. Logue, and Daniel Benjamin Schwarcz, "Understanding Insurance Anti-Discrimination Laws," *Law & Economics Working Papers* 52 (2013), http://repository.law.umich.edu/law_econ_current/52.

19. Calculation based on the data in Jiaquan Xu, Sherry L. Murphy, Kenneth D. Kochanek, and Brigham A. Bastian, "Deaths: Final Data for 2013," *National Vital Statistics Reports* 64, no. 2 (2016), table 18, www.cdc.gov/nchs/data/nvsr/nvsr64/nvsr64_02.pdf.

20. Avraham, Logue, and Schwarcz, "Understanding Insurance Anti-Discrimination Laws," 52.

21. Mary L. Heen, "Ending Jim Crow Life Insurance Rates," *Northwestern Journal of Law and Social Policy* 4, no. 2 (2009): 360–99, http://scholarlycommons.law.northwestern.edu/njlsp/vol4/iss2/3.

22. Businessdictionary.com, s.v. "cross subsidization," accessed September 30, 2019, www.businessdictionary.com/definition/cross-subsidization.html.

23. Ashley Durham, "2014 Insurance Barometer Study: Supplemental Data," LIMRA, table 19: 27.

24. Ibid.

25. Michael J. Sandel, *What Money Can't Buy: The Moral Limits of Markets* (New York: Farrar, Straus, and Giroux, 2013), 134.

CHAPTER 7. TO BE YOUNG AGAIN

1. *CNN*, "Law Background on the Schiavo Case," March 25, 2005, accessed January 10, 2018, www.cnn.com/2005/LAW/03/25/schiavo.qa.

2. Jonathan Weisman and Ceci Connolly, "Schiavo Case Puts Face on Rising Medical Costs; GOP Leaders Try to Cut Spending as They Fight to Save One of

Program's Patients," *Washington Post*, March 23, 2005, www.washingtonpost .com/wp-dyn/articles/A58069-2005Mar22.html.

3. Broader definitions of health exist, such as the one from the World Health Organization, which states that "health is a state of complete physical, mental and social well-being and not merely the absence of disease or infirmity." Preamble to the Constitution of the World Health Organization, signed at the International Health Conference, New York, July 22, 1946, www.who.int/governance/eb/who_constitution_en.pdf.

4. A summary of healthy choices for living appears at the Centers for Disease Control and Prevention, "Tips for a Safe and Healthy Life," www.cdc.gov/family/tips.

5. The United States President's Emergency Plan for AIDS Relief, "United States Government Global Health Initiative Strategy Document," accessed October 7, 2019, www.state.gov/pepfar.

6. World Bank, *World Development Report 1993: Investing in Health* (New York: Oxford University Press, 1993), https://openknowledge.worldbank.org /handle/10986/5976.

7. Karin Stenberg Henrik Axelson, Peter Sheehan, Ian Anderson,A. Metin Gülmezoglu,Marleen Temmerman, Elizabeth Mason, et al., "Advancing Social and Economic Development by Investing in Women's and Children's Health: A New Global Investment Framework," *The Lancet* 383, no. 9925 (2014): 1333–54.

8. Agency for Toxic Substances and Disease Registry, "Arsenic Toxicity: What Are the Physiologic Effects of Arsenic Exposure?," last updated January 15, 2010, www.atsdr.cdc.gov/csem/csem.asp?csem=1&po=11.

9. United States Environmental Protection Agency, "Sulfur Dioxide (SO2) Pollution," accessed October 7, 2019, www.epa.gov/so2-pollution.

10. In addition to QALYs, disability-adjusted life years (DALYs) are often used as a measure of population health. DALYs for a disease or health condition are calculated as the sum of the years of life lost (YLL) due to premature mortality in the population and the years lost due to disability (YLD) for people living with the health condition or its consequences. DALYs convert into a single unit the years lost due to the early loss of life or the lower quality of life associated with illness and disability. Similar to QALYs, DALYs combine disease and early death into a single number by using a scale from 1 (death) to 0 (perfect health).

11. World Health Organization, "Health Statistics and Information Systems: Disability Weights, Discounting and Age Weighting of DALYs," accessed October 7, 2019, www.who.int/healthinfo/global_burden_disease/daly_disability_weight/en.

12. Joshua A. Salomon, Juanita A. Haagsma, Adrian Davis, Charline Maertens de Noordhout, Suzanne Polinder, Arie H. Havelaar, Alessandro Cassini, et al., "Disability Weights for the Global Burden of Disease 2013 Study," *The Lancet Global Health* 3, no. 11 (2015): e712–23.

13. Centers for Medicare and Medicaid Services, "U.S. Personal Health Care Spending by Age and Gender: 2010 Highlights," accessed October 7, 2019, www

.cms.gov/Research-Statistics-Data-and-Systems/Statistics-Trends-and-Reports/NationalHealthExpendData/Downloads/2010AgeandGenderHighlights.pdf.

14. V. Fuchs, "Provide, Provide: The Economics of Aging" (NBER working paper no. 6642, National Bureau of Economic Research, Cambridge, MA, 1998).

15. Christopher Hogan, June Lunney, Jon Gabel and Joanne Lynn, "Medicare Beneficiaries' Costs of Care in the Last Year of Life," *Health Affairs* 20, no. 4 (July 2001): 188–95.

16. For an overview of the concept of quality-adjusted life years and other basic health economics concepts, see M. F. Drummond, M. J. Sculpher, G. W. Torrance, B. J. O'Brien, and G. L. Stoddart, *Methods for the Economic Evaluation of Health Care Programmes* (Oxford: Oxford University Press, 2005).

17. Some health situations are considered by health economists to be worse than death and therefore have negative QALYs.

18. National Institute for Health and Care Excellence, Glossary, s.v. "quality-adjusted life year," accessed October 7, 2019, www.nice.org.uk/glossary?letter=q.

19. EuroQol, "EQ-5D User Guide Version 2.0," 2009, accessed October 7, 2019, https://euroqol.org/wp-content/uploads/2019/09/EQ-5D-5L-English-User-Guide_version-3.0-Sept-2019-secured.pdf.

20. M. C. Weinstein, G. Torrance, and A. McGuire, "QALYs: The Basics," in "Moving the QALY Forward: Building a Pragmatic Road," special issue, *Value in Health* 12, no. S1 (2009): S5–9, http://onlinelibrary.wiley.com/doi/10.1111/j.1524-4733.2009.00515.x/epdf.

21. E. Nord, J. L. Pinto, J. Richardson, P. Menzel, and P. Ubel, "Incorporating Societal Concerns for Fairness in Numerical Valuations of Health Programmes," *Health Economics* 8, no. 1 (1999): 25–39; J. Coast, "Is Economic Evaluation in Touch with Society's Health Values?," *BMJ* 329 (2004): 1233–36, www.med.mcgill.ca/epidemiology/courses/EPIB654/Summer2010/Policy/Coast%20BMJ%202004.pdf.

22. M. L. Berger, K. Bingefors, E. C. Hedblom, C. L. Pashos, and G. W. Torrance, *Health Care Cost, Quality, and Outcomes: ISPOR Book of Terms* (Lawrenceville, NJ: ISPOR, 2003).

23. K. Arrow, R. Solow, P. R. Portney, E. E. Leamer, R. Radner, and H. Schuman, "Report of the NOAA Panel on Contingent Valuation," *Federal Register* 58, no. 10 (1993): 4601–14, www.economia.unimib.it/DATA/moduli/7_6067/materiale/noaa%20report.pdf.

24. Centers for Disease Control and Prevention, "National Health Expenditures Fact Sheet," last modified April 26, 2019, www.cms.gov/research-statistics-data-and-systems/statistics-trends-and-reports/nationalhealthexpenddata/nhe-fact-sheet.html.

25. OECD, "Health Spending," 2017, https://data.oecd.org/healthres/health-spending.htm. It should be noted that it has generally been shown that health spending takes up an increasing share of national economies as countries become

wealthier. See William Baumol, *The Cost Disease* (New Haven CT: Yale University Press, 2013).

26. *Fortune,* "Fortune 500," http://fortune.com/fortune500.

27. Henry J. Kaiser Family Foundation, "Key Facts about the Uninsured Population,"December12,2018,www.kff.org/uninsured/fact-sheet/key-facts-about-the-uninsured-population.

28. OECD, "Measuring Health Coverage," accessed October 7, 2019, www.oecd.org/els/health-systems/measuring-health-coverage.htm.

29. OECD, "Social Expenditure Update," November 2014, www.oecd.org/els/soc/OECD2014-Social-Expenditure-Update-Nov2014-8pages.pdf.

30. OECD, "Life Expectancy at Birth," accessed October 7, 2019, https://data.oecd.org/healthstat/life-expectancy-at-birth.htm.

31. Ibid.

32. World Bank, "Maternal Mortality Ratio (Modeled Estimate, per 100,000 Live Births)," accessed October 7, 2019, http://data.worldbank.org/indicator/SH.STA.MMRT?order=wbapi_data_value_2015+wbapi_data_value+wbapi_data_value-last&sort=asc.

33. Christopher J. L. Murray, Sandeep C. Kulkarni, Catherine Michaud, Niels Tomijima, Maria T. Bulzacchelli, and Terrell J. Iandiorio, Majid Ezzati, "Eight Americas: Investigating Mortality Disparities across Races, Counties, and Race-Counties in the United States," *PLOS Medicine* 3, no. 9 (2006): e260, http://journals.plos.org/plosmedicine/article?id=10.1371/journal.pmed.0030260.

34. For a more detailed discussion, see Howard Steven Friedman, *Measure of a Nation* (New York: Prometheus Books, 2012)

35. T. J. Mathews and M. F. MacDorman, "Infant Mortality Statistics from the 2010 Period Linked Birth/Infant Death Data Set," *National Vital Statistics Reports* 62, no. 8 (2013), www.cdc.gov/mmwr/preview/mmwrhtml/mm6301a9.htm; Centers for Disease Prevention and Control, "Pregnancy Mortality Surveillance System," last reviewed June 4, 2019, www.cdc.gov/reproductivehealth/maternalinfanthealth/pmss.html.

36. McKinsey Global Institute, "Accounting for the Cost of U.S. Healthcare: A New Look at Why Americans Spend More," December 2008, www.mckinsey.com/mgi/publications/us_healthcare/index.asp.

37. Laura D. Hermer and Howard Brody, "Defensive Medicine, Cost Containment, and Reform," *Journal of General Internal Medicine* 25, no. 5 (2010): 470–73. www.ncbi.nlm.nih.gov/pmc/articles/PMC2855004.

38. For an overview of the Affordable Care Act, see U.S. Department of Health and Human Services, "Health Care," accessed October 7, 2019, www.hhs.gov/healthcare/about-the-aca/index.html.

39. H. A. Glick, S. McElligott, M. V. Pauly, R.J. Willke, H. Bergquist, J. Doshi, L. A. Fleisher et al., "Comparative Effectiveness and Cost-Effectiveness Analyses Frequently Agree on Value," *Health Affairs* 34, no. 5 (2015 May): 805–11.

40. Persad Govind, "Priority Setting, Cost-Effectiveness, and the Affordable Care Act," *American Journal of Law and Medicine* 41, no. 1 (2015): 119–66, http://scholarship.law.georgetown.edu/cgi/viewcontent.cgi?article=2521&context=facpub.

41. Soneji Samir and Yang JaeWon, "New Analysis Reexamines the Value of Cancer Care in the United States Compared to Western Europe," *Health Affairs (Project Hope)* 34 no. 3 (2015): 390–97.

42. National Institute for Health and Care Excellence, "The Guidelines Manual: Process and Methods; 7 Assessing Cost Effectiveness," November 2012, www.nice.org.uk/article/pmg6/chapter/7-assessing-cost-effectiveness.

43. Usa Chaikledkaew and Kankamon Kittrongsiri, "Guidelines for Health Technology Assessment in Thailand (Second Edition)—The Development Process," *Journal of the Medical Association of Thailand* 97, suppl. 5 (2014): S4–9.

44. World Health Organization, "Tracking Universal Health Coverage: First Global Monitoring Report," 2015, http://apps.who.int/iris/bitstream/10665/174536/1/9789241564977_eng.pdf.

45. Avik Roy, "Conservative Think Tank: 10 Countries with Universal Health Care Have Freer Economies Than the U.S.," *Forbes*, January 27, 2015, www.forbes.com/sites/theapothecary/2015/01/27/conservative-think-tank-10-countries-with-universal-health-care-are-economically-freer-than-the-u-s.

46. Healthcare.gov, "Essential Health Benefits," accessed October 7, 2019, www.healthcare.gov/glossary/essential-health-benefits.

47. David U. Himmelstein, Deborah Thorne, Elizabeth Warren, and Steffie Woolhandler, "Medical Bankruptcy in the United States, 2007: Results of a National Study," *American Journal of Medicine* 122, no. 8 (2009): 741–46, www.pnhp.org/new_bankruptcy_study/Bankruptcy-2009.pdf.

48. Henry J. Kaiser Family Foundation, "Key Facts."

49. Zack Cooper, Stuart Craig, Martin Gaynor, and John Van Reenen, "The Price Ain't Right? Hospital Prices and Health Spending on the Privately Insured," (NBER working paper no. 21815, National Bureau of Economic Research, Cambridge, MA, December 2015), www.healthcarepricingproject.org/sites/default/files/pricing_variation_manuscript_0.pdf.

50. Yosuke Shimazono, "The State of the International Organ Trade: A Provisional Picture Based on Integration of Available Information," *Bulletin of the World Health Organization* 85, no. 12 (December 2007): 955–62, www.who.int/bulletin/volumes/85/12/06-039370/en.

CHAPTER 8. CAN WE AFFORD A LITTLE ONE?

1. Mark Lino, "Expenditures on Children by Families, 2013," United States Department of Agriculture, Center for Nutrition Policy and Promotion, Miscellaneous

Publication No. 1528-2003, April 2004, https://fns-prod.azureedge.net/sites/default/files/expenditures_on_children_by_families/crc2003.pdf. A middle-class household is defined as having a before-tax income of between $61,530 to $106,540.

2. A key exception is the roughly half a million American children working on their family's farms, where there are minimal restrictions on child labor. United States Department of Labor, "Youth and Labor: Agricultural Employment," accessed October 7, 2019, www.dol.gov/dol/topic/youthlabor/agricultural employment.htm; United States Department of Labor, "Agricultural Operations," Occupational Safety and Health Administration, accessed October 7, 2019, www.osha.gov/dsg/topics/agriculturaloperations.

3. University of Iowa Labor Center, "Child Labor Public Education Project: Child Labor in U.S. History," accessed October 7, 2019, https://laborcenter.uiowa.edu/special-projects/child-labor-public-education-project/about-child-labor/child-labor-us-history.

4. A critical turning point in the United States was the Fair Labor Standards Act (1938), which regulated the hours that a child could legally work. This transition in children's rights was globally formalized in the Convention of the Rights of a Child (1989), a human rights treaty that defines the civil, political, economic, social, health, and cultural rights of minors. Convention on the Rights of the Child, 1577 U.N.T.S. 3 (1989), www.ohchr.org/en/professionalinterest/pages/crc.aspx. As of 2016, every member of the United Nations is a party to the convention except the United States. See United Nations Human Rights Office of the High Commissioner, "Convention on the Rights of the Child," accessed October 7, 2019, www.ohchr.org/en/professionalinterest/pages/crc.aspx .

5. Fertility treatments are more common among women in their late thirties and early forties, as infertility rates increase sharply for women at the latter end of their reproductive age window. American Society for Reproductive Medicine, "Age and Fertility: A Guide for Patients," 2012, www.reproductivefacts.org/globalassets/rf/news-and-publications/bookletsfact-sheets/english-fact-sheets-and-info-booklets/Age_and_Fertility.pdf.

6. Cost of in vitro fertilization estimated assuming an average cost of a fertilization cycle of around $12,000, additional costs for medications that can run up to $5,000, and $6,000 for a preimplantation genetic diagnosis. Jennifer Gerson Uffalussy, "The Cost of IVF: 4 Things I Learned While Battling Infertility," *Forbes Personal Finance*, February 6, 2014, www.forbes.com/sites/learnvest/2014/02/06/the-cost-of-ivf-4-things-i-learned-while-battling-infertility.

7. The carrier often earns less than half that amount; the majority of the revenue is claimed by the agency and for legal fees. West Coast Surrogacy, "Surrogate Mother Costs," accessed October 7, 2019, www.westcoastsurrogacy.com/surrogate-program-for-intended-parents/surrogate-mother-cost; WebMD, "Using a Surrogate Mother: What You Need to Know," accessed October 7, 2019, www.webmd.com/infertility-and-reproduction/guide/using-surrogate-mother?page=2.

8. Michael Sandel, *Justice: What's the Right Thing to Do?* (New York: Farrar, Straus, and Giroux, 2008).

9. U.S. Department of Health and Human Services, Child Welfare Information Gateway, "Foster Care Statistics 2017," accessed October 7, 2019, www.childwelfare.gov/pubPDFs/foster.pdf.

10. U.S. Department of Health and Human Services, Centers for Disease Control and Prevention, "Effectiveness of Family Planning Methods," accessed October 7, 2019, www.cdc.gov/reproductivehealth/unintendedpregnancy/pdf/contraceptive_methods_508.pdf.

11. William C. Shiel Jr., "Medical Definition of Spontaneous Abortion," Medicinenet, reviewed December 11, 2018, www.medicinenet.com/script/main/art.asp?articlekey=17774.

12. Center for Reproductive Rights, "The World's Abortion Laws," last updated April 26, 2019, http://worldabortionlaws.com.

13. One state allowed abortions if the women's life was endangered or if the pregnancy was a result of rape.

14. Rachel Benson Gold, "Lessons from before Roe: Will Past Be Prologue?," *Guttmacher Report on Public Policy* 6, no. 1 (March 2003): 8–11, www.guttmacher.org/pubs/tgr/06/1/gr060108.html.

15. Roe v. Wade, 410 U.S. 113 (1973), www.law.cornell.edu/supremecourt/text/410/113.

16. I. Seri and J. Evans, "Limits of Viability: Definition of the Gray Zone," in "Proceedings of the 4th Annual Conference 'Evidence vs Experience in Neonatal Practice,'" supplement, *Journal of Perinatology* 28 no. S1 (May 2008): S4–8.

17. H.C. Glass, A.T. Costarino, S.A. Stayer, C.M. Brett, F. Cladis, and P.J. Davis, "Outcomes for Extremely Premature Infants," *Anesthesia & Analgesia* 120, no. 6 (2015): 1337–51.

18. Canwest News Service, "Miracle Child," February 11, 2006.

19. Lydia Saad, "Trimesters Still Key to U.S. Abortion Views," Gallup Politics, June 13, 2018, https://news.gallup.com/poll/235469/trimesters-key-abortion-views.aspx.

20. Guttmacher Institute, "State Policies in Brief: Abortion Bans in Cases of Sex or Race Selection or Genetic Anomaly," last updated October 1, 2019, www.guttmacher.org/state-policy/explore/abortion-bans-cases-sex-or-race-selection-or-genetic-anomaly.

21. FindLaw, "Aggravated Assault," accessed October 7, 2019, http://criminal.findlaw.com/criminal-charges/aggravated-assault.html.

22. National Conference of State Legislators, "State Laws on Fetal Homicide and Penalty-Enhancement for Crimes Against Pregnant Women," May 1, 2018, www.ncsl.org/research/health/fetal-homicide-state-laws.aspx.

23. Cal. Pen. Code § 187-199, https://leginfo.legislature.ca.gov/faces/codes_displayText.xhtml?lawCode=PEN&division=&title=8.&part=1.&chapter=1.&article.

24. R.I. Gen. Laws § 11-23-5, http://webserver.rilin.state.ri.us/Statutes/title11/11-23/11-23-5.htm.

25. Webster v. Reproductive Health Services, 492 US 490 (1989), www.law.cornell.edu/supremecourt/text/492/490.

26. Jaime L. Natoli, Deborah L. Ackerman, Suzanne McDermott, Janice G. Edwards, "Prenatal Diagnosis of Down Syndrome: A Systematic Review of Termination Rates (1995–2011)," *Prenatal Diagnosis* 32, no. 2 (2012): 142–53; Centers for Disease Control and Prevention, "Reproductive Health Data and Statistics," last reviewed September 24, 2019, www.cdc.gov/reproductivehealth/data_stats.

27. David Plotz, "The 'Genius Babies,' and How They Grew," *Slate*, February 8, 2001, www.slate.com/articles/life/seed/2001/02/the_genius_babies_and_how_they_grew.html.

28. Addgene, "CRISPR Guide," accessed October 7, 2019, www.addgene.org/CRISPR/guide.

29. Julia Belluz, "Is the CRISPR Baby Controversy the Start of a Terrifying New Chapter in Gene Editing?," *Vox*, December 3, 2018, www.vox.com/science-and-health/2018/11/30/18119589/crispr-technology-he-jiankui.

30. While in some cultures there is a daughter preference rather than a son preference, the far more pervasive situation involves the selective abortion of girls, and so that is the focus in this discussion.

31. Woojin Chung and Monica Das Gupta, "Why Is Son Preference Declining in South Korea?" (World Bank Policy Research Working Paper No. 4373, World Bank Development Research Group, Human Development and Public Services Team, October 2007); Klaus Deininger, Aparajita Goyal, and Hari Nagarajan, "Inheritance Law Reform and Women's Access to Capital: Evidence from India's Hindu Succession Act" (World Bank Policy Research Working Paper No. 5338, June 1, 2010).

32. World Bank, "Fertility Rate, Total (Births per Woman)," accessed October 7, 2019, http://data.worldbank.org/indicator/SP.DYN.TFRT.IN.

33. For a comprehensive discussion of the impacts of sex selection and excessive female mortality, see John Bongaarts and Christophe Z. Guilmoto, "How Many More Missing Women? Excess Female Mortality and Prenatal Sex Selection, 1970–2050," *Population and Development Review* 41, no. 2 (June 2015): 241–69, http://onlinelibrary.wiley.com/doi/10.1111/j.1728-4457.2015.00046.x/pdf.

34. L. S. Vishwanath, "Female Infanticide, Property and the Colonial State," in *Sex-Selective Abortion in India: Gender, Society and New Reproductive Technologies*, ed. Tulsi Patel, 269–85 (New Delhi, India: SAGE Publications India, 2007); D. E. Mungello, *Drowning Girls in China: Female Infanticide in China since 1650* (Lanham, MD: Rowman & Littlefield, 2008).

35. Shuzhuo Li, "Imbalanced Sex Ratio at Birth and Comprehensive Intervention in China" (report presented at the 4th Asia Pacific Conference on Reproduc-

tive and Sexual Health and Rights, October 29–31, 2007, Hyderabad, India), www.unfpa.org/gender/docs/studies/china.pdf.

36. Ministry of Health of the Socialist Republic of Vietnam and the United Nations Population Fund, "Report of the International Workshop on Skewed Sex Ratios at Birth: Addressing the Issue and the Way Forward" (conference report, International Workshop on Skewed Sex Ratios at Birth, United Nations Population Fund, Ha Noi, Vietnam, October 5–6, 2011), www.unfpa.org/webdav/site/global/shared/documents/publications/2012/Report_SexRatios_2012.pdf.

37. In Eastern European countries, elevated male to female sex ratios are sometimes associated with the need in those countries to replace men who have emigrated and to produce more men for military service.

38. World Bank, "Sex Ratio at Birth, (Male Births per Female Births)," accessed October 7, 2019, https://data.worldbank.org/indicator/SP.POP.BRTH.MF.

39. In China, there are some suggestions that the official sex ratio at birth may be distorted slightly due to parents underreporting births to avoid having to pay penalties for violating the One Child Policy. The magnitude and impact of this is not certain.

40. Christophe Guilmoto, "Characteristics of Sex-Ratio Imbalance in India and Future Scenarios" (report presented at the 4th Asia Pacific Conference on Reproductive and Sexual Health and Rights, October 29–31, 2007, Hyderabad, India), www.unfpa.org/gender/docs/studies/india.pdf. Note that Punjab's GDP per capita is only slighter higher than the national average.

41. Shuzhuo Li, "Imbalanced Sex Ratio at Birth and Comprehensive Intervention in China" (report presented at the 4th Asia Pacific Conference on Reproductive and Sexual Health and Rights, October 29–31, 2007, Hyderabad, India), www.unfpa.org/gender/docs/studies/china.pdf.

42. Chung and Gupta, "Why Is Son Preference Declining in South Korea?"

43. Ministry of Health of the Socialist Republic of Vietnam and the United Nations Population Fund, "Report of the International Workshop on Skewed Sex Ratios at Birth."

44. W.C. Tse, K.Y. Leung, and Beatrice K.M. Hung, "Trend of Sex Ratio at Birth in a Public Hospital in Hong Kong from 2001 to 2010," *Hong Kong Medical Journal* 19, no. 4 (2013): 305–10, www.hkmj.org/system/files/hkm1308p305.pdf; *Sex Ratio at Birth: Imbalances in Vietnam* (Hanoi: UNFPA Viet Nam, 2010), https://vietnam.unfpa.org/en/publications/sex-ratio-birth-imbalances-viet-nam.

45. James F.X. Egan, Winston A. Campbell, Audrey Chapman, Alireza A. Shamshirsaz, Padmalatha Gurram, and Peter A. Ben, "Distortions of Sex Ratios at Birth in the United States; Evidence for Prenatal Gender Selection," *Prenatal Diagnosis* 31 (2011): 560–65, www.nrlc.org/uploads/sexselectionabortion/UofCT-PrenatalDiagnosisStudy.pdf.

46. Lisa Wong Macabasco, "Many Asian American Women Accept Abortion as a Practical Way out of an Unwanted Situation," *Hyphen*, April 16, 2010, www.hyphenmagazine.com/magazine/issue-20-insideout/choice-made.

47. Christophe Z. Guilmoto, "The Sex Ratio Transition in Asia," *Population and Development Review* 35, no. 3 (September 2009): 519–49.

48. Ministry of Health of the Socialist Republic of Vietnam and the United Nations Population Fund, "Report of the International Workshop on Skewed Sex Ratios at Birth."

49. Pre-Natal Diagnostic Techniques (Regulation and Prevention of Misuse) Act, 1994, Act No. 57 of 1994, http://chdslsa.gov.in/right_menu/act/pdf/PNDT.pdf.

50. The states that have banned sex-selective abortions are Arizona, Arkansas, Kansas, Missouri, North Carolina, North Dakota, Oklahoma, Pennsylvania, and South Dakota. National Asian Pacific American Women's Forum, "Race and Sex Selective Abortion Bans: Wolves in Sheep's Clothing," July 2013, https://aapr.hkspublications.org/2014/06/03/wolves-in-sheeps-clothing-the-impact-of-sex-selective-abortion-bans-on-asian-american-and-pacific-islander-women.

51. John Bongaarts, "The Implementation of Preferences for Male Offspring," *Population and Development Review* 39, no. 2 (June 2013: 185–208.

52. Ibid.

53. Mara Hvistendahl, *Unnatural Selection: Choosing Boys over Girls, and the Consequences of a World Full of Men* (New York: PublicAffairs, 2012), 225.

54. Danièle Bélanger and Hong-Zen Wang, "Transnationalism from Below: Evidence from Vietnam-Taiwan Cross-Border Marriages," *Asian and Pacific Migration Journal* 21, no. 3 (2012): 291–316.

55. United Nations, "We Can End Poverty: Millennium Development Goals and Beyond 2015," accessed October 21, 2019, www.un.org/millenniumgoals/gender.shtml.

56. John Bongaarts, "The Causes of Educational Differences in Fertility in Sub-Saharan Africa," *Education and Demography* 8 (2010), 31–50; Anrudh K. Jain, "The Effect of Female Education on Fertility: A Simple Explanation," *Demography* 18, no. 4 (November 1981): 577–95. A Pearson correlation of -0.72 was computed between the country-level total fertility rate (Central Intelligence Agency, "World Factbook," accessed January 10, 2019, www.cia.gov/library/publications/the-world-factbook/rankorder/2127rank.html) and the country-level expected number of years of education (United Nations, "International Human Development Indicators," accessed January 10, 2019, http://hdr.undp.org/en/data).

57. United Nations Population Division, "World Population Prospects 2017," accessed October 7, 2019, https://population.un.org/wpp/Publications/Files/WPP2017_DataBooklet.pdf.

CHAPTER 9. BROKEN CALCULATORS

1. Institute for Health Metrics and Evaluation, "GBD Compare," accessed October 10, 2019, http://vizhub.healthdata.org/gbd-compare.

2. Daniel Kahneman and Amos Tversky, "Prospect Theory: An Analysis of Decision under Risk," *Econometrica* 47, no. 2 (March 1979): 263–91, www.its.caltech.edu/~camerer/Ec101/ProspectTheory.pdf.

3. National Research Council, *Improving Risk Communication* (Washington, DC: National Academy Press, 1989); D. A. Small, and G. Loewenstein, "Helping the Victim or Helping a Victim: Altruism and Identifiability," *Journal of Risk and Uncertainty* 26, no. 1 (2003): 5–16.

4. Quote Investigator, "A Single Death is a Tragedy; a Million Deaths is a Statistic," May 21, 2010, http://quoteinvestigator.com/2010/05/21/death-statistic.

5. Paul Slovic, "If I Look at the Mass I Will Never Act: Psychic Numbing and Genocide," *Judgment and Decision Making* 2, no. 2 (2007): 79–95.

6. Computed based on the International Labor Organization's estimation of approximately twelve thousand annual mining deaths, cited in Olivia Lang, "The Dangers of Mining around the World," *BBC News,* October 14, 2010, www.bbc.com/news/world-latin-america-11533349.

7. *CNN,* "Syrian Civil War Fast Facts," May 3, 2018, www.cnn.com/2013/08/27/world/meast/syria-civil-war-fast-facts/index.html.

8. Helena Smith, "Shocking Images of Drowned Syrian Boy Show Tragic Plight of Refugees," *Guardian,* September 2, 2015, www.theguardian.com/world/2015/sep/02/shocking-image-of-drowned-syrian-boy-shows-tragic-plight-of-refugees.

9. Quoted in *Fog of War: Eleven Lessons from the Life of Robert S. McNamara,* directed by Errol Morris, released May 21, 2003, transcript accessed October 10, 2019, www.errolmorris.com/film/fow_transcript.html.

10. The power of moving from statistics to discussing individuals was also displayed in the media response to the September 11 attacks. The victims were individuals who had families, friends, and dreams. To help the world appreciate the loss, their biographies were published in a *New York Times* series called Portraits of Grief. "9/11: The Reckoning," *New York Times,* accessed October 10, 2019, www.nytimes.com/interactive/us/sept-11-reckoning/portraits-of-grief.html.

11. Paul Bloom, *Against Empathy* (New York: HarperCollins, 2016)

12. For more, see Richard Dawkins, *The Selfish Gene,* 30th anniversary ed. (Oxford: Oxford University Press, 2006).

13. Some have argued that moral progress involves continuing to expand our concern outward, presumably until we are concerned about all humans both alive today and yet to be born. It is possible to envision a future world in which this circle expands even beyond humans to include all sentient beings, all

animals, or even all living things. Jeremy Rifkin, *The Empathic Civilization: The Race to Global Consciousness in a World in Crisis* (New York: Penguin, 2009); Paul R. Ehrlich and Robert E. Ornstein, *Humanity on a Tightrope* (New York: Rowman and Littlefield, 2010).

14. Domestically, during World War II, tens of thousands of American citizens of Japanese descent were placed in internment camps.

15. Tom Brokaw, *The Greatest Generation* (New York: Random House, 1998).

16. History.com, "Bombing of Dresden," November 9, 2009, www.history.com/topics/world-war-ii/battle-of-dresden.

17. Iris Chang, *The Rape of Nanking: The Forgotten Holocaust of World War II* (New York: Basic Books, 1997). Nanjing Massacre Memorial Hall in Nanjing, China, displays Japanese media coverage of a contest between Japanese military leaders for who could cut off the most Chinese heads.

18. National World War II Museum, "Research Starters: Worldwide Deaths in World War II," accessed October 10, 2019, www.nationalww2museum.org/learn/education/for-students/ww2-history/ww2-by-the-numbers/world-wide-deaths.html.

19. Charles Hirshman, Samuel Preston, and Vu Mahn Loi, "Vietnamese Casualties during the American War: A New Estimate," *Population and Development Review* 21, no. 4 (December 1995): 783–812, https://faculty.washington.edu/charles/new%20PUBS/A77.pdf. The official Vietnamese estimate published in 1995 was 3.1 million deaths (1.1 million military, 2 million civilian), according to Philip Shenon, "20 Years after Victory, Vietnamese Communists Ponder How to Celebrate," *New York Times*, April 23, 1995, www.nytimes.com/1995/04/23/world/20-years-after-victory-vietnamese-communists-ponder-how-to-celebrate.html.

20. Theodore H. Draper, "The True History of the Gulf War," *New York Review of Books*, January 30, 1992, www.nybooks.com/articles/1992/01/30/the-true-history-of-the-gulf-war.

21. Joseph Stiglitz and Linda Bilmes, *The Three Trillion Dollar War* (New York: W.W. Norton, 2008).

22. A. Hagopian, A.D. Flaxman, T.K. Takaro, A.I. Esa, S.A. Shatari, J. Rajaratnam, S. Becker, et al., "Mortality in Iraq Associated with the 2003–2011 War and Occupation: Findings from a National Cluster Sample Survey by the University Collaborative Iraq Mortality Study," *PLOS Medicine* 10, no. 10 (2013): e1001533, http://journals.plos.org/plosmedicine/article?id=10.1371/journal.pmed.1001533.

23. American Civil Liberties Union, "Al-Aulaqi V. Panetta—Constitutional Challenge to Killing of Three U.S. Citizens," June 4, 2014, www.aclu.org/cases/al-aulaqi-v-panetta-constitutional-challenge-killing-three-us-citizens.

24. Jeremy Scahill, "The Assassination Complex," *The Intercept*, October 15, 2015, https://theintercept.com/drone-papers/the-assassination-complex.

25. Micah Zenko, *Reforming U.S. Drone Strike Policies* (New York: Council on Foreign Relations, January 2013), www.cfr.org/report/reforming-us-drone-strike-policies.

26. For politicians, authorizing military campaigns is often a depersonalized experience. Few national elected officials have served in the armed forces, and even fewer have experienced military engagement. This was not always the case. From 1945 to 1979, every U.S. president had some military service. Since Reagan was elected in 1980, the only commander in chief with combat experience has been George H. W. Bush. This shift reflects the broader change in the American military from a conscription to a volunteer force, as well as the passing of the generations who were drafted to support America's effort in the world wars.

This lack of direct military experience is also mirrored in the families of elected officials. During the run-up to the 2003 war in Iraq, there was only one U.S. senator who had a child in the military. The children of senators and congresspersons do not generally serve in the military, and the children of upper-middle and upper-class parents rarely do either. As a result, those who are most likely to influence foreign policy are those most removed from the realities facing soldiers.

From a politician's point of view, these military deaths are mostly unidentified deaths, so they carry less weight in the eyes of a given policymaker than lives he or she can more easily identify with. Imagine a potential war scenario where the president knew, going in, the names and faces of every serviceperson who would be killed. What if, on making the decision to go to war, Congress and the president immediately had to personally apologize to all of these people and their families for causing their deaths? Would war still occur?

27. Eric Schmitt and Charlie Savage, "Bowe Bergdahl, American Soldier, Freed by Taliban in Prisoner Trade," *New York Times*, May 31, 2014, www.nytimes.com/2014/06/01/us/bowe-bergdahl-american-soldier-is-freed-by-taliban.html.

28. Michael Ames, "What the Army Doesn't Want You to Know about Bowe Bergdahl," *Newsweek*, January 27, 2016, www.newsweek.com/2016/02/05/serial-bowe-bergdahl-mystery-pow-419962.html.

29. Ben Quinn, "Gilad Shalit Freed in Exchange for Palestinian Prisoners," *Guardian*, October 18, 2011, www.theguardian.com/world/2011/oct/18/gilad-shalit-palestine-prisoners-freed; Ethan Bronner, "Israel and Hamas Agree to Swap Prisoners for Soldier," *New York Times*, October 10, 2017, www.nytimes.com/2011/10/12/world/middleeast/possible-deal-near-to-free-captive-israeli-soldier.html.

30. Centers for Disease Control and Prevention, "2014 Ebola Outbreak in West Africa Epidemic Curves," last reviewed April 3, 2019, www.cdc.gov/vhf/ebola/outbreaks/2014-west-africa/cumulative-cases-graphs.html.

31. World Health Organization, "Ebola Situation Reports," accessed October 10, 2019, http://apps.who.int/ebola/ebola-situation-reports.

32. Google search trends show a major spike in Americans searching for Ebola starting in the last week of July 2014.

33. Data on international tourism indicate that the countries hit hardest by Ebola (Sierra Leone, Liberia, and Guinea) reported having less than two hundred thousand tourists annually. World Bank, "International Tourism, Number of Arrivals," accessed October 10, 2019, http://data.worldbank.org/indicator/ST.INT.ARVL.

34. *RTÉ News*, "Paris Attacks Death Toll Rises to 130," November 20, 2015, www.rte.ie/news/2015/1120/747897-paris.

35. U.S. Department of Commerce, International Trade Administration, "Profile of U.S. Resident Travelers Visiting Overseas Destinations: 2014 Outbound," accessed October 10, 2019, http://travel.trade.gov/outreachpages/download_data_table/2014_Outbound_Profile.pdf.

36. Liz O'Connor, Gus Lubin, and Dina Spector, "The Largest Ancestry Groups in the United States," *Business Insider*, August 13, 2013, www.businessinsider.com/largest-ethnic-groups-in-america-2013-8.

37. Part of this diminished empathy and response is likely related to the current Myanmar government's approach to the international community.

38. Maria Konnikova, "The Limits of Friendship," *New Yorker*, October 7, 2014, www.newyorker.com/science/maria-konnikova/social-media-affect-math-dunbar-number-friendships.

39. Top solutions for Kaggle's *Titanic* machine learning competition identified these variables as being most important in predictive modeling of the survivors. See Kaggle, "Titanic: Machine Learning from Disaster," accessed October 10, 2019, www.kaggle.com/c/titanic.

40. Titanic Facts, "Titanic Survivors," accessed October 10, 2019, www.titanicfacts.net/titanic-survivors.html.

41. Amos Tversky and Daniel Kahneman, "The Framing of Decisions and the Psychology of Choice," *Science*, n.s., 211, no. 4481 (January 1981): 453–58, http://psych.hanover.edu/classes/cognition/papers/tversky81.pdf.

42. Kahneman and Tversky, "Prospect Theory."

43. Paul Slovic, Melissa Finucane, Ellen Peters, and Donald G. MacGregor, "The Affect Heuristic," in *Heuristics and Biases: The Psychology of Intuitive Judgement*, ed. Thomas Gilovich, Dale W. Griffin, and Daniel Kahneman, 397–420 (Cambridge: Cambridge University Press, 2002), 408.

44. William H. Desvousges, F. Reed Johnson, Richard W. Dunford, Sara P. Hudson, K. Nicole Wilson, and Kevin J. Boyle, "Measuring Natural Resource Damages with Contingent Valuation: Tests of Validity and Reliability," in *Contingent Valuation: A Critical Assessment*, ed. Jerry A. Hausman (Amsterdam: North-Holland, 1993), 91–114, www.emeraldinsight.com/doi/pdfplus/10.1108/S0573-8555(1993)0000220006.

45. W. Kip Viscusi, *Pricing Lives* (Princeton: Princeton University Press, 2018), 56.

46. Kendra Cherry, "How the Availability Heuristic Affects Decision Making," Verywell Mind, last updated September 5, 2019, http://psychology.about.com/od/aindex/g/availability-heuristic.htm.

47. Steven Pinker, *The Better Angels of Our Nature: Why Violence Has Declined* (New York: Penguin Books, 2012).

48. Philippa Foot, *The Problem of Abortion and the Doctrine of the Double Effect in Virtues and Vices* (Oxford: Basil Blackwell, 1978).

49. April Bleske-Rechek, Lyndsay A. Nelson, Jonathan P. Baker, Mark W. Remiker, and Sarah J. Brandt, "Evolution and the Trolley Problem: People Save Five over One Unless the One Is Young, Genetically Related, or a Romantic Partner," *Journal of Social, Evolutionary, and Cultural Psychology* 4, no. 3 (September 2010): 115–27 www.bleske-rechek.com/April%20Website%20Files/BleskeRechek%20et%20al.%202010%20JSEC%20Trolley%20Problem.pdf.

CHAPTER 10. WHAT'S NEXT?

1. Isaiah Berlin Virtual Library, "Quotations from Isaiah Berlin," accessed October 10, 2019, http://berlin.wolf.ox.ac.uk/lists/quotations/quotations_from_ib.html; Nicholas Kristof, "Mizzou, Yale and Free Speech," *New York Times*, November 11, 2015, www.nytimes.com/2015/11/12/opinion/mizzou-yale-and-free-speech.html.

2. Frank Ackerman and Lisa Heinzerling, *Priceless: On Knowing the Price of Everything and the Value of Nothing* (New York: New Press, 2005).

3. Mark Zuckerberg, "A Letter to Our Daughter," December 1, 2015, www.facebook.com/notes/mark-zuckerberg/a-letter-to-our-daughter/10153375081581634.

4. Bill and Melinda Gates Foundation, "Who We Are," accessed January 8, 2019, www.gatesfoundation.org/Who-We-Are.

5. Howard Friedman, *Measure of a Nation* (New York: Prometheus Press, 2012).

6. United Nations General Assembly, Universal Declaration of Human Rights, December 10, 1948, www.un.org/en/universal-declaration-human-rights.

7. World Bank, "Forty Years Later: The Extraordinary River Blindness Partnership Sets Its Sights on New Goals," July 3, 2014, www.worldbank.org/en/news/feature/2014/07/03/forty-years-later-the-extraordinary-river-blindness-partnership-sets-its-sights-on-new-goals.

8. Bjorn Thylefors, "Onchocerciasis: Impact of Interventions," *Community Eye Health* 14, no. 38 (2001): 17–19, www.ncbi.nlm.nih.gov/pmc/articles/PMC1705922.

Further Reading

This book introduces a broad set of topics. Those interested in further reading may wish to consider the following books.

COST-BENEFIT ANALYSIS

Ackerman, Frank. *Poisoned for Pennies: The Economics of Toxics and Precaution.* Washington, DC: Island Press, 2008.

Ackerman, Frank, and Lisa Heinzerling. *Priceless: On Knowing the Price of Everything and the Value Of Nothing.* New York: New Press, 2005.

Boardman, Anthony, David Greenberg, Aidan Vining, and David Weimer. *Cost-Benefit Analysis Concepts and Practice.* London: Pearson Publishing, 2011.

Sunstein, Cass R. *The Cost-Benefit Revolution.* Cambridge, MA: MIT Press, 2018.

———. *Valuing Life: Humanizing the Regulatory State.* Chicago: University of Chicago Press, 2014.

VICTIM COMPENSATION

Feinberg, Kenneth R. *What Is Life Worth? The Inside Story of the 9/11 Fund and Its Effort to Compensate the Victims of September 11th.* New York: PublicAffairs, 2006.

———. *Who Gets What?* New York: PublicAffairs, 2012.

COGNITIVE SCIENCE AND BEHAVIORAL ECONOMICS

Bloom, Paul. *Against Empathy.* New York: Ecco, 2016.

Kahneman, Daniel. *Thinking, Fast and Slow.* New York: Farrar, Straus and Giroux, 2011.

FAMILY PLANNING

Connelly, Matthew. *Fatal Misconceptions.* Cambridge, MA: Belknap Press, 2008.

PHILOSOPHY

Sandel, Michael. *Justice: What's the Right Thing to Do?* New York: Farrar, Straus and Giroux, 2008.

———. *What Money Can't Buy: The Moral Limits of Markets.* New York: Farrar, Straus and Giroux, 2013.

OTHER

Pinker, Steven. *Better Angels or Our Nature.* New York: Penguin Random House Books, 2012.

Acknowledgments

This book has traveled a long distance from the original concept to the final product. There have been many highs and lows throughout the journey of conceptualizing, researching, drafting, editing, editing, editing . . . editing a little more, and then finalizing this work. The writing of this book involved learning a great deal about science, history, ethics, and writing, and it also gave me some important reminders about work and life itself.

I am tremendously grateful to all of those who have provided feedback, guidance, support, and encouragement throughout the process.

I would like to start by thanking the people who battled their way through the very first drafts of my writing. Alan Friedman (my father), Jerrold Friedman (my brother), and Ann Friedman (my mother) were all kind enough to read the roughest of rough drafts and provide constructive feedback.

I received excellent research and writing support from Phil Bastian, who also served as a terrific brainstorming partner.

Other helpful feedback was provided by Jeffrey Chen, Nabeel Qureshi, Paul Veldman, Chris Eshleman, Stan Bernstein, Scott Walsh, Jeff Volinski, Sarah Wilson Hou, Holly Berkley Fletcher, Peter Steinmetz, Michael Friedman, Nicholas O'Brien, Ralph Hakkert, Julio Ruiz, Carole Biau, Gabriela Armenta, Jeremy Friedman, Laura Agosta, Kevin Fletcher, Christos Constantinidis, Jason Bloom, Danilo Moura, A Heather Coyne, Boon Pin, Sameer Sampat, Josh Krulewitz, Skye Silverstein-Vitale, and a very special member of the NYC Police Department.

My agent, James Levine, and my editor, Naomi Schneider, provided excellent guidance as we moved from a draft to a final, polished product. Genevieve Thurston was most helpful in improving the text and ensuring that the concepts were expressed clearly.

I greatly appreciate the encouragement of many key people, including Andrea Hurst, Alice Martell, Angela Baggetta, Bridget Flannery-McCoy, Matthew Connelly, Sasha Abramsky, Charles Kenny, and Andrew Bacevich, and the specific guidance and support I received from Steven Pinker and Jared Diamond.

Arthur Goldwag was a terrific friend, guide, and mentor throughout the process of writing this book.

I am thankful to the reviewers who dedicated a great deal of time to this project, including Eva Weissman, Paul Thurman, and Kim Sweeney.

I wish to recognize my much, much better half, Shui Chen, who patiently supported this work and served as a sounding board.

Lastly, I want to recognize Prakash Navaratnam. He has been a great friend, scientific collaborator, business partner, and brainstorming partner for many years. This book would never have come to life without his discussions, friendship, and partnership.

Index